WHY HISTORY MATTERS

WHY HISTORY MATTERS

Life and Thought

GERDA LERNER

OXFORD UNIVERSITY PRESS
NEW YORK   OXFORD

OXFORD UNIVERSITY PRESS

Oxford   New York
Athens   Auckland   Bangkok   Bogotá   Bombay
Buenos Aires   Calcutta   Cape Town   Dar es Salaam
Delhi   Florence   Hong Kong   Istanbul   Karachi
Kuala Lumpur   Madras   Madrid   Melbourne
Mexico City   Nairobi   Paris   Singapore
Taipei   Tokyo   Toronto   Warsaw

and associated companies in
Berlin   Ibadan

Published by Oxford University Press, Inc.
198 Madison Avenue, New York, New York 10016

First published by Oxford University Press, Inc., 1997
First issued as an Oxford University Press paperback, 1998

Oxford is a registered trademark of Oxford University Press

Library of Congress Cataloging-in-Publication Data
Lerner, Gerda, 1920–
Why history matters : life and thought / Gerda Lerner.
p.   cm.   Includes bibliographical references and index.
ISBN 0–19–504644–7
ISBN 0–19–512289–5 (Pbk.)
1. History—Philosophy.
2. Lerner, Gerda, 1920–
3. Women—Social conditions.
4. College teachers—United States—Biography.
I. Title.
D16.8.L377   1997   901—dc20   96–41288

1   3   5   7   9   8   6   4   2

Printed in the United States of America

For Stephanie

her courage
her goodness
her wisdom

Acknowledgments and Note on Usage

The period of the writing of these essays coincides with my work and tenure at the University of Wisconsin-Madison. The generous support for my scholarly work given by this institution in the form of research funds and research leaves has been immensely helpful to me and has been publicly acknowledged in my earlier books. This support has also enabled me to engage talented and knowledgeable research assistants who facilitated my work in innumerable ways. Of these, the most recent are Ann Spurgeon and Angela Nissing. I especially want here to thank them for their patient and reliable support of my work.

For several decades Sheldon Meyer has functioned as my editor, critic, and literary mentor. His broad knowledge of history, his fine critical skills and his patient support have strengthened me and allowed me to do my work under the best conditions. His involvement in the books has continued even after their publication, which, in today's climate in the publishing business, is a rare and remarkable occurrence and one I greatly appreciate. I am deeply grateful for his unwavering confidence in me and for his steady support of my work.

It has been my privilege and good fortune to have a working relationship with Leona Capeless which has extended over nearly twenty years. This is the fourth book of mine she has copyedited. Her superb knowledge of the rules and usage of English, combined with her flexibility in occasionally breaking the rules, her vast store of general information, and her respect for the style of the author and the meaning of the work have transformed a technical process into artistic cooperation. She has challenged me and I have learned a great deal from her. The work undoubtedly is the better for it, for which I thank her and with gratitude acknowledge her contribution.

A NOTE ON USAGE

The terms of reference by which African-Americans have referred to themselves have changed in the course of history. At any given time there has usually been a range of differences among them in how they prefer to be designated. I have followed the practice of using the designation chosen by the author or by the group in question during a particular historical period. (Thus: "Negro Women's club movement," but "Black Liberation.") African-Americans have struggled for over a hundred years to have the term used to designate them be capitalized, as are the designations for other ethnic or racial groups ("Italian, Spanish, Negro"). Thus, whenever the noun "Black" is used as a substitute for "African-American" or "Negro" it should be spelled with a capital B. There is a great deal of variation about the spelling of the adjective "black." One can reason both ways—"Black women and Italian women," both designating group adherence, or "black and white women," both designating skin color, hence lower-case. I usually capitalize the noun and lower-case the adjective, but I recognize that this usage is in transition.

A major point of my essay "Rethinking the Paradigm: I. Class, II. Race" is that the term "race" is itself a racist construct. (See Chapter 11, pp. 184–97, for the full argument and rationale behind this position.) I will therefore *in the future* join others in putting the word in quotes, in order to alert the reader to its essential inappropriateness. In this collection of essays, however, there are a number of essays written earlier in which the term is used without qualifications. As a historian, I cannot bring myself to alter earlier documents in order to conform to later insights. Since it might be confusing to the reader to see the term used with and without quotes in the same book, I have reluctantly decided to stay with the earlier usage of the word in this volume.

The reader should be mindful of the fact that "race" and "racial" are scientifically questionable and thoroughly inadequate terms for a number of concepts, for which the terms racial formation, experience of racism, experience of discrimination, and others might better be used.

G. L.

Contents

Introduction

In my first volume of essays, *The Majority Finds Its Past: Placing Women in History*, I traced my development as a feminist thinker and a historian from 1960 to 1979.[1] The present volume continues this endeavor, including work done from 1980 to the present.

In these sixteen years the field of Women's History has grown spectacularly, both in institutional and in intellectual terms. Tens of thousands of Women's History courses have become a regular part of university and college curricula. Women's Studies, an interdisciplinary specialization, also grew by leaps and bounds. The broad appeal of Women's History can be gauged by the number of college and university positions held by specialists in this field. In 1972, when I founded and, with Joan Kelly, directed the first Women's History Master's degree program in the country, we were lonely pioneers. By 1988, some 202 institutions of higher education offering doctoral training reported having at least one faculty member specializing in the history of American women. In the past decade the field has continued to grow, with a number of institutions now offering training in European, Asian and Latin-American Women's History in addition to the American specialization. My own career reflects this development: in 1980 I accepted a position at the University of Wisconsin-Madison with the express mandate to create a Ph.D. program in Women's History.

Women's History has become one of the "frontiers" of historical scholarship. In the process of documenting and interpreting the female past, valuable monographic work began to fill in the blank spaces. A virtual avalanche of biographies of "forgotten and neglected women" of the past appeared on the list of scholarly publishers and stocked the shelves of bookstores to meet an ever increasing demand for such work. Almanacs, encyclopedias, reference works about women, flooded the market.

Interest in the history of women has spread to the K-12 system, to communities and libraries. The National Women's History Project, an organization in existence since 1977, distributes teaching materials, posters, books and videos in Women's History to its 20,000 subscribers. It initiates and supplies materials for the celebration of Women's History Month (March) in tens of thousands of communities across the country.

Historians of women's history have in the past fifteen years challenged the conceptual framework and the methods of traditional history with new categories, with new questions and with interdisciplinary work. The concept "gender," the social construction of the differing roles deemed appropriate to the sexes, has found wide acceptance as a tool of analysis among scholars in a number of specialties.

African-American, Latina and lesbian historians challenged Women's History for making false generalizations about women on the basis of studies which focused only on white heterosexual women. Such accusations of false universalization challenged historians to examine their categories more closely and with more self-awareness. A lively, still ongoing debate among scholars of different races and ethnicities has helped to define more clearly the ways in which gender, race, class and ethnicities interact in history and theory. All in all, the vitality of Women's History as a field, and its ability to critique and constructively challenge established theory, has been proven over and over again. My own work has been grounded and enriched by my being part of this process.

In 1979 I wrote: "The two aspects of my own consciousness, that of the citizen and that of the woman scholar, had finally fused: I am a feminist scholar." The essays in the current volume trace another expansion of consciousness: the fusing of my own life experience as a Jewish woman refugee with my work as a scholar concerned with race, class and gender. I trace the stages of my coming to consciousness as a Jewish woman in the first three essays in this volume. In Chapter 1

I deal with my conflicted and ambivalent definition of my own Jewish-ness and try to explain to myself why I spent over thirty years documenting and studying the history of American women and of black women and never thought of studying the history of Jewish women.

In Chapter 2 I come to terms with my reaction to my first visit to the democratic Germany of the postwar period. The visit was occasioned by the publication in Germany of my book *The Creation of Patriarchy*. I was doing a book tour, covering fourteen cities, giving book talks in German, despite not having spoken the language for nearly fifty years.

Since that book tour three more of my books have appeared in German editions. I worked closely with the translator, and by the end of that process I had regained fluency in and mastery of the German language. It seems that only after regaining my lost mother tongue could I begin to deal honestly and consciously with the fact that I am a bilingual citizen of two cultures. I write about the problems of losing one's mother tongue in Chapter 3. It was through language that I was able to begin the process of healing from the hidden cost of my life as a refugee.

Chapter 4 is a speech I gave on the occasion of receiving a prize from the Austrian government for my work in Women's History. Chronologically, this award followed upon two periods of teaching and lecturing, first in Germany, then in Austria, in 1994 and 1995. I wrote that speech in German, the first writing in the German language I had done since 1939, and then translated it into English. It seems to me to incorporate quite accurately the weave of connections between the different identities and expressions of my life and my scholarship.

The same theme is expressed in a more scholarly format in Chapter 9, which is my Presidential Address to the Organization of American Historians. The themes struck in this address represent the various strands of my intellectual work in history.

Chapter 5, one of the earliest in this collection, derived from my research on abolition and the early 19th-century woman's movement. I was intrigued by the discovery that the practice of nonviolent resistance had originated in the United States abolition movement and been successfully used by female abolitionists. It struck me as odd, that when the practice of nonviolent resistance reappeared in the United States over a hundred years later in the civil rights movement, its origin was credited to Gandhi and Tolstoy, but not to American female abolitionists. The connection between ideas and action, thought and social commitment, has always intrigued me. It was of lively concern to me during the period when I changed from being a political activist to becoming a teacher and analyst of social institutions. Was there a discernible pattern to the way ideas related to social movements? Did theory shape practice or did practice affect theory? By studying the complex evolution of the idea of non-violent resistance and tracing its transformations through both practice and theory I was able to answer the questions to my own satisfaction. The essay, which started out as an endowed lecture, was then published in a few hundred copies by the sponsoring university, and it appears here for the first time for a wider reading public. It has always been one of my favorites.

Chapter 6 was a commissioned position paper, part of a debate on issues of multiculturalism initiated by the American Jewish Congress. It made me think about the broader patterns of American values and ideas. The concept that contradictions are deeply embedded in American thought became useful as an explanatory device and as a teaching tool. The article has not previously been published.

Chapters 7 and 8 are conceptually connected even though they were written six years apart. They follow, as did Chapter 6, my twelve-year-long immersion in "long history," represented by my two-volume *Women and History*. By looking at the history of women over the long duration—a span of three millennia—certain patterns of social construction and institutional formation became visible, which had previously been invisible, mystified. Both articles challenged me to think about women trans-culturally, world-wide and in a futuristic way. Chapter 7 is based on two reports I gave at a conference in Vancouver, British Columbia, in which I was asked to sum up the situation of women world-wide during the 20th century. At first unenthusiastic about what seemed to me an unrealistically broad assignment, I found that certain patterns of development emerged quite clearly. My finding—that, indeed, the 20th century marked a watershed in the history of women, and that "progress" on certain issues had been world-wide—surprised me, since I had anticipated finding uneven progress, favoring women in the highly industrialized nations only.

Chapter 8 was written in English and translated into German for a book published in Germany on the subject "The Year 2000." Here, too, I was challenged by the publishers to speculate in a futuristic way. I used the opportunity to discuss feminism as a worldview, a subject on which I had often lectured, but never published. The two futuristic essays seem to me to fit quite neatly into the questions raised by Chapters 5 and 9. The connection between theorizing about the emancipation of women and conceptualizing a feminism that is securely practical and political was becoming clearer and clearer in my mind. Enthusiastic audience responses at my lectures, both in the United States and in Europe whenever I struck these themes, seemed to me to indicate that other people, too, were seeking such connections. Writing history and thinking about women could lead to transformative politics rooted in both thought and experience.

Part III, "Re-visioning History," aims to go beyond the recognition that "differences" among people—race, class, gender, ethnicity and others—are constructed categories and beyond the additive approach commonly used to discuss them. In Chapter 10, "Differences Among Women," I offer an integrated, holistic model for dealing with these categories. I define the creation of categories of "deviants" as an essential, necessary instrument for the maintenance of oppressive, hierarchical systems of governance, and I stress the inter-relatedness of these various aspects of dominance. Race, class and gender oppression are inseparable; they construct, reinforce and support one another.

Chapter 11, "Re-thinking the Paradigm: I. Class, II. Race," in a way connects my earliest work with my latest. It rests upon over thirty years of my work on *class* and *race*. The questions I posed in my 1969 article "The Lady and the Mill Girl" and in my 1973 essay "Black Women in the United States: A Problem in Historiography and Interpretation" are here answered, at least to my satisfaction. The debate on these issues has broadened and deepened in the past fifteen years, and I have greatly benefited from the work of the scholars cited in the sources. Still, in the earlier drafts of this essay, which go back to 1985, and even in the latest draft, late in 1995, my definitions did not advance much over those stated in my essay on "Differences." I could see inter-relatedness and connections between the categories, but I still saw them as "things, "entities" with specific boundaries and three dimensions. It was only when I began to think comparatively and to apply concrete comparisons across time and space that the more radical definition I offer here—namely, that we are dealing with a series of processes over time—opened up to me as I wrote the final draft of this essay.

Earlier, I had planned on doing two separate essays, one on *class* and one on *race*. But with my new definition this proved impossible: the form had to reflect the new content. Thus the essay is written in two parts, *class* and *race*. Its overarching purpose is to deconstruct the "mantra"—sex, race, ethnicity, class—and re-define the relations between the various aspects of dominance in a holistic, functional way. As regards *class*, I move away from a categorization which reifies the concept and makes it appear as a fixed entity which stands in dialectical opposition to other "classes." I liken this system of classification to "sorting categories into vertical boxes," and I show how it prevents us from seeing the fluidity of boundaries (they are not rigid, nor vertically separated) and how it misleads us into regarding *class* as a fixed category, a thing, when in fact it is a process constantly in formation and adjustment. I focus on the process whereby class is first constituted historically and then maintained over time, and show that this process always involves gendered relationships. Surveying these gendered relationships—homogamous marriages, gendered inheritances and unequal obligations of families that favor sons over daughters—I re-define class as a process over time through which hierarchical relations are created and maintained in a patriarchal system.

In the second half of the essay, "Rethinking the Paradigm: II. Race," I analyze the ways in which the construction of *race* differs from other constructed categories. Then I reverse the process and look at the way dominance is constructed and institutionalized through the creation of deviant out-groups. By looking at the process in terms of its function one can at once see great similarities among the elements of the "mantra." I then re-define the elements as aspects of one integrated system that functions in a predictable, quite rational manner. I believe that these re-definitions not only are more accurate than others now in use, but that they also have great transformative power.

The final essay, Chapter 12, is my effort to explain why my work and quest of the past thirty-five years has been passionate and deeply fulfilling. It is written at a time when there is a virtual "culture war" being fought about the meanings of history, when the history of oppressed and marginalized groups is being challenged for its very existence by those who see history as the property of ruling elites and as a vehicle for the justification of states and other institutions of power. It is a time, too, when some radical thinkers have gone so far in their deconstructionist zeal as to subordinate reality to symbol, politics to meaning. At such a time it is necessary for historians to think about meanings and definitions in a deeper way. We can no longer take for granted that what we are doing and professing has general validity. I hope that the essays in this volume will make a contribution toward documenting and elucidating the work of the historian and its significance. In the final analysis, after a lifetime spent as a writer and as a historian, I must take a stand in my own right. History matters to me, for the many and complex reasons that are documented in this volume, and I feel the need to find a proper form for expressing why it does.

Madison, Wisconsin   G. L.
May 1996

PART I

HISTORY AS MEMORY

1

A Weave of Connections

In these days of the agony of the state of Israel, its native-born citizens and that large group of survivors from every part of the globe who have found refuge there—all of us as Jews in the diaspora—are forced to examine our relationship with the fact of being Jewish. What does it mean to us? What burdens and responsibilities does it pose for us? What values do we derive from this accident of birth or this chosen allegiance?

These are very personal questions that do not lend themselves easily to meaningful generalization. They are ancient questions which, it seems, are posed anew to each generation of Jews. Simple existence, the acceptance of one's being as normal and secure and unchallengeable, has not been possible for Jews. We have had to live consciously, with awareness, and by making choices. This is so because everywhere, since the days of the destruction of the Temple, since the days of the onset of the diaspora, Jews have not only been defined by themselves as "different," but they have been everywhere defined by non-Jews as "the Other," the outsider, the deviant. Among equals there is no category of "Otherness." The very act of categorizing another implies oppression. The one who does the categorizing sets himself up as the norm, the defining subject, while the one being categorized becomes the deviant from the norm, the defined object. Being so defined forces one to take a position, to assert or deny, who one is.

Let me illustrate what I mean by being "the Other" from my own

This essay is a revised version of two earlier lectures: one, a paper given at the conference "Developing Images: "Representations of Jewish Women in American Culture," at Brandeis University, March 14–15, 1993; the other, the Sam and Helen Stahl Jewish Heritage Lecture, "The Jew as 'Other' in Western Civilization," April 8, 1991, University of Wisconsin-Madison.

experience. I grew up in Vienna, Austria, after World War I, in a comfortable middle-class family. We were "assimilated" Jews, that is, we did not keep a kosher home, although my grandmother did; we were raised in the best traditions of German culture and regarded ourselves as liberal Austrians. Still, I was sent to Sabbath services in the orthodox synagogue and we kept the religious holidays in the traditional way, going to synagogue and celebrating at home. Strangely, it was not at Sabbath school that I learned that I was a Jew and what that meant— it was in a number of subtle lessons my family taught me.

In elementary school, a public school, I met a girl I wanted to be my special friend, but my father forbade it because she was not Jewish. I then tried making friends with a Jewish girl. All was well as long as she visited me in my home. When I was invited to hers I encountered a traditional Jewish home in which Yiddish was spoken and kosher food was served. At age eight or nine, this was a novelty for me on which I reported enthusiastically at home. After a few questions my father elicited the fact from me that the girl's father was the local kosher butcher, whereupon he categorically forbade me ever to visit that home again. It was all right for the girl to come to my home, but not the other way around. I am still not sure whether this edict was due to class or cultural prejudice, but the result was that the friendship ended abruptly, when the girl refused to accept these conditions and informed me I was a stuck-up goose. My family, it seemed, mixed neither with non-Jews nor with Yiddish-speaking Jews. True, mine was a peculiar family, but the friends and neighbors of my childhood were all homogeneous in class, education and religion. We lived in self-chosen affinity groups, in which for a long time, one could exist without having to confront most of the actual negative conditions of one's existence.

Yet when, one day in high school, I brought home the first B grade I had ever earned, my father reacted as though the world were coming to an end. I was berated, scolded, punished. When finally I objected meekly that, after all, I had so far earned nothing but A's and the other children in my class got C's and D's, I was told in no uncertain terms, "Jews don't get B's."

I never did get one thereafter. So we were the chosen people, intellectually superior, more disciplined, more conscious of the need to achieve. Excellence was the mark of the tribe and each of us had better live up to that standard. Even though it was a good preparation for achievement, it was a burden too heavy for a child to bear. And worse, it only further separated one from the other group. Scholastic excellence, prized by parents as a guarantee of future success, meant for Jewish children, especially female children, that they were only further marked off as being different in a world where being different was definitely not good.

In public school there was a crucifix on the wall in every classroom. On Wednesday afternoons students were required to take religious instruction and the class divided into two groups—*them*, thirty or more Christians; and *us*, three or four embarrassed Jewish children who were gathered in a separate room with the Jewish children from the other grades so that we might be instructed by a Rabbi imported for that purpose. The Rabbi was an ardent Zionist and preached politics to us. I disliked him and his message. I was an Austrian, a normal person, I was not going to allow him to make me into some sort of foreign misfit, dedicated to setting up a so-called Jewish homeland in some distant desert area in the Mideast. I read Goethe and Schiller, I formed my views of the world from German fairy tales and heroic sagas of the Norse people. I was, as it happened, blue-eyed with light brown hair and was constantly mistaken for one of *them*, which was not unpleasant to me. On the other hand, there were my black-haired, yellow-complexioned mother and sister—I always explained that they looked Hungarian, which my mother was by birth. Strangely, it was my blue-eyed father and his family who kept up the Jewish tradition, while my more Jewish-looking mother was a modern European and world citizen who wanted nothing to do with "Otherness." When we went on summer vacations in the beautiful mountain resorts of Austria, my father impressed us with the need not to "act Jewish," that is, we were not to speak with our hands, not to raise our voices, not to be noisy or too lively or too inquisitive. The message again backfired—it told me we were outsiders and ought to try to hide our deviant, disgraceful status as best as we could.

I have sometimes been asked, "How has your being Jewish influenced your work in Women's History?"

The simplest way I can answer this question is, I am a historian because of my Jewish experience. With the Covenant story in the Book of Genesis, Jews invented teleological history, the concept that the God-given purpose of existence is the fulfillment of a distant goal defined in the Covenant. It is not individual fate that matters, but the historical promise of people, land and prosperity in some distant future which is implicit in the Covenant between God and Abram. With it history as the unfolding of God's promise begins. After the destruction of the Temple, and with the beginning of the diaspora, this unfolding of historical events included the promised return of the people of Israel to their homeland. Thus every Jew is born into a historical world, and a consciousness of being linked to other members of the Jewish community. How to define that collectivity becomes a crucial and disturbing question. In the Bible the Jews are referred to as the "chosen people," a nation set off from others because of its special relationship with God. I never could accept this, even when I still believed in God. Since the diaspora that chosen flock had not been a nation. Was it "a people"? But it came in different colors, nationalities, spoke different languages, lived in vastly different cultures. Was it then merely a group of religious believers, united by that belief and by nothing else? Where I grew up, such thoughts about the nature of Jews and the origins of their history were forced upon us by daily experience.

What I learned from that comfortable, sheltered life I led in a country in which Catholicism was the state religion and antisemitism was an honored political tradition, was that being Jewish set one apart. Jews were not "normal," we were not right, we were different. And that difference had something to do with our inescapable, compelling history.

Was our history different because we were the "chosen people"? Were we different because of our history of persecution and suffering? Had we shaped our history by our refusal to be like other nations, by clinging to customs and habits that inevitably set us off from those among whom we lived? Assimilated Jews in Central Europe, like my birth family, accepted that explanation. If it was true, then the more we became like those among whom we lived, the less would our difference be offensive. We spoke High German, not Yiddish; in appearance, clothing and education we were not to be distinguished from the gentiles, except for those inescapable physical characteristics that identified some of us immediately as Jews—the dark hair, a certain kind of nose, the intense, vivid gestures. Self-hatred was a necessary component of assimilation, a self-hatred so subtle we never admitted it, even to ourselves, but still it operated as a corrosive poison, setting family members against each other. We reinforced it by keeping our distance from those not interested in assimilation—the orthodox, the Yiddish-speaking Jews. We were different, different from the gentiles, different from "those" Jews.

Assimilated Jews did not wish to dwell on the actuality of European Jewish history. There were biblical times and there was the present. What was forgotten and silenced out of existence was the long, bitter, repetitive history of persecution. There was no good news in it. As a child I once heard a story of how in the Middle Ages the Jews of certain German cities had been forced onto leaky boats to float down the Rhine river and drown to the last man, woman and child. Such stories made me feel the shame of belonging to a group so thoroughly victimized. Victims internalize the guilt for their victimization; they become contemptible for being available to victimization. Did they never fight back? Did they go like sheep? Today, I know innumerable instances of Jewish heroism, resistance, fighting back in the series of medieval antisemitic disasters which led to the 15th-century holocaust which destroyed two-thirds of the Jewish communities of western Europe and ended with the expulsion of all Jews from Portugal and Spain. I never heard of this history, not at school, not at home, not in the synagogue, any more than I heard of the existence of a women's history. Had I been a boy and studied Talmud, I would have learned Jewish history in a positive way. I would have learned about the existence of wise rabbis and great leaders; I would have studied that mysterious mental construct which held the community together for all these persecuted millennia. I was a girl, and the life-line of Jewish learning—Talmud, Mishna, Midrash—was out of my reach. All I got was indoctrination in gender restrictions and a thorough exposure to the great silences—the denial of the past, the suppressed voices, the absence of heroines.

Thus, historical consciousness grew together with consciousness of gender, but all the process yielded were baffling questions, no answers. Why did women and girls have to sit upstairs in the balcony in the synagogue, while men and boys sat below? Why could men speak and act during the services, reading the daily portion of the Torah, swaying dramatically over their prayer books, chanting their Hebrew lines in ragged unison, while we upstairs sat in stiff silence, at best following the words with our fingers in the Hebrew text. And when the Torah was lifted from the ark and carried on the shoulders of two of the elders in a sort of procession through the synagogue, so that each man might touch his finger, wrapped in the *tallis*, reverently to the scroll and then kiss it, why were the women allowed only to stretch out their fingers into the air reaching for the Torah without seeing or touching it? These were questions I asked repeatedly and the answers were never satisfactory. I was told that it was the tradition; and when I asked where was it written in the Bible, there was no answer other than that the rabbis had so interpreted it for thousands of years. Thus I became a Jew and a Jewish woman and double difference became imprinted on me—not pride, but embarrassment; not collectivity, but exclusion. I did not have the words for it at the time, but I know that my discomfort at being part of the religious Jewish community was based not so much on theological differences as on my unwillingness to accept the role this community assigned to women.

I soon stopped stretching out my hand in search of the Torah during services, a cheap and inconspicuous refusal. More difficult and public was my refusal, four weeks before the appointed date, to go through with my *Bat-Mitzvah* on the ground that since I no longer believed in God nor in what I was taught in religious instruction, it would be hypocritical for me to go through the ceremony. This provoked a family crisis, much noise, anger and pressure of various sorts, but in the end I prevailed. But more—I refused to set foot in a synagogue again and kept to that refusal for over fifty years. As I look back on these events, these small steps taken for reasons not entirely understood at the time, I can now name them differently: my first feminist actions came out of my experiences as a Jewish woman.

What is left to a Jew who refuses the religious community? Antisemitism and history. In short order I experienced plenty of both.

※

On March 11, 1938, German troops, meeting no resistance, occupied Austria and were greeted enthusiastically by millions of wildly cheering Austrians. The *Anschluss* was quickly followed by outbursts of violence against Jews that exceeded anything that had been inflicted in Germany since 1933. Gangs of armed Nazis terrorized Jewish pedestrians. Jewish men and women were forced to scrub the streets, walls and toilets in

8

police barracks with their bare hands or with toothbrushes to the amusement of crowds of bystanders. Raids on homes and businesses, followed by theft of property by Nazi gangs, were commonplace despite their illegality. In the streets and Jewish communities of Vienna there was open season on Jews for anyone with a Nazi insignia on his lapel. Jewish businesses were forced to close their doors; Jews were dismissed from their jobs and official positions; the University was closed to Jewish students and faculty within six weeks of the *Anschluss*. The legal and administrative regulations to legalize these excesses were soon enacted.

Violent antisemitism came naturally to Austrians, who had a long history of antisemitic political parties and movements. The Germans had to be led into violent antisemitism; in Austrians it erupted spontaneously. Within weeks of the *Anschluss* the situation of Jews in Austria was worse than that of Jews in Germany six years after the Nazi takeover.[1]

Right from the start, a reign of terror was instituted. Prominent Jewish leaders and businessmen, the heads of various Jewish organizations, doctors and university professors, journalists and politicians were arrested without any charges against them and held for weeks and months in jail or in the Dachau concentration camp. Jewish playwrights, actors and directors were barred from the stage, and many prominent writers and actors were arrested. A Jewish orphanage was closed, the orphans thrown out and the building turned into a Nazi barracks. SA troops forced their way into the biggest Jewish synagogue during evening services, arrested all present and desecrated the premises by singing the Horst-Wessel song. All government employees were forced to take a loyalty oath to Hitler; those unwilling to do so were summarily dismissed. By the end of April a decree of the Education Department assured that all school and university sessions would open and close with students and faculty giving the Hitler salute.[2] Everywhere, former Nazi sympathizers and "illegal" Nazis* now emerged proudly with new power and status. In the private school I attended, which had many Jewish teachers and a Jewish director, a number of the teachers turned out to have been underground members of the

---

*From 1939 on, ever since the assassination of the Austrian Chancellor by Austrian Nazis, the Nazi party was illegal in Austria.

Nazi party. The Jewish director was replaced by one of these illegal Nazis before the end of the school term.

My father fled the country after being warned by a "friendly" Nazi that his name was on a list of people to be arrested. He thought of course his absence would be temporary, but it proved permanent. A few weeks after my father's flight, twelve fully armed stormtroopers raided our apartment, put a gun at my twelve-year-old sister's chest, demanding to know where my father was, tore up the furniture with bayonets and generally terrorized us for hours while they pretended to search the apartment for hidden gold. In the end they took me and my mother to jail. We were taken to regular prison, separated from each other, and for six weeks we were forgotten, not accused, not indicted, not tried. We were, in fact, held as hostages for my father and were released only after he finally signed away all his property and his business. We were then forced to sign our own deportation orders.

I lived for another six months in Nazi Austria after that, because we could not get the various permits necessary to leave. Each week we had to report to the police, who threatened to throw us in a concentration camp if by the next week we were still here. During these months, the persecution and daily harassment of Jews increased. Destitute families doubled up in apartments, and many people never left their homes for fear of arrest during the random street raids that were a daily occurrence. The number of Jewish suicides increased from five in January to more than a hundred during each month of that summer. In our circle, each family had its own horror stories; everyone had heard of some acquaintance who had committed suicide rather than be taken to jail. This was long before the "final solution," long before any of these persecutions were cloaked in the mantle of legality. The Austrian treatment of Jews was improvised on the spot; its versatility, ingenuity and brutality were then unprecedented.

Legally and theoretically, it was then still possible for Jews to leave the country. In actuality, all borders in Europe and most other countries of the world were closed against refugees from Nazi persecution and only a lucky few had the connections or money to escape. Since by newly enacted legislation, Jews leaving Austria were permitted to take only the equivalent of $10—in cash and their household goods and clothing—money or connections were essential for survival abroad. In April approximately 25,000 Viennese Jews applied to the U.S. consulate for immigration visas; at the time the quota for immigrants from Austria was fixed at 1413 per year.[3]

With the aid of "Aryan" lawyers and by signing over all our property and assets, finally, one week before *Kristallnacht*, my mother, my sister and I secured all the necessary papers and were able to join my father in Liechtenstein, a tiny country on the Austrian border. We had residence permits for Liechtenstein because my father had established a business there in 1934. This fact saved his and our lives. He was also able to rescue his mother and adopted sister, while most of our relatives remained in the death trap.

An emigrant now, awaiting my U.S. immigration visa, I had become virtually a stateless person. With a German passport which marked me as a Jew, return to Germany meant certain death. Being stateless, a Jew and destitute change one's view of what it means to be part of an establishment: my outsider status from then on was firmly fixed. Even after coming to America, I never felt secure in front of anyone connected with an establishment—bureaucrat, policeman, soldier or lawyer.

During World War II the U.S. government forced me and other Jewish immigrants like me to register once a month at the post office as "enemy aliens." Still, I did eventually become an American citizen. Insofar as I now had citizen's rights I could trust, this fact changed my outsider status. But I was different, marked by my experience; I was carrying my "Otherness" within me.

A few years after the end of the war, when the full extent of the horror in which some of my family members had perished had become known, the sense of the difference of my own experience became sharper. My mother had died at age fifty, a death hastened by the hardships of emigration. Still, I was among the very fortunate; most of my close relatives had survived. But the personal loss was dwarfed by the enormity of the loss of a people, of communities, of one's own past.

Sometimes, when you walk up a mountain, the views of the valley below are clear and sharp. Then the weather changes, a cloud of fog settles into the valley and the view vanishes. There is nothing beneath one's feet except gray mist. It is eerie, like the terror of nightmares, one is cut off and cast off and the very place from which one came, what once was home, has vanished. When this happens, on the mountain, one can console oneself in the knowledge that the place in the valley is still there; it is as it always was and one will see it when the fog lifts. But for the refugee such consolation does not exist. The city in which I had grown up, the circle in which I moved during the years of my childhood no longer existed. Of the 176,000 Jews of Vienna, over 9 percent of its total population in 1934, only 4746 survived in 1944, a few months before the liberation of the city. More than 65,000 Austrian Jews died in the ghettoes and concentration camps of Nazi Europe. The others, who had been deported or forced to emigrate survived scattered all over the world.[4] I have visited Vienna six times in the past fifty years. The buildings are restored, some of them are more beautiful than they ever were. But what I notice most, as I walk through the streets of the city is the absence of Jews, an absence I think only a survivor could notice. For me, there is no one left to go back to; there is no place to go back to except a place of hatred and bad memories. There is only one life-line left—memory, personal and historical. After the Holocaust, history for me was no longer something outside myself, which I needed to comprehend and use to illuminate my own life and times. Those of us who survived carried a charge to keep memory alive in order to resist the total destruction of our people. History had become an obligation.

Like all immigrants, I did not think this through or find such fancy words for it. I had to struggle for existence and survival and if I gave any thought to the matter at the time, it was how to become a good American. I tried to erase whatever I could of my foreign characteristics. I worked hard at acquiring as pure an English as I possibly could. I shed my indestructible European clothes, as soon as I could afford to replace them with throw-away American fashions. I tried to make friends with Americans and be accepted by them. It is no accident that decades later when I began to prepare for an academic career I chose the field of American history, not European. I still wanted, as I had in Austria, to be a "normal" person. Yet, from the start I chose a deviant field, in fact, a then non-existing field, that of Women's History. My "Otherness" was obvious from the moment I entered graduate school— too old (over forty), a foreign-born woman, a Jew, insisting on specializing in a field of history my professors considered "exotic" and weird. I will skip over the years of struggling for the legitimation of this new field of inquiry. It was only when I came to Madison, by then a well-established historian of fairly advanced age, that for the first time I began to feel accepted, an insider. The University gave me recognition, honors, support for my work and clear signs of their appreciation. The advances made in my embattled field—Women's History—had brought some measure of respectability and, while some colleagues still considered me a deviant sort and not quite up to their measure, my general experience was of having finally made it. I was now an insider and began to worry about being corrupted by that unaccustomed state. Then, a few years ago in April, there was a swastika smeared on a poster on my office door. In August there were forty-one antisemitic incidents in Madison and one, not reported and thus not included in that number, a threatening antisemitic phone message left on my answering machine. Back to square one. The Jew remains "the Other."

My story illustrates quite well the effect on Jews of being designated a deviant out-group. There are essentially three major response patterns: cultural separatism, denial through assimilation, and acculturation.

Cultural separatism means affirming one's "Otherness" as a positive good. We are the chosen people, smarter, better, morally superior and somehow purified by our history of suffering. We prefer to live in self-selected ghettoes, confine our social contact to people like ourselves and cultivate our separate institutions.

Denial through assimilation is an effort to fuse with the majority and ultimately to give up all distinctiveness. For many Jews of the generation between the wars in both Central Europe and in America this took the form of adopting a philosophy of modernism, of anti-nationalism and internationalism, of a desire to find a new form of community which would embrace different cultures, religions and nationalities. This was my mother's philosophy and for a long time it was mine. We abhorred all nationalism and all theories of hierarchy and dominance. Tolerance and a "new humanism" would take the place of the old separations, hatreds and differences.

I married a second-generation American. My husband's family represented another response, in its *shtetl* culture in the Jewish ghetto of Philadelphia. His parents were immigrants from Russia who had come to the U.S. to escape the infamous Kishinev pogroms. They were working-class people who spoke Yiddish and were proudly affiliated with their synagogue, their *Landsmannschaft* and their Yiddish culture. They were as unassimilated as Americans as one can be and they were wonderful, loving people who took me in as their own, even though at first glance I seemed to them to be a *shikse*. Living in solid, tightly knit networks of families, they were mutually supportive, but resisted the tendency of the younger generation—the first-generation Americans—to partake of the general culture, to accommodate to the values of tolerance, multi-culturalism and internationalism. To this younger generation, the old folks seemed hopelessly limited and limiting. The horizontal mobility of first-generation Americans—out of the ethnic working-class ghettoes—into ethnic suburban ghettoes—illustrates this process of "Americanization."

The third response, "acculturation," is both more adaptive and more realistic than the other two. It embraces the demand for integration in regard to rights and opportunities—one wants to be an Austrian or an American with full equality—yet one does not want to lose one's group identity. Integration *and* difference is the goal. Jews with that stance will privatize their Jewishness and separate its communal function within their group from their public roles. Jews would adopt the external behavior and standards of the dominant culture but retain their emotional, psychological affinities to their own group. They might, as in America in the third generation, move into integrated upper-class neighborhoods, attend elite colleges and vote not on the basis of ethnicity but of class, yet their social life would be within a like-minded circle of Jews. My father represented that stance in its European version.

The irony of these choices is that antisemitism would not recognize any difference between the separatist, the assimilated, the acculturated Jew. Hitler's Nuremberg laws defined Jews by "genetic" inheritance into the third generation, and lifestyle choices meant nothing. Similarly, the person who put a swastika on my door in Madison, Wisconsin, fifty years later cared not one bit as to what kind of a Jew I was or I am. I was a Jew, that was sufficient.

Each of us has over a lifetime struggled with choices representing these different positions. And as we choose, we take on ourselves the guilt over our existence. If we choose right, we and the people will be spared. If we get all A's, we will be among the saved. If we choose wrong, the holocaust is our fault. It is a cruel bind, which blames the victim and obscures the actuality of the situation in which he or she exists. What it obscures is that it is not difference, but the designation of difference as inferiority which has created the evil.

The psychological effect on Jews, as on other out-groups designated as deviant, is that they internalize guilt for their being "different" and spend their lives choosing between various forms of adaptations to the constraints placed upon them. But what is really oppressing us is not our choice of adaptation or our nature as a group designated as "different," it is having our definition of self made not by ourselves but by others.

To be a Jew means to live in history. The history of the Jews is a history of one holocaust after another with short intervals of peaceful assimilation or acculturation. Most of us never study this long and bitter history and yet we live with it and it shapes our lives. We live from pogrom to pogrom, one of my friends recently said. What it means to be a Jew—having to look over your shoulder and have your bags packed.

It is only in the light of this history that we can understand the significance of the existence of the state of Israel and even the idiosyncratic behavior of the leaders of the state. It is not always a sign of paranoia to think that one is surrounded by enemies. For many religious Jews, Eretz Yisroel, the land of Israel, means the fulfillment of biblical promise and the re-establishment of their rightful place in a land from which they were driven. But for millions of nonreligious and secular Jews the state of Israel, means that for the first time in two thousand years Jews no longer will allow themselves to be defined by others and scapegoated by them. I think that this particular meaning should be important as well to every non-Jew who believes in the right of people to self-determination and freedom.

It was this understanding of the problem of "Otherness" and of the denial of self-definition which led me to the study of the history of women. For women have, for longer than any other human group, been defined by others and have been defined as "the Other." Women have, for longer than any other group, been deprived of a knowledge of their own history. I have, for the past thirty-five years, tried to comprehend analytically what I experienced and learned as a prototypical outsider—a woman, a Jew, an exile.

There is a third strand to this weave of connections Why did I spend years helping to develop the then nonexistent field of Black Women's History and never, until recently, study the history of Jewish women?

As one who chose to be an American, I had to accept the problematic in my newly adopted home together with the good. Race was the crucial issue in America. The relative freedom of the American Jewish community compared with Jews in other countries, and its long existence under conditions of tolerance and open access to the resources of the society, is no doubt due to the existence of the American Constitution and its protections, but it is also due to the existence of racially defined minorities which are the primary target for discrimination, hatred and scapegoating. This is not to minimize the existence of a history of antisemitic discrimination. We must recognize that, whether we like it or not, as Jews and as whites we have had privileges and benefits from the racially segmented labor market and from housing and job discrimination against people of color, just as have non-Jewish whites. Moreover, the way the system of competing outgroups works, there is an incentive for members of one minority group to display their assimilation, their Americanism as it were, by participating in institutionalized racism. Thus some European Jewish immigrants, who in all their lives had never seen a person of color, learned racism in short order once they assimilated to American society. I wanted to be an American but I did not want to assimilate to the evil of racism, here any more than there. It was logical for me as a scholar to focus on the issue of race in American history and because of my interest in women, on the history of black women.

There was another reason why I could not then focus on Jewish women. Coming out of my own experience of fascism, I had become convinced that nationalism of any kind could only lead to conflict and war. It was this conviction that made me unable for a long time to accept the ideological premise of Zionism. I wanted to get away from nationalistic allegiances; I wanted to transcend differences of race, ethnicity, religion and nationality. I saw my choice as "either-or." Now I am more aware of the complex weave of connections, of multiple causes, of interdependencies.

None of us can be defined simply as being members of one group or another. We are Jewish, Christian or Muslim, women or men, immigrants or fifth generation, we may be differently abled or differently acculturated by being rich or poor, we may be lesbians or married heterosexual women, battered or independent, educated or deprived of education. And all of us, ultimately, will join one of the most despised, neglected and abused groups in our society—the old and the sick. As Jews we know the frailty and unreliability of acquired status and privilege. It may be here today but gone tomorrow. We know the perils of being defined by others and of being stigmatized. We know the pain and the invisibility, the fickleness of friends and the conformity of enemies. Our history of suffering has taught us patience and survival skills.

But now, what must survive is no longer the small group, the kin, the *shtetl*, the *Landsmannshaft*, even the nation. All of us must survive in a world in which difference is the norm and no longer serves as an excuse for dominance or we will not survive at all. And in order to survive in this interconnected global village we must learn and learn very quickly to respect others who are different from us and, ultimately, to grant to others the autonomy we demand for ourselves. In short, celebrate difference and banish hatred.

2

In the Footsteps of the Cathars

This year I did something I have avoided doing for more than fifty years—I spent six weeks in Germany. I was born and raised in Austria. I am Jewish, and I left Vienna just a few weeks before the *Kristallnacht* of 1938. I have been to Vienna a number of times since World War II, and each time I swore I would never go back again; then, something or other would come up and I would change my mind. But I did draw the line on going to Germany.

I still have the German passport with which I traveled to the United States in 1939. It is, of course, decorated with a swastika. A few years later, all Jews issued a German passport would find that their names had been altered—each female was given the middle name Sarah; each male was given the middle name Israel. I was among the lucky ones to have escaped before this way of identifying Jews had been enacted. In my German passport, my family name was underlined twice—this was the "secret" way I was marked as a Jew for the benefit of frontier guards or anyone else who might care to harass me. I used to say, when people asked me whether I was German, "No, I'm Austrian. I've never been to Germany—Germany came to get me." With such sentiments, sharpened by what happened to members of my family who could not escape in time, it is not surprising that for fifty years I avoided going to Germany. Over those decades, I hardly ever spoke German, and I even gave up reading German literature.

Now I am old and reconciliation is on my mind. One cannot live with hatred. Besides, after the A-bomb and the H-bomb and the Viet-

This essay first appeared in *The Progressive*, vol. 58, #3 (March 1994), pp. 18–22.

nam war, I carry war guilt on my shoulders as an American, even though I always opposed those weapons and that abominable and despicable war. I am no longer on such firm ground in condemning Germans for the deeds of the Nazis. I feel more strongly than ever that to transcend hatred bred of racism and ethnic prejudice, one must at least make an attempt to distinguish between the guilty and the others. One must strive for reconciliation.

On all my trips to Austria I had gone as an American. For years, I was accompanied by my American-born husband: later, as a widow, I was still resolutely an American visiting Europe. My German, while perfect in idiom and diction, was hopelessly outdated, lacking fifty years of vocabulary; I stumbled over common words and could not pronounce many of the typically German combination words—three to five nouns strung together for more precise meaning. I thought and dreamt in English, and my German was literally an instant translation. On those few occasions when I gave a lecture, I had it translated from my English into German and read it aloud. It seemed a shame to have to go through such a process as a native German-speaker, but I accepted it as a reality over which I had no control.

Then one of my books was published in Germany, followed by three more. The first two were translated into German by a capable professional, but I had a contractual right to supervise the translation and make suggestions for changes. The process of doing this with the first book was exhausting—I sat with a German-English dictionary and first had to look up every tenth word or so. By the end of the book, I no longer used the dictionary, and while I was working on the translation I found myself thinking in German. By the time I was working on the second book, I had regained my old assurance in the use of the language and was only occasionally stymied by an unfamiliar "modern" word. During the research for this book, I had spent many months reading German sources, and found my competence coming back. When my publisher suggested a book tour in Germany, I not only agreed, but decided to lecture entirely in German.

So it was actually through my books that I began the process of return. As it happened, a German university invited me at about the same time to become a visiting professor for a semester. I declined the offer of a semester but, on an impulse, agreed to come for two weeks and deliver a few lectures. I also offered to give an intensive graduate seminar on racism, sexism, and antisemitism. My offer was enthusiastically accepted before I had time to think it over, and so, almost inadvertently, I entered a process of reconciliation.

Before going to Germany, I vacationed for two weeks in France with my sister, who lives in Israel. We traveled by car, driving north from Toulouse, visiting the *bastides*, medieval fortified towns that had been strongholds of a group of heretics called the Cathars. Every tourist office had maps of the "Road of the Cathars," with information about their persecution and heroic resistance. The Cathar or Albigensian heresy flourished during the 11th century among the nobility and artisans of the Languedoc towns. It persisted for two centuries despite severe Church persecution, but the Albigensian Crusade, launched in 1209, took a severe toll. For decades, Cathars in their isolated *bastides* fought heroic rear-guard actions against much superior forces. With the fall of the Castle of Montsegur in 1243, the Cathar cause was decisively defeated. More than two hundred male and female Cathars were burned alive on a great pyre in Montsegur: their children were placed into convents and raised as good Catholics.

My sister and I had read the Cathars' history, and I have even taught about them, citing them as a rare example of a group that was isolated, persecuted, and totally destroyed. Most groups targeted for persecution survive as some sort of remnant. Not the Cathars. They stuck to their simple and powerful creed, kept their faith, and in defeat chose suicide rather than conversion. And so they perished.

For days we had been following the Cathars' trail of tears and defiance, taking notice of the sturdiness of the walls behind which they hid, the integrity of their convictions, the heroism with which they died. Now that the Cathars are 750 years dead and gone, they have been resurrected as martyred emblems and have become grist for the tourist mills. We visited the scenes of their martyrdom and admired the sparse artifacts of their existence.

At Gaillac, near Albi, I took a short walk one evening, straight across the bridge in front of the lovely medieval square on which we were staying. Enjoying the view from the bridge over the rapidly flowing Tarn. I then followed a country road lined with shade trees. In the distance, there were open fields and a blue evening sky gradually turning purple. I had hardly gone fifty steps when I noticed a small stone with an inscription set before a closed iron gate that seemed to fence in an abandoned farm with several barns and decaying buildings. The inscription read, HERE WERE IMPRISONED IN A CONCENTRATION CAMP, TOGETHER WITH FRENCH ANTIFASCISTS AND FIGHTERS IN THE UNDERGROUND, WOMEN WHO HAD SOUGHT REFUGE IN OUR COUNTRY. FROM HERE, ON THE TWENTY-SIXTH OF AUGUST 1942, GERMAN AND POLISH WOMEN WERE DEPORTED TO AUSCHWITZ, FROM WHERE NONE OF THEM RETURNED. HONOR TO THEIR MEMORY. Beneath the stone were two plastic wreaths, apparently placed there by a local group whose name I could not discern.

I looked into the overgrown yard, into the barracks with their open doors that suddenly seemed to be full of the straw mattresses of the women of Gurs, the French internment camp for foreigners in which my mother had been imprisoned. No, my mother was already safely in Liechtenstein on the date of that deportation, but I could see the others and could suddenly feel their presence. This place where I stood was the last they saw; here they had the view I now saw, that pure uncluttered horizon, the farms, the tree-lined road leading north. There was barbed wire around it now, probably the same as then. And when they turned they saw the medieval towers of the church with its open-armed Christ on top, the town walls, the little tower of our idyllic vacation home. They could not see the river but they could hear it, and how many of them attempted to flee down those steep banks?

The friendly French farmers in their picturesque *bastides*, the ones we complimented so often in our conversation for their respect for tradition, for their old houses, their lovely gardens—their parents were here when these women slowly starved to death. This *camp de concentration* is small, perhaps not two acres, in all a cozy place of horror, and yes, I am immensely grateful for the memorial stone. And yes, I notice that it says "German and Polish women" when, in fact, they were Jews.

That must not be said, even in memorial, just as it was not said on the tablet in the Jewish quarter of Paris—the formerly Jewish quarter of Paris—where the passerby learns that several thousand (I forget the exact number) of French children were taken from there to Polish camps, never to return. These were Jewish children, and they were French Jewish children, but the memorialists have a wonderful instinct for forgetting what was the worst of it, the genocide, and reducing the victims to a mere casualty of war.

I stood a long time in front of the rusty iron gate before I finally noticed the cement tower way over to the right. It could have been a water tower, but there was a ladder going up to it and it could as well have been a guard tower. It certainly looked like the typical guard tower in prison movies. I felt as I did two years ago when an unknown person scrawled a swastika on my door in Madison, Wisconsin: It never ends, it just gets worse with each repetition.

The map of the internment camps for refugees in southern France, which I had worked with for months now while writing about Gurs, appeared before me in its inexorable, insistent pattern. Over the verdant fields, the gentle pink and yellow landscape so lovingly preserved, so carefully nurtured, there is that layer of the markings of terror.

There were so many of these camps dotting the landscape of beautiful southern France, dotting the countries of Europe, spreading leprosy and decay over the fields of Poland—just like the maps we gather admiringly from the tourist offices here, maps with dots almost as frequent lying over that same landscape, the maps of the castles and fortifications of the Cathars. But the hatred that killed them has taken cover in these stone walls, has settled in the ground and sprouted afresh each season, seeking its victims. It lives under these trees and among these picturesque ruins, and ever so often, every century or so, its fungus-like tentacles erupt from the soil and the walls and the purest of pure skies, and engulf yet another group of victims.

The women in the *camps de concentration* at Gaillac probably did not hear the voices of the Cathar women, men, and children who perished among these same stones. And we, survivors, inheritors, pensioners of our good fortunes, walk among these ghosts again with our selective forgetting. Each generation forgets selectively, and so the circle of death continues. We come to drink wine and celebrate the memory of the Cathars—and those of our own who died instead of us sprout up among the weeds on the brick walks and cry to heaven. "And they never returned. Honor to their memory."

After my first week in Germany, I spent a weekend in Berlin. The train on which I traveled stopped at a small suburban station, Wannsee. A few commuters got on and off; the town seemed peaceful and somewhat sleepy. Here, in 1942, during the Wannsee Conference, the Nazis planned and set into operation their "final solution," the plan for the destruction of European Jewry. I could hardly breathe as the train pulled out of the station. How can people stand to live in that town? How come they have not at least changed its name? I was still new to Germany—I had not yet passed through a tourist attraction called Dachau Concentration Camp, the real place, now a memorial. After all these years and after all my acquired knowledge of German history and current German politics, I was naive.

But I really wanted to know, to experience, the better Germany. Thus, on a Saturday, I joined a walking tour that had been recommended by my local hostess, a tour of Jewish Berlin. At our meeting place, the square in front of the Red Rathaus, there were enough police to handle a major emergency. The disturbance that occasioned this display of force turned out to be a pitiful demonstration of unemployed and shantytown dwellers in a few trucks, their supporters straggling along in the steady, cold rain. The square is Marx-Engelsplatz, with a huge statue of the pair in the center. To the right is the neo-Gothic Red Rathaus—red, red brick, built in 1869. Ahead is a monstrous radio-TV-lookout tower, and to the left medieval *Margaretenkirche*. Somewhere in the back looms a huge, baroque church. The contrasts are fitting—the incongruities are, obviously, what makes this city work.

The man leading the tour, whose name I could not understand, worked for a *Volksbildungsinstitut* and this was the last part of a four-session course on Jews in Berlin. He looked a bit like Trotsky and had beautiful thin long hands. He was bareheaded and refused to acknowledge the rain, though he shivered continuously. He spoke with great intensity and conviction and I had the feeling he was an old politico—I thought East German, but was told West.

First he showed us the frieze on the Rathaus, which celebrated the arrival of the Huguenots who had been called to Brandenburg to help in its modernization in the 1860s. They were welcomed and immediately granted all the rights of citizens. Ha, he said, but the eighty Jewish families who had also been invited were denied rights and isolated in the housing quarters for the poor. They do not appear on the frieze, he said. Then, pointing to St. Margaret's Church, he talked of the 130 Jews who had been burned in front of it in the 14th century. He made us walk across the square to the spot, and then to a street still called Jüdengasse—they were called Jüden, not Juden—where the eighty families who came in 1868 had settled.

We walked through the courtyards of tenement buildings that had provided both living and working quarters for Jews. They were of a later date, faintly Art Deco, but neglected. I asked about some holes in the walls. Yes, our guide confirmed. These were World War II rifle shells or bomb splinters. Nothing in this part of town—formerly East Berlin—has been restored. He told us of one gentile businessman who had employed fifty blind Jewish men in his shop in this tenement and had saved them from death through his connections with high Nazi officials, somewhat like the hero of *Schindler's List*.

The courtyards were fenced and faced a wall and some trees—all that was left of the old Jewish cemetery. We walked there next—it's now a plot of grass between two buildings and it has two plaques— one to the philosopher Moses Mendelssohn, who lies buried there. The other states, HERE WAS THE OLD JEWISH CEMETERY. IT WAS DESTROYED AND DESECRATED BY THE NAZIS IN 1939. THIS BUILDING THEN BECAME A SAMMELLAGER FROM WHICH WOMEN AND CHILDREN WERE DEPORTED TO AUSCHWITZ AND RAVENSBRÜCK, THERE TO BE TORTURED AND MURDERED. DO NOT FORGET. The building in back was formerly a Jewish boys' school; the guide pointed out the sign that said so, and told us it is one of only two signs with the word "Jewish" that remain in Berlin. The Nazis missed it.

Next to the boys' school was a Lutheran orphan asylum and across the street a Catholic charity school, formerly a hospital. In that hospital, doctors and nurses saved seventeen Jews from death. Behind it, another charitable institution bore a plaque: THIS WAS A SAMMELLAGER WHERE 50,000 OLD PEOPLE WERE COLLECTED TO AWAIT DEPORTATION TO THEIR DEATH IN 1943. FIGHT AGAINST WAR; HONOR PEACE. DO NOT FORGET.

On to Rosengasse. A "Litfass-Säule" memorial, with photos and inscriptions. This, our guide said, was the scene of the single known act of effective resistance inside Berlin. As the war was ending, after the battle of Stalingrad, the Gestapo ordered several thousand Jewish men whose lives had been spared because they were married to gentile women to be taken from the forced labor they were doing in war factories and collected into a newly established *Sammellager* right there in Rosengasse. Several truckloads of them had already been taken to Auschwitz when the wives of these men began standing in front of the building, round the clock, demanding the release of their husbands. Police and SS arrived with machine guns, but the women stood fast. After a few days of this, the men were released and those already in Auschwitz were returned. An amazing event.

Our tour continued through several more streets in which only plaques or memories remained of the Jews who had lived there. Finally, we came to a grandiose, gilded building with a golden cupola—the Jewish synagogue. This ostentatious building had been constructed late in the 19th century by the flourishing Jewish community. Amazingly, it survived the *Kristallnacht* destruction. It was set on fire, its front destroyed, as were the other nearby Jewish-owned buildings. Storm troopers and police stood by, watching. Firefighters ignored the burning synagogue but watered down neighboring houses to keep them from being damaged. Then a police captain appeared with several of his men, waving papers at the other police and demanding, in the name of the law, that the fire be stopped. The papers he held showed that the building was under police protection as a national monument, and he intended to do his duty. The storm troopers retreated and the fire company put out the synagogue fire; the building was saved. This decent police captain's deed earned him a marker in Yad Vashem, the Israeli Holocaust memorial, as a "righteous gentile." Still, during the war the building was badly damaged. It was one of the few buildings in East Germany that the Bonn Government decided to subsidize for reconstruction at this time of economic tightening.

I was the only Jew taking the tour, and my response to it was mixed. Certainly it was good to see that all these upright Germans were interested enough to have taken a four-day seminar on Jews. One of them told me they had seen the inside of a synagogue and met with a Rabbi who explained the Jewish service. They had been to the large Jewish cemetery and to the Jewish museum. I felt that I and all the Jews had become some sort of museum piece to be admired, stared at, have their graves honored, their memorials marked. Somehow, it connected with what I had seen in France regarding the Cathars—a dead culture, dead people reified into something other than what they had been, all for the edification of future generations.

Our dedicated lecturer, undoubtedly earnest and sincere, had managed to mention acts of resistance only by gentiles. He had informed us, probably quite accurately, that it took seven Aryans to keep one Jew alive during the war. Put this together with the desolate plot of grass that once was the cemetery of a living community, the desecrated schools, the synagogue saved by a gentile and restored by gentiles—and you had a sense of devastation and pervasive victimization. Dead Jews are now extolled as victims, but they are deader than dead, since the meaning of their lives and that of their communities to the building of a German state and of German culture are lost.

Over the next few days I saw five more monuments to the victims of fascism, to the Jews murdered by Nazis, to the victims of Soviet persecution. At the moment, a fierce political battle is raging over yet another monument: Should it list separately each group that had been destroyed? Should it lump Jews together with victims of Soviet persecution? Should it use a "neutral" all-purpose inscription to the dead? Our guide had told us that the two biggest department stores in Berlin had been owned by Jews and had never been restored to their owners or their owners' heirs. I went to see them, Bloomie's and Altman's—stolen property.

The city is full of life, building, buying and selling, producing and consuming. It puts up memorials for the dead whatever and wherever. In some ways, all of this vitality is admirable—but it is also obscene. They have made monuments out of concentration camps and tourist sites out of *Sammellager*.

From what I can gather, most of the Jews in Berlin are the very old, who can live here better on their pensions and their restitution money, or those who have fled from acute persecution elsewhere. Many of the friendly, engaged Christians I met turned out to be the children or grandchildren of mixed marriages. The rest go their own way.

In Munich, I walked to the old Rathaus, all medieval gingerbread and really ugly. A large pedestrian mall with elegant shops extends over more than ten city blocks and is always crowded with pedestrians. I went to a Rathskeller for lunch—the usual Bavarian beer-garden decor, very crowded. The waiter directed me to a table at which three other patrons were already seated, and I sat down opposite a middle-aged man who exchanged a few friendly words with me. He was clean and neatly dressed, and looked like a minor bureaucrat or a prosperous artisan.

"Where do you come from?"

America.

"How come you speak such good German?"

It is my mother tongue.

I should have stopped right there, for I noticed an expression of eager cunning in his eyes, which I instantly disliked. But his attitude was friendly, and I didn't see how I could break off without being offensive. I took my time ordering and opened my *International Herald Tribune*.

"When did you come to America?"

In 1939.

"The year I was born."

Then you're lucky, I said.

"Why?" suspiciously.

Because you were spared a lot of bad times.

"*No ja. Der Hitler der war ja ein Verrückter, was er mit die Juden gemacht hat, das war ja net recht.*" Hitler was crazy; what he did with the Jews was not right.

I tried to change the subject to Austria and the city of Vienna. He pursued it with interest. He had been there only once—a very nice city. I said it had been the capital of a great empire that was now just a small country, but it still had all the big buildings and squares.

"When did it become so small?" he asked.

In 1918.

"Aha," he said, "the monarchy. No, that was all because of the war. They lost everything because of the war."

Hoping to keep the diversion going, I gave a small lecture on the history of the monarchy and its territorial holdings. He revealed vast ignorance of history and seemed, on the whole, satisfied with the information I offered.

"What was the frontier with Germany?" he wanted to know, "Austria and Germany?"

I explained.

"And when was that made?"

At the time the German nation was formed. 1870. Didn't you learn that in school?

"*Na*, we didn't learn history, only Hitler history. About the destruction of Germany by the Allies."

That sounded hopeful. Apparently, he wasn't entirely satisfied with what he learned at school and showed some skepticism.

"Was it hard to get to America?" he asked.

Yes, quite hard. I didn't feel like elaborating.

"They didn't want them either, the Americans. Not the English, either."

I said nothing.

"*Die Juden*. Nobody wanted *die Juden*. Maybe 10,000 of them were turned back on the high seas because the Americans didn't want them. Did you know thousands of them drowned in the Atlantic. *Keiner wollte die Juden*. Nobody wanted the Jews."

Considering his ignorance of geography and history, I thought he might simply be misinformed, so I straightened him out. The Americans took Jews and all other refugees, I said, but only in accord with the regular immigration laws. They were wrong not to change those laws to save more Jews, but they went according to their regular laws.

"*Ja, ja*," he repeated. "Nobody wanted the Jews."

I came to America according to the regular laws, I explained. You needed a sponsor and a waiting period, and then you were admitted.

But he was off on another tack, as though I had inadvertently connected a certain circuit in his brain and now there was no stopping it.

"*Die Polaken*," he offered mournfully, using the derogatory epithet for Poles, "*die Polaken, jetzt will die auch keiner*. Now nobody wants them, either. But they keep coming here, you can't stop them. Do you know they stole 10,000 cars in Germany last year, *die Polaken*?"

Maybe so many come here because there is no work in their country, I said in what I hoped was a reasonable tone. After all, they suffered a lot of destruction in the war and since the war.

"*Nein, nein*—with them it wasn't so bad in the war. I know a Polak and he told me, they didn't have it so bad in the war."

I thought of the Poles killed in German concentration camps, of the tens of thousands of slave laborers imported into Germany. I bit my tongue.

"I saw a show on television," he offered as the final proof. "The Polaks did not have it bad."

I opened my newspaper and began reading. My dinner arrived and I started eating. But he was not to be deterred. In some way, he had a dialogue with words I had not spoken. I was simply the prompt for the monologue in his head.

"*Der Hitler der war ja auch ein Oesterreicher.* He wasn't a German, he was an Austrian."

I refused the bait.

"He was wrong about the Jews, but he helped the Germans. Did you know what unemployment was like in Germany in 1933? Millions of people had no work. When you can't feed your family, you can't feed the children—anybody gives you work, you take it and you're grateful. He built roads, that gave work to a lot of people. It's all the fault of the Allies. We would never have lost the war [he must have been referring to World War I] if the Amis [Americans] hadn't come in with all the weapons and all the stuff they have. No wonder they defeated Germany. And they took our land, they took all the colonies, and we had to spend millions on reparations—no wonder people were dissatisfied. It's all the fault of the Americans—the same way they came in to the Second World War—the last minute. . . ."

I had had just about enough. You're giving me straight Hitler history, I said, the kind you learned in school. You're truly uninformed—your facts are wrong and you believe everything the Nazis told you.

He looked at me in some bewilderment, then got stiff-necked. "*Wieso*? I saw it on television. The Allies betrayed us; the Treaty of Versailles is what got us Hitler; it was all inevitable once we got that treaty."

A message was being sent me by the younger couple at the other end of the table. I could not understand it right away, until I gathered they were speaking English to me. "That was a fine argument," they said.

What, I said, that drivel?

"No, no, you gave him a good argument," they applauded.

The man was trying to win back my attention. He laughed good-naturedly, to show he meant no harm. He began telling me a joke.

"The Jew goes to a store to buy a radio. The German salesman asks what he wants. A radio. A radio, says the German. Don't you know how to spell? *R-Raus A-aus D-Deutschland I-Juden O-Osten.* Out of Germany, Jews, to the East. The Jew says, don't you know we spell backwards: *O-Ohne I-Juden D-Deutschland A-armes R-Reich*. Without Jews, Germany poor country."

Against my better judgment I had to laugh at this Nazi anti-Nazi joke. He seemed totally unaware that he had followed the straight Nazi line in making a distinction between the Jew (obviously a German Jew) and the German. To him, a Jew was no German, and could never have been one.

I was beginning to choke on my food and just wanted to get out. His self-confidence, beliefs, self-importance, were untouched and untouchable. Nothing I could say would have the slightest impact. On the other hand, I did not want to give him the satisfaction of having chased me away. I could just hear him telling his buddies. "So I says to this American Jew . . ."

It would be good to see the Germans take some responsibility for what Hitler did, instead of blaming it on everybody else.

"*Der Hitler war ja nix wert.* Hitler wasn't any good. He was bad for the peasants, too. I come from a little village, 250 people, and we were on the list to be transferred to the Ukraine. The whole village. If they hadn't stopped him—-Hitler—we would've all been moved. And about the Jews he was wrong."

I paid my bill.

"But what Morgenthau wanted to do to the Germans, that was wrong, too," he said triumphantly, playing his trump card. "That was terrible."

Well, I said soothingly, what Henry Morgenthau [Franklin D. Roosevelt's Secretary of the Treasury] wanted didn't happen. Nobody listened to him.

"Do you know why? Because he was a Jew. He wasn't an American, that's why."

I left hastily, fearing I would throw up. The voice, the tone, the language, the content—all of it I could have heard in Vienna in 1938. All of it I *did* hear in Vienna in 1938. Here it was again, unchanged, undefeated, unreconstructed. Good-natured, humorous, kindly evil. *Gemütlich* evil. He knew how to sniff out a Jew. He knew how to handle a Jew. Humor her, attack her, isolate her. The Jew is no German; Morgenthau isn't an American, he is a Jew. *Keiner will die Juden.*

It took me all afternoon, walking through hall after hall of raging, brilliant, furious paintings by Max Beckmann, a German gentile forced to flee his country, before I could recover some balance. It took a long talk with a decent German art historian, before I could stop feeling nauseated and defiled.

❧

I taught for two weeks after these incidents. My students were much like the ones I teach at home—progressive, politically active graduate students in history, many of them feminists. They were young enough to be the grandchildren of the Nazis, and yet they wrestled with their burden of collective guilt. There was reconciliation in my offering to teach them about racism, sexism, and antisemitism—I was offering them the best I knew; I was giving them the benefit of what life had taught me. They responded in a way that was healing for me. But even in the open and trusting atmosphere of our classroom, there was the reality that most of them had never had any close contact with a Jewish person nor were they likely to have such contact, except when foreigners came to visit.

Everything functions beautifully in this modern German state. The railroads run on time. The streets are much cleaner than the streets of American cities. There are beggars and homeless people, but their numbers are few, and they do not appear in the most obvious public spaces. Most of the people one sees in the towns are well-dressed. The crowds in the shopping mall show that despite high unemployment people are buying and consuming.

What is wrong here is the homogeneity of the population. There are few people of color visible—just a few *Ausländer* types. Turkish men, women in colorful kerchiefs. No Jews. They exist, a small Jewish community of fewer than 30,000 people in all of Germany. The average German has no contact with living Jews; to my students, with all their good will and finely honed consciences, Jews are abstractions.

It is now fifty years since the Holocaust. I have read all there is to read about it; my memories and nightmares are unrelenting I was among the lucky survivors; the list of my personal dead is not as long as that of others. I did not think that at my age there was anything I could learn about these events. What I discovered in Germany or this trip really should not have surprised me. Still, it chokes off my breath and makes my head feel curiously empty and light.

They have succeeded. Germany is *judenrein*. They have succeeded in annihilating my people. I was hurt in France because the monuments to the World War II dead did not mention that some of them were dead only because they were Jews. The French have claimed all their Jews as French. I wanted them to recognize that they were Jews, too. But the Germans, even in memory—especially in memory—have retained the racist categories. What is more, they have obliterated our history, so that all they and anyone else remembers is the end, the dying, the murders. They have excised the history of German Jews in such a way that even to well-meaning contemporaries, there are Germans and there were Jews, but there are no Jewish Germans and never have been. Inside Germany, in the heart of Europe, we are as nonexistent as the Cathars. That is the meaning of genocide.

I knew it, of course. I've known it for fifty years, but I've never felt it before. Now that I have walked in the footsteps of the Cathars, I do.

3

Living in Translation

Dedicated to my sister Nora

When I came to the United States in 1939 as a refugee from Hitler fascism, I had, like all refugees, a very problematic relationship with the English language. On the one hand, I wanted desperately to learn English and to speak it well. This was my meal ticket, absolutely essential if I was to get work. On the other hand I felt a responsibility to uphold, treasure and keep intact the integrity of the German language which fascism had stolen from me, as it had stolen all my worldly possessions. The Nazis spoke a language of their own—first a jargon of slogans and buzz words; later the language of force and tyranny. Words no longer meant what they said; they meant what the Nazis intended them to mean, and so, gradually, they became empty of meaning. Like banners flapping forever in the wind, they flapped around the skeleton of German speech until all that could be heard was the clattering words pretending to meaning they could not encompass. Seen in that light, it was the obligation of every antifascist German-speaking refugee to uphold the old language, so that some day it might be restored.

I had, in the last two years before my emigration, studied English with a private tutor. The results were pathetic. The book from which I studied must have been more than fifty years old. It operated on the assumption that the manners, habits and customs of English gentlemen constituted a universal norm. One learned some vocabulary and, most importantly, a dozen or so phrases which presumably equipped one to enter into polite British society.

"Will you come and have tea at my home?"

"I shall be delighted."

"May I introduce you to my good friend Roger Forsythe?"

To which the proper reply was: "Delighted to make your acquaintance, sir."

If one were seated in front of someone, it was essential to lean back toward the person behind one and say politely: "Please excuse my back." Or, as the occasion warranted, one might make use of the phrase "Please excuse my glove." Unclear was whether what one was apologizing for was having or not having a glove.

The phrase book, carefully memorized, would equip the German-speaker to navigate through the quaint old-fashioned British village, purchase a few choice items at the greengrocer's (the book was heavy on the use of the Saxon genitive), exchange a few polite phrases at the fishmonger's and return to one's hostelry where the crucial question: "Where's the Ladies?" was never to be asked. One was simply to observe where the Ladies was. With the important distiction between "will" and "shall" obsessively fixed in one's mind one was supposed to be able to announce: "I shall be taking the 8:20 train to London" and instruct the ubiquitous servants to "fetch my trunk from my room."

All of which was worse than useless in giving instructions to a New York City cabbie or in understanding his growling response to any question. Fishmongers and greengrocers refused to make an appearance, and servants, such as could be identified, had no intention of fetching anything without a tip which exceeded the immigrant's means and comprehension. One gestured one's way through the first weeks and learned that a firm "no" and "buzz off" were more valuable than any of the learned phrases.

"Please, I desire a job," was a declaration which was certain to land the applicant in a plastic chair in the employment agency, to wait all morning to be called while watching other applicants get their referral slips.

"Excuse please, lady, your newspaper announcement said there was job as 'lady's aide' and I wait all morning why never you call me?"

"There's nothing for you today. Come back tomorrow."

"Please I desire—"

"You got no references. You can't speak English. You got no experience. This ain't the welfare."

Learning English, the kind spoken in New York City with its multiple accents, innumerable slang words, abbreviations, elisions, swallowed syllables and exploding expletives, was a bare bones necessity.

I listened to the radio for hours a day, especially to the advertisements, which usually had longer sentences than the rest of the show. One could go to the movies for twenty-five cents, and I spent many evenings studying language at the movies. I listened with intense attention to people's speech and I read my way through the Children's Books section of the Public Library, gradually advancing to Young Adolescents.

English was a simple language, compared with German, French and Latin. The verbs had simple endings, if any; one did not add adjectives and adjectival constructs to nouns in long chains ("The no longer quite youthful, but otherwise still good-looking, pipe smoking general etc."). The beginner learned to rely on the auxiliary verbs—to be, to have, to do. I kept book on the hundreds of meanings of the verb "to do" and learned at least fifty ways of using "to get." Since the finer shadings of syntax and vocabulary eluded me, I thought of the language as blunt and utilitarian, and devoid of subtlety.

Living in translation and lacking both an adequate vocabulary and sense of the rhythm of the language it was as though my adult knowledge had to be transposed into the vocabulary of a six-year-old. It does not take long to learn to get by in English; to master the language takes years.

I began to write poetry in English before I could properly speak or write. Since I wrote free verse in ordinary speech, patterning my style after Bertolt Brecht, and getting effects by sharply contrasting images and striking sound patterns, I could achieve some sort of effect with the most primitive means. Writing poetry was then my way of venturing out into a higher level of language connection, but I deliberately stayed primitive, fearing to make a fool of myself if I tried to be poetic.

For nearly two years, I managed on that level of crude communication, while my thoughts and dreams went on unperturbed in German. I forced myself to read only in English. Whether I read newspapers, magazines or books, I always had a dictionary nearby. I would look up each word I did not know; for a while I kept a small notebook with words and definitions. I was quite aware of the fact I was living a split life, thinking in one language and speaking in another. I could not find adequate words for the thoughts I wanted to express. I said things, and people rephrased them, translating for themselves. More and more, as I began to move among English-speakers, I lived with an overwhelming sense of inadequacy and frustration.

What made matters worse was that I had aspired to become a linguist in German. I studied Old German and Middle High German in Gymnasium and had done a year's work on my honors thesis, which was a close textual analysis of a dozen German ballads. I was fascinated with languages and had hoped to go to the University to study comparative languages. For at least four years prior to my graduation I had been an acolyte of the writer Karl Kraus, whose every work I had read and re-read and whom I considered my foremost teacher.

Karl Kraus was an essayist, satirist, playwright and, in the opinion of many literary critics, the finest poet writing in German in the 20th century. His monumental drama "for a Martian theatre," *The Last Days of Mankind*, written after World War I, was perhaps the outstanding pacifist work created out of that terrible European cataclysm. As editor of the satirical journal *Die Fackel* (The Torch), Kraus held up a mirror to his contemporaries, exposing their follies, cruelties and self-serving hypocrisy in savage, brilliant essays and aphorisms. He regarded himself as the last of the German "Classics" and as the upholder of a humanistic tradition of form, style and language in a world deaf to its own speech and forgetful of its history. Kraus was fanatic about the German language, which he mastered in all its complexities of dialects and intonations. He wrote long essays about two lines of poetry and devoted one celebrated issue of his journal to a 200-page essay on the subject of "The Comma." To read Kraus, study his essays and attend his remarkable "Readings"—performances at which he not only read his own works but put on complete dramas such as *King Lear*, reading all the parts in the play—these were formative experiences for a young person interested in language. Kraus presented a constant challenge—being one of his disciples one learned to watch one's speech and one's writing. Meaning was to be found, as Kraus put it, "by tapping along the guiding rope of language." Young writers coming under Kraus's spell either gave up altogether or attempted to write in his voice, until at last they found their own.

Kraus, a Jew born in Czechoslovakia, then part of the Austro-Hungarian empire, was antisemitic, arrogant, elitist and in the last five years of his life, politically reactionary. Earlier, he was a savage critic of bourgeois life, of greed, corruption and exploitation. He had excoriated the military, complacent politicians and shoddy literati and espoused the causes of down-trodden workers, exploited peasants and victimized prostitutes. At the time I came under his influence, he had made his peace with the semi-fascist totalitarianism of Chancellor Dollfuss's government which he defended out of disgust with the failings of weak liberalism and corrupt democracy. I was totally opposed to Dollfuss and his government and my politics were more radically left than Kraus's had ever been, yet I managed to disregard his turn to conservatism, even his betrayal of his own beliefs, because of his impact on my artistic and linguistic sensibilities. I attended each of his Readings and his many lectures, read his work and every work he recommended, honed my own writings on his demanding essays on language and worshipped at his feet. In 1936 I attended his funeral and cried bitterly, as though he had been a personal friend. In all my life, no single writer has ever influenced me as profoundly as did Karl Kraus.

One of his incredible accomplishments was to "translate" Shakespeare without knowing English. He had read the several current German Shakespeare translations, the chief one by Tieck, representing a German Romanticist rewrite of Shakespeare, and found them wanting. Having read all the French translations and putting these beside the German versions and then, word for word, comparing them with the English version, he had sensed what was missing: the Anglo-Saxon structure and bluntness of Shakespeare's speech and his poetry, which could not be rendered adequately in the words and rhythms of German Romantic poetry. Kraus undertook his own "translation"—one might better call it an intuitive adaptation in German and it was these versions he used in his Shakespeare readings. I think I have never read Shakespeare in better German than in these free adaptations. Kraus got Shakespeare right. Thinking about his accomplishment and the way he went about it gave me new insights into the art of translation. A translator might get the literal meaning, and yet miss the other layers of meanings, all the resonances conveyed to hearer and reader in the original. She might miss the richness of ambiguity, the force that stretches a word's meaning beyond its formal definition, the pulse and vibrations of tone that resonate over and above mere content. It seemed to me then and it does now, after I have worked for years on translations and lived for decades in translation, that the overtones and resonances are more significant than the literal meaning. If a choice has to be made, I would chose texture over mere information.

To come from the speech of Karl Kraus to the imbecile stammerings of an immigrant American was a fall, indeed, symbolic of all the rest of it—the loss of economic security, of status, of potential, of opportunity. All refugees experienced that fall, and many, perhaps most, never got over it. They lived their lives in the new land either as temporary exiles or constantly in denial. The world they had lost became more attractive, more worthy, the longer they were away from it. In New York City's Washington Heights they created a small *Mittel-Europa* of familiar shops, coffeehouses and organizations. Their cynical stance toward the USA gave them a sense of continuity; they were and would remain Europeans transplanted against their will into an alien environment.

When I made the decision, in my second year here, to become an American writer, I made the decision to abandon such attitudes, to become, in fact, a voluntary emigrant from Europe. I embraced America with gratitude and fascination, as I embraced its primary language. If that meant suppressing and denying some of my European habits in thought and attitude, so be it. I was young enough to start anew. There are many gains in such an enterprise, not the least of it, citizenship and familiarity in a formerly alien culture. But there is a cost to it, greater than I ever wanted to admit to myself. I am trying to reckon up that cost, at last, after fifty years and more.

In an irony of fate, the very first paid "job" I had in the United States was as a translator of a rather esoteric sort. I had nearly gone under in the first eight months as an immigrant, unable to find work, due mostly to the fact that employers of casual labor and domestic work found me "overqualified," and I was too afraid of getting in trouble with the Immigration Service to seek even private assistance. Then, an orthopedist I had met through one of my refugee friends required the services of someone able to translate from Latin to English. I volunteered and, for five dollars an hour, translated a medical treatise on the hip joint from Latin into English. I earned enough to support myself for two weeks and to regain some sense of self-respect. My fancy classical education, might, after all, equip me for self-support. In fact, it did not, not for another twenty years, when it was finally useful in allowing me to continue my academic education.

If you are forced to give up your mother tongue, what is lost? In a way, losing one's mother tongue is inconceivable—one assumes one can always return to it. But that is not so. Language is not a dead body of knowledge; language changes year by year, minute by minute; it lives and grows. In order to remain adequate it must be spoken and it must be read. When you lose your language, you lose the sound, the rhythm, the forms of your unconscious. Deep memories, resonances, sounds of childhood come through the mother tongue—when these are missing the brain cuts off connections. Language communicates much more than literal meaning. It gives us timbre, tone, a rich undercurrent of resonances and shadings, multiple and ambiguous crosscurrents. But in the early years of speaking the learned language one knows nothing of those complexities; the new language stays linear and flat. Inflection adds layers of meaning to what is spoken, but the immigrant has no ear for inflections. Translating meaning from another circle of culture, she constantly makes mistakes and is given to misperceptions.

German, like most European languages which developed through centuries of feudalism, has a rich variety of dialects and intonations, which mark not only region but also class. British English of the upper classes and the Cockney speech of the lower classes retain that function, but English in America reflects region more than class. Still, there are class markers in speech, but they are immensely complicated by the effect of immigration—the millions of Americans who speak English as a second language have created a number of creolized varieties of speech. In all this the newcomer finds it hard to become oriented.

I was always aware of the awkwardness of my position as an immigrant. Normally, I'm quick to a fault—I catch the meaning of what a person says often before the speaker finishes, which leads me to interrupt the speaker with my answer. A very unattractive trait, one that over the years I have tried to unlearn, but it is indicative of the way my mind works. Living in translation I usually could not catch the exact meaning without doing the translation. Therefore, from being fast to a fault, I now appeared slow, if not slow-witted. Lacking the information usually transmitted by dialect or speech patterns and body signals, I had to guess at the whole meaning or rather I had to be satisfied with an approximate meaning. For a person like me, who is committed to precise definition and precise expression, this was a form of torture.

Living in translation is like skating on wobbly skates over thin ice. There is no sure footing; there are no clear-cut markers; no obvious signposts. It helps to trust in one's balance, to swing free and make leaps of the imagination. I suppose what I am saying is that it is immensely strenuous. Quite apart from being alienating.

Two years after I came to the United States, the country was at war. Speaking German in public exposed the speaker to hostile looks and remarks. I'm a noncomformist by inclination, so public disapproval would not have been enough to discourage me from speaking German. The truth was, I no longer wanted to speak German; I was repelled by the sound of it; for me as for other Americans it had become the language of the enemy. These expressions of mindless patriotism are not sentiments of which, in the abstract, I can approve. In practice, however, they were just what I felt. I ceased speaking German altogether.

By then, I was married to an American-born man and all my friends were American-born. Still retaining enough of my European heritage to think that every child should learn one or more foreign languages, I wanted my children to be raised in such a way that they would easily learn foreign languages. Yet I did not speak German to them, because of the attitude I held at the time. I did sing them German lullabies, because they were the only lullabies I knew. Later, I taught them the rudiments of French.

It took several years before I began to think in English. It was exciting when it actually happened and it made a qualitiative difference in the way I lived. I began to be able to express myself with the speed and precision characteristic of me and most of the time I could find the word I needed without resorting to a dictionary. There came a night when I dreamt in English and after that, I thought I had made it.

But it is one thing to speak and think and even dream in a second language; it is quite another to be able to write in it as a creative writer. My decision to become "an American writer" had been made long before my language proficiency entitled me to such a claim. Nevertheless, I wrote short stories and articles, although I felt quite inadequate to the task. I had great difficulty getting dialogue right; my characters all talked the same way, since I was incapable of creating individual speech patterns. Awareness of my shortcomings was of little help. I felt like a tone-deaf person trying to compose a symphony. Carrying a notebook with me everywhere, I jotted down the speech fragments I heard. I read books on the craft of writing and on "style." Nothing seemed to help. One of my favorite exercises was to compose a paragraph in the style of a famous writer. That was useful, but I still had no style of my own. That should not have surprised me—I already knew then that form is the shape of content. But it is not some ideal abstract "shape"—it is content as shaped by the creating artist, content filtered through the prism of the artist's entire life experience. And I was then a broken prism—a refugee without language, between cultures, belonging to neither the old nor the new.

I took another translation job which I found quite satisfying. I translated the jacket copy and the texts of a collection of German folksongs appearing on a two-disk LP. The folksongs were all well known to me; to give a poetic and not just a literal translation was a challenge, which in the end I felt I met. I contemplated a career as a translator, but I quickly gave it up. What I wanted to be was a writer.

At one point during this initial apprenticeship I decided to stay with my Austrian culture, to write only of what I knew. My first two short stories written in English were descriptions of my experience in Nazi Germany. In one of the stories, I did the interior monologues of five Nazi soldiers, caught in a tense battle situation on the Russian front. In both stories I avoided having to do English dialogue. Both were published immediately: the first one in a small, cultural journal, the second one in the best fiction magazine then in existence, *Story* magazine. This quick and unexpected "success" spurred my literary ambition but did nothing to improve my language skills. Daringly, I wrote three short stories with American locale and characters—none of which aroused the slightest interest in publishers. Once again, I returned to my earlier decision to write about what I knew best and I began to work on a semi-autobiographical novel. It described the four years 1934–38 in which Austria made the transition from a democracy to an authoritarian clerical government and finally to Nazi fascism, as experienced by a teenage girl.

In a sense, this novel was my apprentice work as a writer of English. It took nearly twelve years to complete it, because I did seven re-writes. Over and over again, I transformed the text from a translation to an original work in English. Even so, the final version still has traces of

German syntax and style. Writing is learned by doing; there is no escaping that. My Sisyphian labor at last produced a book with which I was satisfied, but by then the topic of antifascism, which had been of such paramount interest in the early forties, had become a drug on the market. I have readers' reports from the various publishing houses that could break your heart. My work was compared to that of Thomas Mann and Thomas Wolfe and the readers expressed high hopes for my literary career, but they did not want to publish this book. In yet another ironic development of my career my novel *No Farewell*, in which I had invested all my best effort to mastering the English language, was first printed in Austria in a German translation in 1954. It was very successful there and this success inspired me to take part in a cooperative publishing venture in the late 1950s, which finally resulted in American publication of the book.

Recently, in trying to think about some of the long-range effects of my refugee status I became aware of something as a problem which I thought was not really a problem for me. I have a German name which is unpronounceable by English speakers and thus is inevitably mispronounced. I accepted that mispronunciation as the proper form of address for me, came to use it myself and have done so for fifty years. I became aware of the disjunction only when I spent some time in German-speaking countries and heard my name pronounced correctly. Each time that happened, it gave me pleasure. That made me realize that it pained me that my own children, my husband, my best friends could never really pronounce my name. I had buried that pain and refused to acknowledge it. It was, so I thought, a trivial matter. I no longer think so, and an examination of my relationship with my only sister confirmed my new insight.

My sister Nora and I were separated through emigration when she was twelve years old and I was eighteen. While I emigrated to the United States, she spent the war years in a school in Switzerland and then settled in England. She eventually became a British subject, but never really felt at home in England. Early in the 1960s she emigrated to Israel, where she still lives.

We were separated by continents, by warfare and finally by poverty. In 1948, when I for the first time after my emigration returned to

Europe, we met briefly in England. By then she was twenty-three years old, independent, self-supporting. I was twenty-eight, married and had a baby and a toddler in tow. Our meeting was difficult, first because of the presence of two overtired and cranky children. We also had trouble communicating with each other—she spoke English with a pronounced British accent; I spoke American English; both of us no longer spoke German. I remember coming away from that meeting with a sense that she had become a stranger to me, in more ways than one, and that she had become "stuck up," different. What I probably reacted to was not a change in her attitude, but the persona she presented to me, that of a young proper English lady. From later conversations I know she had similar feelings toward me.

We met again in 1957, when she came to visit us in New York. We both wanted very much to have "a good visit," to recapture our old intimacy. By then both of our parents were dead, we were the only close family for one another and we sincerely wanted to find a common ground for friendship. We loved each other and showed it in many ways, but our daily interaction was stiff, formal and full of mutual irritation. We simply seemed to get on each other's nerves—and ostensibly there was no good reason for it. From my point of view, I found her mannerisms, her mode of behavior, difficult and in some profound way incomprehensible. The fact that my beloved little sister had turned into a cultural stranger never ceased to outrage me, but I could not learn how to deal with it.

It was on her second visit to New York, eight years later, that an incident occurred which suddenly illuminated our difficulties. We were in my apartment, washing the dishes after dinner. My husband and the children were not with us at the time, and so perhaps we had a moment of quiet. One of us, I don't know which one, began to hum an Austrian folksong, and then to sing it, in German. The other chimed in, and we found ourselves singing in two voices, the way we had often sung in our childhood. One song followed another—from somewhere long-forgotten by both of us, the childhood songs welled up and broke to the surface. We were not doing it consciously; we were not even aware of what was happening, but when we finished we were smiling and hugged each other with the spontaneity that had been missing all those years. I felt as though suddenly all the barriers between us had broken down; we were children together, as we had always been, and what separated us—the shifts in cultures, the different lifestyles, the separate hard struggles for survival and reconstruction—all of that fell off our shoulders as the common language at last united us.

Nevertheless, during our infrequent visits—about once every two or three years—and in our correspondence we mostly stayed with English. I think this was largely due to my often expressed insistence that I no longer thought in German and therefore could not express anything significant in that language. I lacked the facility, I said. I would often start a letter to Nora in German and give it up after a few lines, switching to English. Nora spoke German continuously with her close friends in Israel, even as she tried to make the language switch to Hebrew, which she found very difficult. So English seemed a mutually satisfactory compromise. I marvel at the fact that even after the incident with the songs, we did not seem to understand the significance of the language barrier between us. It took another incident to make it crystal clear.

This occurred in 1973, in Sicily. My husband had died a few months earlier, and I wanted and needed to be with my sister. We had a wonderful week together in Sicily, and most of the time that week we spoke in German. We celebrated our feeling of closeness by a fine dinner in a fancy restaurant. My sister has never learned to be a social drinker, and at the most will take a glass of wine. That night I insisted on her drinking along with me and between us we emptied a bottle of fine wine. I was pleasantly warm and lively, but she was definitely tipsy. Two middle-aged women in a foreign city, we left the restaurant noisily chattering and decided to rest by sitting down at the curb of the street. We were giggling and laughing and suddenly my sister started telling jokes—ancient jokes which we used to tell each other as children. They concerned a male figure famous as the butt of Viennese humor, a certain mythical Count Bobby. Count Bobby was stupid, arrogant, self-satisfied and endlessly duped by others. He spoke Viennese dialect in the nasal twang characteristic of the nobility and that was the way my sister told the joke. I immediately topped it with another Count Bobby joke, also in dialect and we both fell into a fit of uncontrolled laughter. The jokes were not that funny and we were not that drunk, but, once again, language unlocked the gates and memory took over. In the Vienna of our childhood, we had learned at least three different ways of speaking German—High German, which was school German, the language one spoke to strangers and to parents; the kitchen dialect one spoke to cooks, servants and lower class people; and Count Bobby's Viennese dialect, which was both accurate and a mockery of the real dialect spoken by upper-class people trying to be "just folks." It is just these kinds of distinctions which are lost in translation. Nora and I finally made it home and into our separate rooms, joking in dialect and getting more infantile with each step, but when we said goodnight to each other there was a deep transformation of feeling between us. Nothing needed to be said; we both knew we had found each other, after all those years. What had done it was the mother tongue, the language going even deeper than formal speech, the actual spoken dialect of childhood.

In the years since then our relationship has improved and deepened. Now we speak German almost all the time; in fact, for nearly a decade, my correspondence with Nora and our biennial meetings were the only times in which I did speak German. It would be nice to be able to report that all estrangement and all difficulties between us have ceased with the change in language, but life is never that simple. Our relationship has remained complex, but deeply meaningful to each of us. We have learned the cost to our intimacy created by cultural separation and by language differences. Our lives have been deeply marked by our fate as refugees and by the happenstance of landing on different shores, on different continents. Each of us paid a heavy price for assimilation into a foreign culture and part of that price was that we, loving sisters, were for decades strangers to each other.

Gradually, assimilation was completed; the past drifted out of sight. There came a time when I felt secure in my command of English, in speech and writing. I did the acrostics in the *New York Times* successfully and usually won at games of anagrams with native English speakers. I proudly developed tricky skills, like being able to read a poem or passage in German, while reading it aloud in English. With a little more effort I might have become a simultaneous translator at the United Nations. But my denial of German had by then gone too far. I never read any German books or newspapers and I lost touch with decades of development in the German-speaking realms. As for my reading in English, I had broadened out to a good knowledge of basic English fiction, poetry since Shakespeare, and modern American literature. I had, by then been an "American writer" for fifteen years, but after that short spurt of early success with the short stories, I had published nothing. Two finished novels and eight or more short stories lay dead in my files, and for the first time in my life I seriously considered giving up writing. Acting in a numb sort of desperation, I decided to take some college level courses and see what would happen.

Looking back on it, there is more than accident in the choice of the first course I was taking at the New School for Social Research. That institution, turned into a university-in-exile by refugee scholars in the late 1930s, is well known for the broad range of scholarship in its faculty. I selected a course in English grammar, taught by a Yugoslavian emigrant with an unpronounceable name. My husband thought I had temporarily lost my mind. As far as he could see I knew more about English grammar than anybody else he knew and why I wanted to take a course in it was beyond his understanding. He kept suggesting other nice courses I could take, but I was unresponsive. "I need to be absolutely certain I know the grammar," I explained lamely. "There are still a few things I'm unsure about and I'm tired of it."

There were seven students in the course, only two of them native-born Americans. The others were one Hispanic and three Chinese. The Americans were the poorest students, while one of the Chinese and I excelled. I enjoyed the course and it gave me a sense of competence and self-confidence which I had lost in my unsuccessful efforts as a writer. In some incomprehensible way it marked the close of one period of my life. The next course I took was in 17th-century British poetry, and after that I decided to resume my academic training and work toward a B.A. This led, by almost imperceptible small steps, to the decision to become a historian and therefore to graduate study. It took me four years of part-time study to earn the B.A. and three years of full-time study to earn the Ph.D. As I now see it, my mastery of the English language had to be followed by mastery of American history before I could truly cease being an immigrant. As a shining reward for all this strenuous effort my writing career began to flourish as soon as I was an academic. It was then by way of American History that I became a successful "American writer."

The story should close with this happy ending, but it does not.

In 1984 I was invited to participate in an international congress of women historians held in Vienna, my hometown. I accepted with many mental reservations and much anxiety. One aspect of it concerned language. I had been asked to offer two papers, but I felt so incompetent in German that I hired a student in the German department of my university to translate my speeches into German. These translations I read from the podium, feeling somewhat like an impostor. My conversational German seemed equally inadequate, since I lacked most of the vocabulary of my recently developed field, Women's History.

In 1986 my book *The Creation of Patriarchy* was published in Germany in translation. My contract with the publishers specified that I had the right to make editorial suggestions in regard to the translation. My editor and the translator were most generous in interpreting this right, and so it came about that I carefully edited the German version, first in manuscript and then again in galleys. The process was very difficult for me and renewed all my insecurities about my knowledge of German. I felt totally incompetent in the academic languages of the various fields on which the book is based—paleontology, anthropology, Ancient Near Eastern studies. Similarly, most of the words for concepts in feminist discourse of the past twenty years were unknown to me. So I sat, once more, surrounded by dictionaries, learning my own mother tongue all over again.

Yet there was something else happening. My "feel" for the language was quite intact and manifested itself in an uncanny sense of style. I always knew when something was wrong in a sentence, but, often, I did not know enough German to fix it. I worked closely with my patient and skillful translator, and I learned a lot in the process.

The publisher invited me for a two-week-long promotion tour in Germany after the book came out. This time, emboldened by the translation work, I decided to attempt to speak about my book in German. I did so with trepidation, and prepared for it as though I were lecturing in a foreign language. Every speech was written out in advance and I mentally prepared answers to the questions I expected would be asked. I always prefaced each public appearance with a statement, which served both as an explanation of my refugee status and as a hedge against linguistic failure. "You may wonder at my peculiar accent, and often at my choice of words. Although I am a native German speaker, I have not really spoken German in fifty years, and I have never before lectured in German." The audience response was good, even though there were moments when I had to use an English word and ask the audience to help me with the translation. After one lecture a woman came up to me and complimented me on my German. I thought she was merely being polite and demurred, but she insisted. "Of course you speak a competent German, but what I admire is that you speak the purest German I have ever heard." "Pure?" "Yes," she said, "uncorrupted by Nazi language and by all the abominations of modern usage." Rip Van Winkle, being complimented on his "pure" speech. How odd . . .

After that lecture tour my interest in German was revived. For the book on which I was then working, *The Creation of Feminist Consciousness,* I made use of many German sources, a few of them in medieval German. As I worked over these sources my old proficiency returned. After all, what I lacked was only the vocabulary of the past fifty years. By the time my work on the translation of the second book started, I felt quite adequate to the task. Now I had many more suggestions for my translator and most of them concerned style. The content was right, but the style was not mine, but hers. We worked on that and corrected it. When my work on the translation of the second book was finished I felt I was truly bilingual.

My new confidence found expression during my second book tour in Germany. While I again carefully prepared my lectures in writing, I soon felt free enough to answer all questions without preparation. In a three-week intense teaching situation in a German university, I taught with only an outline of notes in German, and finally, looking at some of my American teaching notes in English, I lectured in German from them.

The Nazis robbed me of my mother tongue, but the rest of the separation, of the violent severing of culture, was my own choice. My writing, my intense drive to become an "American writer" had pushed me into leaving the language of my childhood behind, never counting the cost. Through my writing, I had found the way back, but now the cost seems enormous. The return of the mother tongue has brought some healing of the other losses, but memory is different now. Before, what was lost, sank into a deep hole of oblivion—one covered it up and built anew forgetting the cost. Now memory includes what was lost and what it cost and what might have been had I been able to be a writer in my own language. Healing the split between feeling and thought, between the conscious learned faculties and the rich vibrations of the unconscious, I might have "tapped my way along the guiding rope of language" and found a richer, more poetic form for what I had to say. In translation, one becomes a trickster, too clever by far and too concerned with mastery. I envy those who live in the power of their own language, who were not deprived of the immediacy by which creativity finds its form.

There are works that cannot be translated. There are wounds that can never heal.

4

Of History and Memory

Käthe Leichter (1895–1942) was a Social Democratic activist and politician in the 1920s and 30s. She was a sociologist by training, a feminist, who devoted most of her life to researching and writing about working-class women and helping to organize them. During the years of clerical fascism in Austria (1934–38), which she spent partially in exile and partially at home, she organized an underground resistance movement. She continued this activity after the Nazi occupation of Austria. Betrayed by a comrade, she was arrested, tried and sent to the concentration camp Ravensbruck, where she continued to be an inspiration to her fellow inmates. She was gassed in 1942.

The State Prize in her name has annually been given to Austrian women historians, most of them quite young. I was the first Jewish refugee from Hitlerism to be awarded this honor, fifty years after my forced exile from Austria. I wrote the acceptance speech in German and translated it into English. This is the first time in fifty years I have written anything in German.

The prize with which you honor me today is doubly meaningful for me: because it honors women and research on women, and because it is given in the name of Käthe Leichter.

Käthe Leichter personifies the highest ideals of feminism—lifelong activity on behalf of all women, but especially of working-class women; conviction that social reforms are only just if they serve the interests of women as well as men; uncompromising struggle against fascism and National Socialism, which cost her her life. In Käthe Leichter's life there was no divide between theory and praxis: she combined her work as a journalist and organizer with her duties as mother and wife, her political leadership role with her research work as a social scientist. Käthe Leichter was heroic in her achievements, for she dared in a time of terror and oppression to organize resistance and to oppose the horrors of Nazi state power with the brave words of humanism on thin leaflets. It was for this she was jailed and finally gassed in the concentration camp Ravensbruck. In honoring other women we remember her and in a way continue her work and her ideals.

The letter which brought me the invitation to the prize award ceremony came from the Chancellor's office on No. 1 Ballhausplatz. The moment I read that address, I saw the square and the beautiful building in front of me, as it was then, in my childhood. And then another strong memory surfaced: on July 25, 1934, the day on which Austrian Nazis murdered Chancellor Dollfuss, I came home towards evening. I knew of the assassination only through the headlines of newspaper special editions. It was almost dark and in many apartments people had placed lighted candles in the windows, one candle to each window. It was done quite spontaneously; nobody organized it, it was simply that there were enough decent people who wanted to mourn and show their solidarity against the Nazi murderers. I remember being so moved that I cried, even though politically I did not agree with Chancellor Dollfuss, whom I regarded as the man who had killed democracy in February 1934 and paved the way for fascism. But the flickering candles in so many windows were a sign not only Engelbert Dollfuss had died, but also the future.

The next picture flashed before my eyes—the 11th of March 1938. That day the sun was shining and out of each window, in each house, the swastika flags were flying and I remembered the candles of that other time, four years earlier, and I knew it was the end, for me, for us Jews, for democracy and a free Austria. That time I did not cry, and not for a long time thereafter, because crying is something you cannot afford to do if you want to survive.

Käthe Leichter did not survive and my aunt, my mother's sister, Dr. Margrit Neuer, a Viennese physician who was gassed at Auschwitz, did not survive. I will not continue enumerating the dead, because it hurts too much. But it has to be said, when today one is celebrated and honored, our dead are always with us. We cannot forget them. I was supposed to perish, just like the others. The only reason I am here today is that, by chance, I was not killed then.

The ritual of awarding a prize in the name of a murdered dead heroine pushes us inexorably toward a consideration of memory and of collective memory through historical writing. Those of us who have experienced first-hand the storm of persecution and of race hatred and have survived it, carry the obligation of remembering it as a heavy burden all our lives. One cannot forget and one must not forget and one must be a witness. But my generation is quite old by now; in twenty years no eye-witnesses will be left. And our memories which we pass on to future generations like a poisoned gift hold a message which is already redundant—the message that in a society which legitimizes evil each human being is capable of committing monstrous deeds. World events, as we see them daily, on our TV screens illustrate the same message, perhaps more effectively than we can do it with our ancient tales. Rwanda and Bosnia, Kashmir and Chechnia—we watch the scenes of horror, we listen to the eye-witnesses and we turn away with the cynical thought that obviously nobody has learned anything from history.

But it is not the function of history to drum ethical lessons into our brains. History is the archives of human experiences and of the thoughts of past generations; history is our collective memory. The only thing one can learn from history is that actions have consequences and that certain actions and certain choices once made are irretrievable. As one can "forget" personal memories and by choosing what to remember—one selects what one *wants* to remembers and leaves out the rest—so it can be done with collective memory. Such collective forgetting of the dark side of events is hurtful to the individual as well as to the entire society, because one cannot heal nor can one make better decisions in the future, if one evades responsibility for the consequences of past actions.

The "great forgetting," selective memory, has a special significance for women. Women are half of humankind; they have always carried out half of the world's work and duties and they have been active agents in history. Yet in recorded history they have appeared only as "marginal" contributors to human development. What we see here is selective memory on the part of male historians which is grounded in the patriarchal values they hold. Such values make the activities of men appear as inherently more important and significant than the activities of women. War and politics are regarded as being more important in the history of humankind than the rearing of children. If one accepts such values as a given, then one commits the basic error of seeing the half as the whole and "forgetting" the other half. The consequence of such thinking is not only unjust to women, but, more importantly, it makes it impossible for women or men to reconstruct a truthful picture of the past.

Women have always lived in history, acted in it and made history. But the history of women was, up until about thirty years ago, distorted in a peculiar way: it came to us refracted through the lens of male observation and distorted through an interpretation based on patriarchal values. The new women's history has undertaken the task of reconstructing the missing half and of putting women as active agents into the center of events in order that recorded history might at last reflect the dual nature of humankind in its true balance, its female and its male aspects.

Women are not the only group which has been "forgotten" in recorded history. Ruling elites everywhere have selectively forgotten and historically marginalized members of the lower classes, slaves and proletarians and colonials. After liberation struggles, members of each group have reconstructed their own history and defined it anew. Seen historically, women are the one group which has remained longest in a subordinate status and which has taken longer than any other group to develop a liberation movement. Yet, within subordinate classes or castes, the position of women was always essentially different from the position of men of that group. Women always have been and are today paid lower wages than men, they are concentrated in occupations carrying low pay and low status; they are exploited as sex-workers and, everywhere, they are the majority of the poor.

When Käthe Leichter researched and wrote about working-class women she attacked both forms of discrimination—that against class and that against sex. Feminist history of the past thirty years continues this work, seeking a holistic worldview in which differences among people are recognized and respected and which records the commonality of human striving in all its variety and complexity. In remembering wholly, without selective forgetting, one can fight the system of distortions and half-truths out of which sexism, classism, racism and antisemitism grow like poisonous weeds.

Experiencing antisemitism and fascism led me to Women's History, for I learned first hand what it means to be defined as "the Other," the deviant. I was a respectable, bourgeois person, with class privileges, a good education, good prospects, a patriotic Austrian who loved Vienna and who considered Austrian culture a model for the world. And then, within weeks I was defined as a Jew, nothing else, "the Other," the outsider, and not much later simply as not more than vermin which could and should be destroyed. No more passport, no more citizenship, no country to which one belongs, suddenly one stands without identity outside of human society, without rights, without protection. Having experienced that one learns the power of social definitions, the power of ruling elites to construct groups as deviant. And one learns how such definitions can be arbitrarily affixed to various target groups—to women defined as biologically inferior, to certain races, certain religions, to foreigners, to those different from the norm. None of us is immune from such definitions. Regardless of the group to which we now belong, we will all at some time get old, or we might become physically impaired, or we might be considered suspect because we think differently than does the majority. Under such circumstances we, too, could become members of a target group defined by the young, the healthy, the majority. There is only one protection against this process of distancing and alienation and that is the understanding that we must abolish the complex system of deviance-formation, discrimination and stigmatization, in whatever form it may manifest itself.

Käthe Leichter remained a feeling, active human being to the last, in prison, in the concentration camp, a person who cared for others. She most likely could have saved her life by fleeing abroad at the time when she heard of her impending arrest. But when she learned that her sick mother was threatened by the Gestapo, she presented herself voluntarily to be arrested on the promise that her mother would be left unharmed. She was, and remains, an example for future generations.

My homeland, which fifty years ago exiled me as an outsider, branded subhuman and deviant, honors me today in the name of this great woman. I assume that such honor signifies new thinking, a search for an all-encompassing memory that includes the dark side with the light. In the name of the long-forgotten women of the past, for women's history and for the ideals of Käthe Leichter, I accept this prize with gratitude and a deep sense of obligation toward those who were forgotten, those who were exiled and hunted, and those who, in the darkest times, acted as human beings.

PART II

HISTORY: THEORY AND PRACTICE

5

Nonviolent Resistance:
The History of an Idea

The concept of nonviolent resistance in the 20th-century United States has been taught and practiced in the civil rights movement and the modern peace movement. In the media and the public mind the practice is generally linked with the names of Martin Luther King, Mohandas Gandhi and Henry David Thoreau. According to the general view, Thoreau furnished the ideas in his essay *Civil Disobedience*, which in time, influenced the two great practitioners of the concept, Gandhi and King. In fact, the history of the idea of nonviolent resistance is much more complex; its roots run deep in the American past; its practice was tested and developed in American soil before it traveled around the world and, almost a century later, returned to the ground from which it sprang.

"America has more often been the teacher than the student in the history of the nonviolent idea," Staughton Lynd states in the introduction to his documentary history of nonviolence.[1] Quite so. Nonviolent resistance, as idea and practice, was developed as much by American women as by men, a fact is seldom remembered in the historical account, where women nonresisters are usually described as followers of male leadership. In tracing the idea and its practice we will be tracing the continuity not only of men's but also of women's activism for social justice and peace for well over 150 years. Finally, there is a larger, more philosophical problem to be considered—how do ideas and political action interrelate? What is the connection between political theory and practice? Nonviolent resistance provides a good model with which to

This article was earlier given as the Harvey Wish Memorial Lecture at Case Western Reserve University on October 26, 1983. It is here printed in a revised form.

study the interaction of theory and practice, and patterns of continuity and rupture in the history of ideas.

The concept of nonviolent resistance to evil is common to Western and Eastern civilizations. It is grounded in the concept of nonresistance to evil that appears in the Old and the New Testament and in the Writings of the Buddha.[2] The terms "nonresistance" and "nonviolent resistance" have often been used interchangeably, but their meanings have, as we will see, undergone shifts in emphasis and have slightly diverged. Some Christians throughout the ages, suffered their bodies to be tortured and violated, accepting martyrdom in mute protest, motivated by their belief in the redemptive force of suffering. Members of most of the religions of the world have at one time or another suffered persecution, imprisonment, torture and death in witness to their faith. In the modern age the radical sects of the Protestant Reformation, with their emphasis on the authority and responsibility of the individual conscience, revitalized the tradition of the Christian martyrs. Some, like the Anabaptists, bore witness to the strength of their faith by stoic suffering in the face of torture and wholesale death. Others, like the Quakers, made suffering and patience under persecution an instrument for converting and influencing their neighbors.

Quakers formed the link between the European tradition and America. In 1656 Ann Austin and Mary Fisher arrived in Boston, determined to save the Massachusetts Bay Colony from sinfully false doctrine and, at the very least, to win toleration for the Quakers. They were promptly deported. More Friends arrived shortly after and openly carried the battle to the Puritans. Despite whippings, trials and increasingly severe punishment they held illegal meetings, distributed their tracts and attempted to preach. They refused to accept banishment, even on pain of death, and returned time and again to the Puritan Commonwealth.

Female Quakers were as assertive and persistent as their male counterparts. Mary Dyer stands chief among them. Born in England, she emigrated with her husband William and her children, and was admitted to a Boston church in 1635. When Ann Hutchinson was excommunicated from that church as a heretic, Mary Dyer was the only person to accompany her out of the building, for which she in turn was excommunicated. The family migrated to Rhode Island, where Dyer became a Quaker. She returned to Boston in 1657, determined to spread her belief and was imprisoned there. Her husband secured her release by promising to keep her out of harm's way until she left the colony. But Mary Dyer returned two years later and was banished once more from Boston under threat of execution, should she return. Feeling a strong call from God, she and two male Quakers returned within a month, determined peacefully to defy "the bloody law against heretics." They were all condemned to death and in October 1659 were led to the gallows through the streets of Boston. Mary Dyer was forced to watch the execution of the two men, then was given a pre-arranged reprieve, due to the intervention of the governor and her son William. Mary Dyer refused her reprieve, arguing instead "like Esther before Ahaverus" that they should repeal their unjust law. Still she was deported to Rhode Island. She was back in Boston in May 1660 "to offer up her life there." This time the death sentence was carried out and she was hanged "as a flag for others to take example by," bearing her witness in death. In her own words: "I came at the Lord's command and go at his command." Mary Dyer chose death as a means of advancing her faith nonviolently. She nearly succeeded. In Massachusetts only one Quaker was executed after her death, and then persecution of Quakers was ended by intervention of the Crown.[3] By 1675 Quakers were meeting freely in Boston—the Puritan colony had learned to tolerate "heretics," and nonviolent resistance had won a major victory.

A hundred years later the Quaker John Woolman set an example for all those bearing personal testimony against the evils of society. Traveling across the South he witnessed against slavery in a quiet personal way. His approach was inoffensive and his methods seemed, at first glance, singularly irrelevant. He reasoned with slaveholders; he tried to persuade them that slavery was sinful. When he stayed at their homes as a guest, he made it his business to give the master money to pay for the services of his slaves. "Conduct is more convincing than language," he said, and he became to hundreds of Southerners a living example of the power of a single righteous conscience. For John Woolman and Anthony Benezet their acts against slavery, their refusal to pay taxes during the French and Indian War, were highly personal expressions of intense religious belief. Their aim was the integration of belief and action, the teaching by example rather than by preachment. They succeeded at least in arousing the consciences of their co-religionists: by 1774 Quakers as a group had ceased holding slaves.[4]

The principle followed by Christian martyrs and Quakers was that of nonresistance to evil. The nonresister follows the Biblical precept "Resist not evil." Instead of resistance with anger and hatred, evil-doing is answered by love. This allows the evil-doer to experience love in his turn; at the very least it shames him into not responding with anger and hatred. The vicious cycle of hostile feelings is broken; the way is opened for reconciliation and redemption. The means, in this concept, loom as large as the end; evil means cannot possibly accomplish good ends.

The antislavery reformers of the 1830s followed in the Woolman tradition, yet in many ways they were a new breed. They shared the traditional view of evangelical reformers in regarding slavery as a sin, comparable to drunkenness and immorality. Since it was a sin there was hope that it could be ended by converting the sinner. Nothing would convert the sinner more readily than moral example, fervent prayer and the willingness to bear martyrdom on his behalf. These reformers lacked understanding of the complex economic and social roots of slavery and did not recognize the powerful interests in every part of the nation which had a stake in the survival of the South's "peculiar institution." But they did understand that to succeed they must create a movement capable of affecting political and legal changes in the nation's government. Abolitionists, in the age of Jackson, started on a new, seemingly doomed crusade to convert millions of non-slaveholding, indifferent, and frequently hostile Americans to their cause.

Their task was enormous and only persons of sturdy conviction would attempt it. The South no longer tolerated the kind of free expression on the slavery question that had existed in John Woolman's day. Northerners were divided and ambivalent on the issue and resented those who made them face it. The willingness to be martyred became more than a rhetorical commitment, it became a position which the individual abolitionist would have ample occasion to test in practice.

Mob attacks on abolitionist meetings were a commonplace occurrence in the North. It took state troops to end the 1834 riots in New York City, which were at first directed against abolitionists, then focused on local Negroes. A riot in Philadelphia left forty-five Negro homes destroyed, many persons wounded, one killed. Elsewhere, abolitionist speakers and organizers were stoned, tarred and feathered, beaten. Antislavery presses were destroyed, meeting halls burned to the ground; citizens sympathetic to these unpopular views were harassed, ostracized, sometimes driven out of town. It was in these years of struggle that abolitionists transformed the concept of nonresistance to evil from a personal, religiously inspired expression of moral conviction into a consciously developed tactic of the weak and outnumbered. Out of several years of pragmatic experience they developed a theory and deliberately applied technique, which became an important political instrument.

The key figure in this development was Theodore Dwight Weld, the "most mobbed man" in America of the 1830s. Weld, Marius Robinson, and Henry Stanton had spent a year "abolitionizing" Ohio, during which time they had had ample occasion to test the efficacy of nonviolent resistance as a political technique. Weld had experimented in village after village and found that a mob, no matter how incensed, would not attack a man who stood with his arms folded. His courage would usually arouse the curiosity of enough people who wanted to find out what manner of man this abolitionist was, so that another hearing would be secured to him. Once he had gained the right to speak, half the battle was won. His cool determination shamed some of his listeners, his arguments persuaded others. Inevitably, the mob helped to increase his audience.

An article in *The Anti-Slavery Record* of July 1836 generalized from this practical experience. Mobs, the article stated, usually were made up of respectable members of the community.

> The true originators of these mobs should be held responsible for them before the world. . . . There should be no unnecessary provocations [on the part of the abolitionists] . . .
>
> Abolitionists should never suffer themselves to be driven from a meeting by the menaces or the noise or the missiles of the mob. . . . Let them [the organizers of the mob] see that nothing short of slaughter will accomplish their purpose, and they will relinquish their wicked attempts.

Firmness in the face of threats demonstrated the seriousness and determination of the abolitionists. It would also discourage mobs from forming in the future. However, abolitionists were cautioned to remain nonviolent at all times.

> There should be no forcible resistance or menace of any kind.
> ... Let the mob have the credit for all the noise and disorder,
> while the friends of human rights retain their position with
> the calmness of reason. ...
>
> The threat of a mob should never prevent a meeting. When
> a right, and above all that right of rights, free discussion is
> called in question, then is the time to exercise it.[5]

The abolitionists had learned that mob action, when met by peaceful resistance, always generated conflict around the free speech question. Such conflict would tend to bring new adherents to the embattled cause and broaden the appeal of the abolitionist message.[6]

The observation was shrewd and its validity was frequently borne out by practical experience. In 1834, a Boston mob dragging William Lloyd Garrison through the streets with a rope around his neck, was observed by the young lawyer Wendell Phillips, offspring of a wealthy and respected family. He was so incensed by the sight that he joined in Garrison's defense and soon became one of the leading and most militant abolitionists. Similarly, the denial of a meeting place to the New York State Anti-Slavery Convention led the wealthy landowner Gerrit Smith to offer his estate to the delegates for their convention. He too, like many others, joined the movement as a result of his involvement with the defense of the civil rights of abolitionists.

In the course of organizing the Niagara County Anti-Slavery Society in upstate New York, Theodore Weld furnished another striking example of the effective use of nonviolence. An angry crowd, headed by the judge and the sheriff, had invaded the organizing meeting and insisted that Weld leave the county forthwith. The abolitionist refused and for four hours the opposition noisily held the floor, preventing the meeting from transacting any business. When their opponents' energies flagged, the abolitionists proceeded to organize their society, despite the presence of the hostile crowd. The job completed, Weld announced that, although earlier he had intended to leave right after the meeting, he had now decided to test the question

> whether they were slaves without rights or men with rights.
> ... Accordingly, with leave of divine Providence, he said he
> should lecture in that house on Monday at 2 o'clock P.M.—
> remarking that if the lecture passed off without interruption,

it would be his last, but if not he should stay in Lockport, and continue to plead for his constitutional liberty . . . till liberty or he was defunct.

The result was that a huge crowd turned out for the Monday meeting. After a long lecture by Weld, "four hundred and eighty new members" joined the abolition society. "There being no disturbances Weld lectured no more and soon left the place."[7]

A year later he was in charge of training a group of forty antislavery agents who would do organizing work throughout the East and Northwest. An important aspect of their training was discussion of the philosophy and practice of nonviolent resistance. Abolitionist thought and practice were influenced by the principles of the American peace movement, which began formally in 1815 with the founding of the peace societies in New York and Massachusetts. Peace activists worked for negotiated settlement of international disputes, for arbitration and the compensated emancipation of slaves.

Independently of them, but working often for the same practical goals, were advocates of nonresistance, who in 1837 formed the New England Non-Resistance Society. Deriving their ideas from the biblical precepts followed by Quakers and Antinomians, the nonresisters preached opposition to all human government and sought a new order of society which would give each individual absolute freedom. Their firm opposition to participation in politics, their refusal to vote, hold office or submit appeals to patriotism set them in opposition to most of their contemporaries, and even to such like-minded reformers as the American Peace Society. Yet their willingness to bear witness and—in their words—"to suffer martyrdom" for their beliefs gave moral force to their arguments for beyond the movement's organizational strength.

Several leading abolitionists, such as William Lloyd Garrison, Edmund Quincy, Maria Chapman and Henry C. Wright were active in the Non-Resistance Society. Although the society as such died out in 1849 its principles lived on. The chief advocate of its principles, who held fast to them during the Civil War, when most of the abolitionist nonresisters gave up theirs, was Adin Ballou. His writings had a powerful influence on future generations, as we shall see.[8]

Religious anarchism, the doctrine of the perfectibility of man and nearly eighty years of the practice of nonresistance and nonviolence by

Quakers and pacifists on American soil, inspired abolitionist tactics as developed in the late 1830s. As a tiny minority bent on converting a hostile or indifferent majority, abolitionists combined the moral strength supplied by religious nonresistance principles and the persuasive power of nonviolent means into a novel, highly flexible tactic. They did not regard their methods as passive, but saw them rather as active, but peaceful means of applying pressure in order to affect a change in the minds of men. Nonviolent resistance to mob action was one aspect of silent moral persuasion. This form of action was particularly suited to women, who were at that time excluded from participation in public affairs and were, as yet, unused to speaking in public. Antislavery women did, however, hold meetings. One of the first of these was the meeting of the Female Anti-Slavery Society in Boston, which was to become famous as the result of the attempted lynching of Garrison. The action of the women deserves at least as much attention as Garrison's ordeal. In the face of an armed and angry crowd, which demanded that they expel the Negroes present at the meeting, the women formed into an orderly procession, black and white women walking side by side through the mob, each woman looking directly into the face of one of the attackers as though to shame him. Their walk through the mob became a moral triumph instead of a retreat and they went unmolested to another place to continue their interrupted meeting.[9]

The Concord Female Anti-Slavery Society, one of the earliest of such societies organized, was proudly aware of this tradition. To this society belonged the female members of Henry Thoreau's household, his mother, aunt, sisters, several neighbors and house guests. One of his close friends, Nathaniel P. Rogers, was editor of the antislavery *Herald of Freedom*. Abolitionist literature was always available in the Thoreau household. The writer was familiar with the Christian anarchism of William Lloyd Garrison, Adin Ballou and Henry C. Wright. Antislavery thought and experience were a vital part of Henry Thoreau's life. Himself a man of practical bent, the pencil-maker and expert woodsman learned more from nature than from books, more from the actions of men than from their words. He braved public hostility in 1845 when he helped to secure a meeting hall in Concord for a scheduled lecture of the controversial Wendell Phillips. When, in 1847, he refused to pay his taxes in the celebrated protest against the Mexican War, he merely followed actions previously taken by Woolman, Benezet, Bronson Alcott and other abolitionists. Why then did this particular tax protest become known the world over—an act strong enough to inspire millions over a hundred years later?

Certainly not because of its practical significance or because it represented a particularly spectacular deed of heroism. Abolitionists had performed much more daring deeds without making a long-range impact; Thoreau himself showed much more courage and took greater risks when in later years he helped a fugitive slave on his way to Canada and, still later, when he defended John Brown publicly before Brown's execution. What made Thoreau's small act of nonviolent resistance so enormously important was, of course, not the act itself but the work of art it inspired. In his essay *Civil Disobedience*, Thoreau fashioned out of the common experience of his time and out of his deepest personal convictions an artistic and philosophical statement of lasting significance and social power.[10]

The idea depended for its spread and impact on the interaction of theory and practice. The essay reached the American public at a time when ideals of nonviolence were unable to compete successfully with the practice of violence in preventing civil war in Kansas and, finally, in the whole nation. With a very few exceptions, abolitionist pacifists reluctantly abandoned their principles to support the war to end slavery, while most Southerners took up arms in what they considered a defense of their homes and their way of life. The bloodshed of the Civil War and the defeat of Reconstruction might have furnished arguments in favor of pacifism, instead it merely contributed to the general war-weariness and disillusionment of the Gilded Age. Thoreau's essay was all but forgotten; the philosophy of nonviolence seemed outdated and irrelevant. We see here one of those examples of discontinuity in history, when ideas which agitated and stirred one generation seemingly sink without a trace.

Yet in distant Russia, despotism, economic misery and social conflict gave rise to various similar ideas and methods for attaining a better society. The doctrine of nonresistance to evil was restored to new life, both in thought and in practice, by Russia's greatest writer, Count Leo Tolstoy. And strangely, it was through his writings that the idea reached America once again.

When Tolstoy wrote his *What I Believe* in 1884, he had formulated his own philosophy of nonresistance from a close reading of the teachings of Jesus, especially the Sermon on the Mount. In arguments which closely resembled those of English and American sectarians and non-resisters, Tolstoy gave a literal reading to the passage, "Resist not evil," from which he formulated a guide for practical living designed to spread love, social justice, and harmony. Tolstoy began to share his inherited wealth with the peasants on his estate; he lived simply by engaging in manual labor, pledged absolute fidelity to his wife and abjured the sensual pleasures taken for granted by men of his class. The results of his experiment do not so much concern us here as does the origin of his ideas. Tolstoy himself wrote later that, in developing his theories he knew "very little of what had previously been done and preached and written on the subject of non-resistance to evil."[11] His book reached America and, in response, he was sent information by American Quakers as to their beliefs. The son of William Lloyd Garrison sent Tolstoy his father's letters and a "Declaration of Sentiments" adopted by the Peace Convention held in Boston in September of 1838, which spelled out the doctrine of "non-resistance to evil" in detail. "Garrison was the first to proclaim this principle as a rule for the organization of man's life," Tolstoy acknowledged, and described the "spiritual joy" with which he discovered the existence of kindred thinkers in Garrison, Ballou and the earlier pacifist William Dymond.[12] Later in his life Tolstoy added to the list of Americans who had influenced him, the names of Emerson, Thoreau and Walt Whitman, among others. He was also influenced in his economic views by Henry George's *Progress and Poverty*.[13]

In turn, Tolstoy exerted a considerable influence on American intellectuals, and his ideas inspired a revitalization of the American peace movement. That movement had persisted organizationally in the American Peace Society (1865–85) and the somewhat more radical Universal Peace Union. American feminists took the lead in attempting to organize a women's international peace organization, first in 1870, again in 1872. Such an organization finally came into existence in 1891.

While the American peace movement maintained organizational continuity it lacked vigor and popular appeal. These were supplied by Tolstoy's literary and philosophical writings which reached America between 1885 and 1890. A generation of progressive reformers, such as William Dean Howells, Edward Everett Hale, Ernest Howard Crosby, Jane Addams, William Jennings Bryan and Clarence Darrow credited him with inspiring their pacifist beliefs and practice. Howells said about Tolstoy: "His writings and his life have meant more to me than any other man's. . . . It has been his mission to give men a bad conscience, to alarm and distress them in the opinions and conventions in which they rested so comfortably."[14] He inspired Howells to protest against the death sentences given to seven radicals unjustly accused of responsibility for the Chicago Haymarket massacre in 1886. The Unitarian minister Edward Everett Hale was inspired by Tolstoy's work to form a Tolstoy Club, which later developed into a settlement house. Hale and Ernest Howard Crosby became the chief popularizers of Tolstoyan principles in the United States. Tolstoy's pacifism, which had profoundly influenced William Jennings Bryan, led Bryan to pursue a sincere search for a peaceful foreign policy in his position as Secretary of State in Woodrow Wilson's first administration. In a display of pacifist spirit, unprecedented for one holding such high diplomatic office, he resigned his post in protest over President Wilson's belligerent response to the sinking of the *Lusitania*.

Another progressive reformer who was greatly influenced by Tolstoy's principles was the lawyer Clarence Darrow, whose book, *Resist Not Evil* spread the doctrine of anarchist nonviolent resistance. But Darrow's pacifism, like that of many of his contemporaries, collapsed with the outbreak of World War I.[15]

It was Jane Addams, the founder of Hull House in Chicago, who most consistently carried Tolstoyan ideas into practice. Addams had visited Tolstoy in Russia and was a lifelong admirer of his work. She well understood the practical implications of his ideas, which she expressed as follows: "Tolstoy would make non-resistance aggressive. He would carry over into the reservoirs of moral influence all the strength which is now spent in coercion and resistance."[16] In his spirit, she advocated "a newer humanitarianism," aggressive in its pursuit of social welfare and international in its reach, as a moral equivalent for war.[17] Addams steadfastly carried these convictions into practice in her peace activities during World War I and her leadership in the postwar Women's International League for Peace and Freedom. She suffered ostracism, vilification and isolation for her pacifism, but she was one of a handful of people who kept the idea and tradition alive in a time of conformity and reaction.

On the other hand, the practice of nonviolent resistance had grown steadily with the growth of the labor movement with its mass strikes and boycotts. Another example of the idea in action was furnished by the militant suffragists during World War I with their mass demonstrations, their picket vigils and their hunger strikes in prison. War resisters during that war, a tiny but staunch band, also rediscovered in practice the tactical usefulness of nonviolent resistance in behalf of the weak and outnumbered. We may say the practice lived on while the idea was subject to a sharp rupture in continuity between the two world wars. Even the post-Depression resurgence of tactics such as the sit-in strikes of the 1930s did not outweigh the impact of Marxist class-struggle ideology and of the prevailing temper of antifascist militancy. Thoreau's ideas seemed slightly irrelevant in the United States of the 1930s. And what nonviolent practice did exist was divorced from theory.

But once again the idea lived on in another part of the world. In South Africa, in 1907, the young Mohandas Gandhi was organizing Indian residents to resist racial oppression. He would later explain:

> My first introduction to Thoreau's writing was, I think, in 1907, or later, when I was in the thick of the passive resistance struggle. A friend sent me the essay on *Civil Disobedience*. It left a deep impression on me. I translated a portion for the readers of *Indian Opinion* in South Africa, which I was then editing.[18]

Gandhi's political practice was determined by his own grounding in the philosophy and teachings of the Buddha. Thoreau's essay provided him with a philosophical statement and a method of struggle grounded in conditions very similar to those he faced in South Africa. Later, in India, he would meet the challenge of organizing a majority of powerless people against a small, but very powerful, group of rulers. Gandhi transformed the Thoreauvian concepts into the tactics and philosophy of a mass movement, transmuted them and infused them with new life. The Indian struggle for independence became the world's proving ground for the effectiveness of the methods of nonviolent resistance in political practice. But it was now a changed theory.[19]

For centuries individuals had asserted the right and duty of placing their own consciences above the will of the majority, even, at times, above the law. A righteous man must resist an evil system by withdrawing his active support from it, Thoreau had declared and predicted confidently that such resistance, even by a minority, would stop the machinery of government. But neither in his own time nor later was this prediction to be realized in his own country. Gandhi furnished the world with proof of the revolutionary potential of nonviolent resistance, provided it became a flexible and consciously used tactic. He transformed the concept of nonresistance to evil into the tactic of *resisting* evil *nonviolently*. This was the same concept Jane Addams had read into Tolstoy's teaching—to make "non-resistance aggressive." Thoreau, Tolstoy and some of his American followers had already given voice to that idea in their writings. American abolitionists had experimented with some success with the practice, but it was left to Gandhi to explore fully its tactical implications in both theory and practice. The difference was in numbers. Nonviolent resistance, when used by the minority, could stir up consciences, advance the raising of issues and might even secure some reforms. When used by the majority against a small ruling group, the method had revolutionary potential. Gandhi's ideas became an inspiration for oppressed groups in many parts of the world.

And so, in the 1950s, the theory and practice of American abolitionists came home by way of India. It happened during the Montgomery, Alabama, bus boycott. The idea of boycotting the buses had originated with some members of a Negro women's organization and had been adopted by community leadership with enthusiasm. When notice of the proposed boycott reached the white community, a newspaper editorial accused the Negroes of using a method which had previously been used by the White Citizens Council to defeat integration.

"Disturbed by the fact that our pending action was being equated with the boycott methods of the White Citizens Council, I was forced for the first time to think seriously on the nature of the boycott," wrote Dr. Martin Luther King, Jr. He came to conclusion that the word "boycott" was a misnomer. What was being proposed in Montgomery was not so much economic pressure as the withdrawing of "cooperation from an evil system." At this point, Dr. King remembered Thoreau's essay *Civil Disobedience*, which had moved him deeply when he had first read it as a college student. "I became convinced that what we were preparing to do in Montgomery was related to what Thoreau had expressed . . . From that moment on, I conceived of our movement as an act of massive non-cooperation."[20]

About a week later, with the bus boycott in full swing, a white woman pointed out another parallel. In a letter to the editor of the local paper she compared the bus protest to the movement of Mohandas Gandhi in India. The idea caught on.

> People who had never heard of the little brown saint of India were now saying his name with an air of familiarity. Nonviolent resistance had emerged as the technique of the movement, while love stood as the regulating idea. In other words, Christ furnished the spirit and motivation, while Gandhi furnished the method.[21]

It is fascinating to notice that in the Montgomery boycott the various strands and origins of the idea of nonviolent resistance fused into a newly invigorated practice and theory of immense power. Dr. Martin Luther King, Jr., although he credited his formulation of "massive non-cooperation" to Thoreau, had been exposed to pacifist thought during his studies under the pacifist Allen Knight Chalmers, who was a Gandhian. Another long-time pacifist, Bayard Rustin, secretary of the Fellowship of Reconciliation since 1935, and later secretary of the War Resisters League, was one of the chief tacticians and organizers of the Montgomery boycott.[22] It was he who counseled the use of nonviolent means at the outset of the boycott. Finally, probably unknown to most of the actors in the drama, there was a precedent for a bus boycott by a black community in the example of the 1892 Memphis, Tennessee, boycott of streetcars by the black community to protest a lynching. This boycott was actively supported by Ida B. Wells-Barnett and was, according to her account, highly effective.[23]

From the early antislavery movement to the mass movement of black men and women, students and pacifists in America of the 1960s the idea of nonviolent resistance has come full circle. The continuity of ideas transcends time and space. Practical experience continuously regenerates ideas which, in turn, have the power to inspire and create a new reality. The abolitionists' and early pacifists' practice could not influence wide circles without the creative impact of individual writers like Thoreau and Tolstoy. Impressed by the practice and reality of their day, these writers transformed it creatively into ideas they shaped in their writings. These ideas in turn, inspired the practical political work of new generations. Mohandas Gandhi lifted the theory to new levels in the test of his practical experience. Martin Luther King, Jr., reached for the appropriate theory, when his practice demanded it and, again, generated a new level of thought and practice, adapted to modern needs.

The fusion of theory and practice expressed in the Montgomery bus boycott inspired a generation of nonviolent resisters who understood that moral force, turned against the aggressor, can become a powerful force for liberation. Once again, with the violence against black and white leaders committed to integration, in the late 1960s, there seemed to occur a rupture, a drawing back, a cultural "forgetting." Yet nonviolent resistance, as idea and practice, has perhaps never been stronger than it is today, as expressed in the world peace movement. Violence and the weapons of violence have reached such proportions that the existence of the earth itself and of all human beings on it is threatened. Perhaps, the idea of a nonviolent alternative, which has such complex and deep roots in the American past, will finally become a liberating concept of our present and future.

6

American Values

In 1620 Virginians met in the first constitutional assembly in the New World, the House of Burgesses. The same year the first African slaves were sold in Virginia. Thus, the establishment of democratic government and the establishment of slavery coincided. These facts are emblematic of the way American values tended to develop in sharply opposed directions.

The very term "American values" embodies several unstated assumptions that represent negative values. One is implied in the use of the term "American" for what should after 1774, actually be "United States"—it is the presumption of U.S. hegemony, by which we make other entities on the American continents invisible. Also there is the unspoken assumption that all "Americans" hold the same values, an assumption by which cultural, racial, ethnic and sexual pluralism is denied. We must begin then by finding a definition for our discussion which does not exclude significant portions of our population from consideration and which does not imply white, male middle-class hegemony over ideas and values.

I will examine "American values" as the values consistently held by large numbers of citizens of the United States of America over a long period of time and I will consider them in terms of pairs of opposites, namely: equality and racism; federalism versus imperialism; individualism and community; open access to opportunity versus elitism and

This article was a contribution to the "American Values" project of the American Jewish Committee, Skirball Institute of Jewish Studies, 635 S. Harvard Blvd., Los Angeles, CA 90005–2511. The project sought to understand the changes and challenges in American values, and the organization used the papers for an educational project on this topic. The paper was commissioned in 1987 and is here reprinted in a revised form.

meritocracy; pluralism versus nativism and racism; faith in technology and unlimited exploitation of natural resources versus conservation and respect for the ecosystem.

By viewing these values in terms of opposites we recognize that for almost every category defined as a universally held value there can be found an opposing value held by a large number of citizens. One of the very basic American values, commitment to a free marketplace of ideas, has led to the coexistence of contrasting and often conflicting viewpoints.

Equality and Racism

Americans have defined equality as the absence of inherited rank and privilege, embodied in the assumption that "all men are created equal" and ever since the adoption of the Constitution, they have taken for granted that political institutions should reflect the equality of all citizens. Some have equated such equality with personal liberty; others with equality of opportunity. The varying concepts embody many contradictions and tensions, but observers and historians have generally agreed that a belief in equality and democracy is a fundamental American value.

Political democracy and racism were institutionalized contemporaneously on the North American continent. From the days of the earliest settlement on, the religious and political ideals of European settlers were in contrast to and in tension with the values and interest of Native Americans, the Hispanic people already settled on the continent and the black slaves forcibly imported from Africa. The Christian churches were too weak and scattered to play the kind of mediating role by which in South America native interests were supported by the Catholic Church. Notions of white superiority brought to the U.S. colonies by the earliest settlers reinforced self-interest to assure that the servitude of African peoples would develop into a system of slavery, whereas the indentured servitude of Europeans would be temporary and lead to upward mobility and social equality. The contradictions between the Christian ideal of white masters and the Christianity of the black men and women they held as slaves were mediated by the racist conviction of the masters that colored people—African-Americans as well as Native Americans—existed on a lower level of civilization than whites and would benefit from servitude and close supervision.

During the period of the writing and adoption of the Constitution the contradictions between libertarian-humanitarian political ideas and the continuation of slavery found expression in sharp conflict between Northern and Southern states. The uneasy compromise regarding slavery embodied in the Constitution laid the basis for the continuation of this conflict well into the 19th century. The abolition of slavery in all of the Northern states after the American Revolution led to the development of two regions as distinct in economic and political interest as they were in culture and values. Regional conflict over slavery became polarized during the antebellum period, making the Civil War virtually inevitable.

While this tragic war once and for all settled constitutional questions of national versus state rights and assured the nationalizing of the United States, it left the essential conflict between democracy and racism unresolved. The end of Southern slavery nationalized racism and brought about its appearance in a variety of new forms, such as state laws disfranchising Blacks in the South in the last decades of the 19th century. The fact that the Civil Rights Act of 1964, although more far-reaching than the earlier legislation, had to enact anew statutes already made law by the Civil Rights Act of 1875 illustrates the persistence and tenacity of racism in U.S. life.

The constant struggle of black Americans for equality and the contradictions of the United States fighting two World Wars for liberty and equal justice, while denying them to African-Americans at home, increased white awareness of racism in the 20th century. The struggles of the civil rights movement of the 1960s challenged racist beliefs and created unbearable tensions between the two opposing traditions of political democracy and racism, with the result that important reforms were enacted with wide popular support. Yet, three decades later many of these reforms are under attack once again. The tension between the polar opposites continues.

In regard to the liberties of Native Americans the record is bleaker. During the 19th century, the relentless expulsion of Native Americans from their ancestral lands and confinement in a few Western enclaves called reservations were, like slavery, based on notions of white supremacy neatly bonded to the economic self-interest of whites. In the 20th century, while treaty rights have been restored to some tribes, the plight of Native Americans and its roots in past injustices have been largely forgotten.

Federalism versus Imperialism

The Constitution of the United States set forth the principles of federalism in its creation of a two-chamber legislature, its various provisions defining the rights of the several states and in the Tenth Amendment to the Constitution. Equally important was the way in which the Northwest Ordinance of 1787 laid down the principles for territorial expansion westward. When there were 5000 settlers (free adult males) in a territory they were to establish a legislature; when the population had reached 60,000 they might constitute themselves a state and be admitted to the Union "on an equal footing with the original states in all respects whatsoever." This principle, in its day quite revolutionary among nations, clearly implied that there was to be no hierarchical ranking among the states in the Union. Those admitted last would have all the rights of the earliest members of the Union; no state would have hegemony over another.

This important concept of democratic growth among equals was opposed to another value embodied in American historical development since the days of the American Revolution which has variously been labeled sense of mission, Manifest Destiny and imperialism. It held that Americans, by their nature, genius, religion and Constitution were entitled to leadership and hegemony over surrounding nations. Individual advocates of the concept emphasized different degrees of obligation toward those other countries. The U.S. mission might be to Christianize the heathen in the process of colonial settlement; to modernize the underdeveloped (as in Latin America, Puerto Rico, Hawaii); to protect populations from the incursions of socialism or communism in countries deemed in need of such protection (Korea, Vietnam, Nicaragua). Advocates of this concept were in sharp conflict with advocates of the principles of federalism and equality, who, beginning with the Spanish-American war, advocated limits to and constraints upon expansionism in whatever name. This conflict is alive and well, although expressed in somewhat different language in the politics and foreign policy issues of our own time.

Individualism versus Community

From the earliest days of settlement on, easy access to cheap land, the absence of constraining feudal institutions and the availability of plentiful natural resources fostered the development of American individualism. The existence, for nearly two hundred years, of a westward moving frontier enhanced the development of self-reliant, assertively independent men. (The commonly made generalization about this being an "American" characteristic disregards the existence of women, whose development toward individualism would have to await the 20th century.) The rugged individualist of the frontier, the Transcendentalist philosopher, the utopian radical, the entrepreneur, the self-made captain of industry, the gun-toting hero of Westerns—all represent this type of American hero.

But the conditions that made for American individualism also made for its opposite—community. Pilgrims and Puritans, Quakers and sectarians, Jews and Huguenots, all depended for their survival on the communities they planted in the wilderness or constituted in the towns and cities. And on the frontier, the ruggedly individualistic fur traders and buffalo hunters blazed the trail for the settled communities of farmers. While individualism was observed as mostly a male phenomenon, it was in the founding and maintaining of communities that American women made their most important and constructive contributions to American development.

This set of opposite values has also given us opposing traditions in regard to solving social problems: individual and communal. Individual solutions to social problems have found expression in innovation, entrepreneurship and politics. In modern society this took the form of resistance to the expansion of state power over individuals, the turning over of federal powers to the states, a resurgence of 19th-century rugged individualism as against the ideology of the welfare state and in the self-centered perfectionism of the "me-first" generation.

The long American tradition of communal solutions for social prob-

lems goes back to the earliest communities with their family-based welfare system, their ethic of social responsibility, their voluntary
organizations to solve a broad range of societal problems. Alexis de
Tocqueville noted the propensity of Americans for joining organizations
and saw in it one of the guarantees for a functioning democracy. The
dis-establishment of religion, which in practice meant a proliferation of
competing beliefs and churches, had as one of its byproducts the spread
of voluntaristic effort for community betterment. Whether prompted by
evangelical fervor and the perception that this activity would ensure one's
own salvation or whether inspired by the need for mutual support centered on a church group, the voluntary movement began in the churches,
largely staffed by women. Throughout the 19th century it spread into
the broader community and was soon one of the major problem-solving
innovations of American society. In the 20th century, voluntary groups
continued to perform these functions with re newed vigor, although
often in new forms, such as community-based drug and rape-crisis centers, self-help groups of people afflicted with various addictions, grass-
roots advocacy groups with a broad range of issues. Voluntarism has
provided one of the strongest checks upon the power of bureaucratic
government and has continued, over the centuries, to refresh the soil
out of which grass-roots political movements could rise.

The tension between individualism and community has also found
expression in the conflict between autonomy and conformity in Amer
ican life. "Don't tread on me," the slogan of the Vermont volunteers
in the American Revolution, expresses this type of American individualism succinctly. The right to privacy and to the inviolability of one's
home and property, the right to bear arms in self-defense, the right
against unauthorized searches, the right against self-incrimination,
these and others embodied in the Bill of Rights express the quintessen-
tially American concept of personal liberty. Liberty is specifically
defined in terms of limits set upon authority and state power and sur-
rounds the individual with a precinct of free space in which to "pursue
happiness" according to his or her own lights. Implicit in this concept
is the obligation to respect the rights, the free space, of others, which
of course proves much more problematic.

Historically, the concept of personal liberty originated in a period
and a society that took communal and religious constraints for granted.
Those who in their expression of personal liberty deviated from com-

munity standards soon found themselves outcasts, such as Anne Hutchinson, Roger Williams and, later, Southern advocates of abolition such as the Grimké sisters and James Birney. In the 20th century, with the erosion of religious and communal constraints on individual behavior and the definition of sexuality as a form of self-expression, the issues surrounding this concept of individual liberty have become ever more complex and controversial.

Personal liberty has also been defined as the quest for autonomy. Liberty is not only the right to be free from interference by others, but also the right to define—define oneself, one's group of affiliation, one's mode of expression. Although this issue has come to the fore most explicitly in the 20th century, it was anticipated by radicals of various sorts in earlier periods. The insistence of sectarians, Quakers for one, on autonomy of self-definition and on rights such as the right to refuse to bear arms or swear oaths, appeared as early as the 1650s in a form found to be heresy in the Puritan commonwealth. The rights of religious sectarians, of Jews, of Catholics, of Mormons became focal points of vexing controversy throughout the 18th and 19th centuries. Members of ethnic groups wanting cultural self-definition, often in the form of the right to use their own language, clashed both with Anglo-Saxon native-born citizens who felt entitled to exercising hegemony over immigrants and with earlier immigrants of their own ethnic group who desired conformity and assimilation. In the 20th century similarly divisive issues have been articulated by members of racial and ethnic minority groups, by women and by homosexuals.

The other side of the dyad, conformity, has helped to bond people into communal structures in the absence of formal and coercive institutions. Foreign observers, from the early 19th century on, noted the tendency of Americans to be both individualistic and conformist, as shown in their outer-directed personalities, their desire to be accepted and to "fit in." Historians and sociologists have explained this phenomenon as being due to the openness and newness of American society, the absence of hierarchical institutions that channel individuals and offer them security, due to upward social mobility, and the availability of horizontal physical mobility across the land on an open frontier. Last, they have pointed to the personal insecurity fostered by rapid social change, mobility and modernization as causes for a desire for conformity.

The pressures toward conformity have often in history led to excesses of bigotry and nativism, such as the 17th-century witchhunts, the rioting and assaults against abolitionists in the 19th century, the persecutions of Catholics, Irish, Blacks, Chinese and other ethnic minorities, the persistence of antisemitism, the assaults upon trade-unionists throughout the Progressive period, the Palmer raids and deportations of alleged anarchists in the 1920s, witchhunting and McCarthyism of the 1950s and the mass hysteria directed at opponents of the Vietnam war in the 1960s. In the modern period, the spread of mass media has made cultural conformity a close ally of consumerism, to the point where being opposed to consumer culture may mark a person as a non-conformist.

Open Access to Opportunity versus Elitism

In the first 150 years of settlement the existence of easily accessible open land provided the actuality of open access to economic opportunity for most white men and women. While there were from the beginning great differences in wealth, income and health standards, living conditions in the colonies were generally superior to those of Europe. With improved living conditions came an undercutting of the institutional constraints that had reinforced European class barriers. There were fixed time limits to indentured servitude but even with them it was difficult for masters to hold recalcitrant servants and apprentices to their contracts, when the open frontier beckoned the enterprising. By the time of the American Revolution, the colonies could be described as composed of yeoman farmers, artisans, workingmen and a thin layer of wealthy merchants and planters at the top, provided one was willing to ignore the existence of Blacks and Native Americans and failed to count women as citizens.

After the adoption of the Constitution and the Bill of Rights, when the principles of equal citizenship had become a birth right of white American males of all classes, equal access to economic opportunity became a powerful political issue. It was expressed in the early 19th century in the struggles around banking, government support of private enterprise, the rights of laboring men in the Jacksonian era, the establishment of public schools, and opposition to corporations. For those at the bottom of the economic ladder, access to education, to credit, to capital and to free markets became rallying cries.

One can view the struggles for an extension of the ballot to the property-less, to women and to African-Americans, and for the extension of education, as struggles of out-groups for equal access to opportunity. In the 20th century many of the issues around which the civil rights movement rallied were of this nature. American women have been engaged in a 175-year-long struggle for equal educational opportunities, which has taken ever-changing forms to overcome constantly shifting obstacles. It is not ended as of this day, as long as hiring and salary differentials in academic employment continue. For minority groups, the quest for open access has meant fighting overt and covert discrimination, educational tracking, discriminatory standards of testing and admission. Recently, the issue has emerged with particular bitterness in regard to seniority rights and affirmative action.

Elitism, the polar opposite of "open access," has respectable and ancient antecedents. Colonial gentry, landed proprietors and the clergymen holding a monopoly of knowledge sought to confine their privileged status to a small elite by setting up obstacles to open access. The sons of the elite were educated in England until several colleges for the education of ministers were established in the colonies in the 17th and 18th centuries. Church and pauper schools, while providing rudimentary instruction in the three R's, did not provide the children of non-elites access to more advanced knowledge, and women's education was further restricted to a few months' of learning each year in Dame schools. In the Southern colonies the absence of public taxation for schools undergirded the development of sharp distinctions of class and status and upheld the planter elite's domination of economics and politics in the region. From the 1830s on to the present, recent immigrant groups, racial minorities and women have had to struggle for equal access to education. When such access could no longer be denied, elites rallied in "defense of excellence." This implied that excellence was more likely to be found among members of elites than among the rest of the population. Advocates of open access considered such an implication profoundly undemocratic, but it persisted with remarkable tenacity, shifting its objects as democratic inroads were made upon educational privilege. Thus, the charge of women's mental inferiority, which upheld male "excellence" in the 19th century, was abandoned in the 20th century in regard to general education, but surfaced in allegations of women's inability to do hard sciences or be the equal of the male professoriate in universities. Where learned opinion in the 19th century could offer "scientific" explanations for the African-American's mental inferiority, the 20th century constructed elaborate theories of cultural and environmental conditioning to maintain elitism.

In contemporary America, with ever increasing government bureaucracies holding power in society and impinging upon the personal liberties of individuals, the concept of meritocracy has displaced the no longer fashionable advocacy of elitism. Supposedly scientific measurement and objective testing are to assure "standards" of merit in public employment and in advancement. In the name of such meritocracy affirmative action goals which would compensate formerly disadvantaged groups for past discrimination have been declared discriminatory themselves and have been the focus of much social conflict.

Elites in America have a long history of success in pitting underprivileged minorities and recent immigrant groups against one another. Nineteenth-century employers were able to delay unionization and the enactment of welfare legislation by such tactics, which continued into the 20th century. The mass migration of impoverished black tenant farmers to the industrial cities of the North in the period from 1912 to the 1940s had the same effect of delaying unionization due to race prejudice. In urban politics, ever since the Progressive period, immigrant groups have become integrated into the economic and political system by gaining entry into local government and into schools, police and welfare bureaucracies. Frequently, in this process recent arrivals are pitted not against representatives of the old elites, which by then had moved upward, but against the group which had most recently worked its way into local power. Thus, in contemporary America, we have seen Jewish and African-American groups pitted against one another in the battle of affirmative action versus meritocracy, which has been presented in the media mostly in racial terms. This is evidence much less of a racial conflict than it is the traditional way by which minority groups integrate into U.S. society. It is a matter of demography, of location and of history. The issues are old; the patterns are repetitive. The conflict and tensions over open access versus elitism are engines of progress in American history, designed to incorporate each new group of immigrants and minorities into the American economy and polity.

Pluralism versus Nativism and Cultural Hegemony

At the time Spaniards, Frenchmen and Englishmen first settled the North American continent, Amerindians had been living there for thousands of years. When the colonies that would later become the United States of America were being founded, the presence of African slaves made the society multiracial and multi-ethnic. Notwithstanding this historic reality, pluralism, as a positive value held by large numbers of Americans did not appear until the end of the 19th century. In the earliest centuries the conviction that white Anglo-Saxon Americans and all Euro-Americans were superior in culture and civilization to other peoples formed the bedrock of popular opinion and of politics. Even those actively working for the abolition of slavery and for the rights of American Indians did so out of a dedication to abstract principles of justice and equity. Their underlying assumption, as that of their contemporaries, was that white Christian Anglo-Saxon Americans would lead the "inferior" races and cultures toward a gradual advance in civilization and with it to the privileges of citizenship. This view was challenged by the arrival of large masses of European immigrants in the last decades of the 19th century which raised the question of their integration into society to a major political issue. Would assimilation of disparate and dissimilar elements of immigrants proceed on the principle of the "melting pot"? Would it proceed on the principle of the "salad bowl"? These metaphors define burning political issues, which in many ways still face us unresolved in today's world. One of the possible solutions to the dilemma—assimilation or cultural separatism—was pluralism.

Euro-Americans much earlier had actually adopted pluralism in the Constitution. The dis-establishment of religion embodied in the First Amendment of the Bill of Rights made a revolutionary break with then current practice in Europe. The dis-establishment of religion guarded

American citizens against a state-sponsored church by expressly forbidding the state to support an establishment of religion or to favor one church over another. Thus, it guaranteed religious pluralism, the coexistence and free marketplace competition of various churches, each free from state support or interference.

Religious pluralism, as it manifested itself throughout the 19th century, led to a proliferation of churches and sects, a dynamic growth in church building and in church-related organizations, a grass-roots movement which checked the tendency of the larger and more prosperous churches to dominate community life. Still, religious pluralism rested upon the hegemony of religious over non-religious belief systems and of Christianity over other religions. Thus, the nation developed as a nation of persons religiously affiliated and predominantly Christian in their affiliation.

There was no fundamental law or constitutional provision to guarantee the peaceful and democratic coexistence of Americans of different races and different ethnic backgrounds. Quite the contrary, the way immigration structured the assimilation of succeeding waves of immigrants into the culture and the body politic maximized conflict. The process began with the immigration of the Irish in the 1840s. As would be the case with succeeding groups, the new immigrants were placed at the bottom of the economic ladder, surrounded by prejudice and hemmed in by discriminatory restrictions. Their entry into the workforce guaranteed the upward mobility of older immigrant groups and their fierce competition with the then lowest-placed group on the economic ladder, free black workers. The pattern would be repeated with increasing intensity. The upward mobility of native-born and assimilated older immigrant groups was made possible by the masses of new immigrants willing to take the bottom-range jobs.

One of the first signs of Americanization for any European immigrant group was to put them into competition with native-born African-Americans and in turn participating in discrimination against them. Education, enlightenment and political sophistication have not essentially altered this pattern in the 20th century. Pluralism and hegemony have long been coexisting tendencies in American life, and have often overlapped in the values of particular groups. Irish, Jews, African-Americans and Hispanics have been firmly dedicated to pluralism, when they found themselves discriminated against and surrounded by culturally created obstacles; but members of these groups have just as firmly adhered to notions of hegemony when they have finally made it into the middle class and the existing political power structure.

Faith in Technology and Unlimited Exploitation of Natural Resources versus Conservation and Respect for the Ecology

American faith in progress has rested upon confidence in the superiority of American technology and unlimited access to natural resources. From the days of the open frontier on, Euro-Americans have decimated forests, exhausted the soil and moved westward to "better" land, slaughtered animals for their furs and their meat, scarred the landscape with open mines and mountains of sludge, and left desolate mining towns for more promising regions of despoilment. They have polluted the air and the rivers and lately, as the result of nuclear technology and the widespread use of chemicals and plastics, they have poisoned the ground and water with waste products of their industrial and technological progress.

True, such carelessness and disregard for limits are characteristic not only of Americans, but of all people in modern technological societies. But on this vast continent, with its long history of freedom from the ravages of war, the disregard for the finiteness of natural resources occurred on a more monumental scale and with perhaps greater intensity than in places where the threat of war and resource shortage was part of the experience of each generation.

In contrast to this set of attitudes and values is the long tradition of Native Americans whose respectful attitude toward the earth and the ecosystem is part of their religious worldview. The skills of former slaves, who learned to live off the land, make use of what others waste and, in the notable case of Dr. George Washington Carver, turn other people's weeds into marketable profit, were of a similar kind. There was also the tradition of newly arrived peasant peoples, with their thrift, their conservative methods of horticulture, their domestic skills. These are practices which vanished with modernization and are seemingly lost, but which nevertheless may offer important guidelines for the future.

Another alternative model was offered by the Mormons in their early settlement of desert land along the 100th meridian. Where other settlers dealt with riparian rights in a land of constant drought by fighting over access to water and competing for private property rights to this precious resource, Mormons took a collective approach and planned their settlements so as to provide optimum, and public, use of scarce water resources.

The contradictions abide. Americans, the "people of plenty," wasteful and insensitive to their despoiling of the landscape, are also the people of conservation. Nowhere else have such vast regions of wilderness been preserved to the public domain, nowhere else has there been such a strong and long-lasting movement for conservation of natural resources and for preservation as a public trust. It was in the United States that the battle against pollution of air, land and water earliest became a live political issue. Today's world-wide ecology movement draws on a strong and vital American tradition.

There are other dyads of American values which could be listed, but I would like to call attention briefly to one hidden assumption underlying all the polarities already discussed—the concept of male superiority. It holds that men and women are essentially different in nature and faculties, and that men because of their superiority are better equipped than women to hold positions of power and leadership. These ideas are reflected in the way American values have been defined. American democratic liberty was so defined that the exclusion of women from political representation and power was not even questioned for nearly 200 years. To this day, after women's seventy-two-year-long struggle for suffrage, women are woefully under-represented in all public bodies and offices, in corporate economic power, in church and academic leadership. American individualism was defined so as to describe the psychological development of males; female autonomy and self-definition were considered subordinate to women's nurturant role as family care-giver and did not even begin to surface as an articulated demand of women until the 20th century. Even the most liberal definition of pluralism did not, until recently, include the possibility that women as a group might have interests, cultural definitions and values dissimilar to those of men of their group (class, ethnicity or race).

Such patriarchal attitudes and values became embedded in American life by the joint actions and decisions of men and women. That is not to say that in regard to certain issues, such as political representation, economic competition and educational opportunities, men did not deliberately and persistently disadvantage women, for they did. But it is to say that the ideas about gender held by both men and women formed the patriarchal matrix within which institutions, values and ideology were formed. It took the massive upheaval and social changes of the postmodern period to bring these assumptions into view and make it possible to conceive of alternatives. The transformation of women's (and some men's) consciousness is one of the major social forces in our time and holds much promise for a positive solution of the crisis in values Americans face today.

The values that have persisted in American life, with all their contradictions, were formed under historical conditions far different from those we live under today. The United States developed on a continent endowed with vast, seemingly limitless natural resources, with wildlife and plentiful water, with generally favorable climatic conditions and nearly two hundred years of an open frontier. The young nation was blessed with what historians have called "free security"—the absence of powerful enemies along its borders and the benefit of protection by the British navy of its maritime frontiers. Although beset from the start by a shortage of labor, the young nation was able to turn this deficit into an advantage by opening its borders to masses of immigrants who brought their education, their skills and their technological knowledge to the new land and helped it to modernize in a remarkably rapid fashion. Several centuries of upward mobility for Americans had given them some reason for their optimistic outlook, their faith in progress and individual resourcefulness. But rapid industrialization, while it greatly contributed to U.S. power and world prestige and to the wealth of its citizenry, also brought with it great social dislocations and struggles that marked the end of the 19th and the beginning of the 20th century.

World Wars I and II brought an end to "free security." New technologies, especially air warfare, made land borders meaningless. Mass communications now spanned the globe—the world had shrunk and national interest was now being re-defined as far outside our physical borders. The major revolutions of the 20th century against colonial and despotic regimes had realigned the power centers in the world. Although U.S. foreign policy has for over seventy years focused on the ideological differences between the capitalist and socialist systems of the world, it can be argued that the real differences are between the rich and the poor. The population explosion and the uneven distribution of the world's resources pose as great if not a greater threat to the security of each developed nation then do regimes with different ideologies. The fact that most of the world is desperately poor, while a small part of the world's population uses up a disproportionately large share of the world's resources, should be cause enough for worry. The fact the poor are mostly people of color and the rich are mostly white, should be more cause for concern.

The loss of "free security" has turned Americans fearful and made them preoccupied with guaranteeing security through military power and through secret espionage networks. The nuclear revolution, which for the past forty years led to the maintenance of peace through deterrence and a balance of terror between the two major powers, has only increased the sense of insecurity in our lives. The fact that destruction of all life on earth is now a technological possibility has entered our nightmares but has not yet affected our political institutions.

The foundations for much of what Americans believed and valued underwent a further series of shocks in the 20th century, creating the sense of bewilderment, catastrophe, despair and anomie that characterizes so much of our current cultural life and discourse. One can view the present as a period of failure and decline. I would rather view it as a period of transition in which we have not yet completed the necessary adaptation of our beliefs and values to the social changes that have already taken place in the world we live in.

Let us now turn to possible answers to the problems posed by these changes. What values then, derived from traditional American values, can be considered appropriate for our grandchildren as they face the 21st century?

Our grandchildren's world has become a global village, a world of mainly colored people living in poverty, with a small segment of mainly white people living in wealth. It is a dangerous world, in which the maldistribution of resources will continue to be a source of conflict and struggle. The communications revolution has not only brought us closer to the developing world, but it has brought knowledge of how we live closer to those who do not enjoy our privileges. This can be a potential for peaceful interaction or it can be a potential source of continuously regenerating conflict.

As citizens of the richest, technologically most highly developed nation, we will find our survival threatened unless we replace racism and the urge toward imperialistic expansion with a firm commitment to political democracy, equality and the concept of a mutuality of equals among nations. We will need to revive the knowledge and skills that helped our forebears build pluralistic communities, a federation of equal states and democratic community institutions. As we move toward improved forms of international cooperation, a crucial leadership role in this endeavor could be played by members of American minority groups, who combine sensitivity to racial and ethnic issues with the technological know-how and skills of a highly developed society.

The inability of big powers to go to war with one another due to the danger of nuclear disaster does not mean the end of international conflicts. On the contrary, many small-scale or regional conflicts will and are becoming substitute arenas for big-power competition. So does ideological warfare, in which competing social systems vie with one another in their ability to gain influence over other nations. In this competition among nations for the best forms of governance, the priceless heritage of our Constitution and its Bill of Rights will give us a decisive advantage over competing systems. Our form of government has the immense advantage over other systems of being self-regulating—its checks and balances and its guarantee of free speech and a free press offer us mechanisms for adaptation and for the correction of errors in judgment and leadership. If we could learn to base our hegemony over other nations on the superiority of our political institutions instead of on our superior wealth and military force, we might in fact win in the battle of ideas.

❦

The gradual and hesitant progression toward finding what William James called "a moral equivalent for war" demands a new style of political and military leadership. Eyeball to eyeball confrontations, bluff and military posturing have become too dangerous in this age of nuclear proliferation to be acceptable as leadership styles. The abilities to negotiate, to build mutual confidence, to make pragmatic adaptations, to substitute peaceful for forceful means are now necessary survival skills which our grandchildren will demand of their leaders. People with experience in community building, in finding social solutions for social problems, in cooperating with others in coalitions, will be more likely to fit the needs of the time than those patterning their leadership type on traditions of rugged individualism. When Geraldine Ferraro, the first female vice-presidential candidate in U.S. history, was asked on television whether she would have the toughness needed to "push the [nuclear] button" she assured the public she would. I am suggesting that such toughness is quite an inappropriate qualification for national leadership for either men or women. Much more important would be the ability to empathize, compromise, negotiate and convince by argument.

As our grandchildren seek new forms of international interaction and new styles of national leadership they may find it advantageous to look for guidance and expertise to people who do not have a vested interest in the traditional ways of doing things. Women as a group have not been tainted or hardened by the exercise of political and military power. Women in the past have had to find alternative ways to power in dealing with problems and may therefore be predisposed to the style of leadership now needed. This is not to say that we should turn only to women for leadership, rather, that the inclusion of women in the pool of talent is an absolute necessity and makes good sense in terms of human survival.

Again, as a matter of national survival, we will need to turn away from unbridled consumerism and the wasting of resources to a practice of conservation, respect for the ecosystem and an acceptance of limits to growth and development. Perhaps the greatest wisdom for the 21st century will be to admit that we should impose limits on what we *can* do and that we should develop the discipline and the humility to know that we must not necessarily do what we are able to do technologically, without regard for the consequences.

In order to draw on the largest possible pool of talent to solve the problems of the 21st century, open access to education and opportunity not only for women but for minorities and the economically disadvantaged is a national necessity. People may have to change jobs and skills several times during their productive years. The span of remunerative work in one's life time may have to become shorter than ever before in history, while the time spent in community service-oriented volunteer work may have to expand over decades. All of this demands new educational goals. Traditional institutionalized forms of education and elitist values implicit in the creation of meritocracies no longer answer the need. In the re-setting of our educational agenda we will have to think of education as the engine that moves society forward and allows the individual to adapt to the rapid changes in modern life. Such education should be a birth right of citizenship, not a reward to be earned or a privilege to be won. People will have to move freely between work and learning at all stages of their lives, not only in youth. Closing the gap between theory and practice in education means changing the value system by which theorizing is considered superior to doing. The citizen of the 21st century will need a new blend of interaction between these two polarities.

As our grandchildren search for values they can use, appropriate to the problems that face them, they need not cast themselves off from tradition and history. In the polarities of traditional American values there is a rich heritage of usable experience and knowledge, which can lead them out of the confusion of this transitional period into the coming new age.

7

The 20th Century:
A Watershed for Women

To help us visualize the significance of the 20th century, let us fix a number of images in our minds: First, the modern airport—a cultural product so homogenized around the world that were it not for the signs and advertisements the traveler would not know which country's airport he had reached. Then, the shopping mall—the emblem of consumerism, appearing in various cultural guises in different parts of the world, but in most of its manifestations, selling goods produced and marketed for international consumption. Whatever local products the mall may feature, there will also be blue jeans, batteries, portable radios and music on cassettes. Then, another image—the Bedouin on his camel in the middle of the desert, listening to a transistor radio. The final image is that of an African woman, barefoot, her infant strapped to her back, a twenty-pound can of water on her head, walking down a dusty road. She is bringing this water to her hut, walking—on the average—twelve to fifteen miles a day. She passes the village bar, or shebeen, where the men of her tribe sit on plastic chairs, drinking Coca-Cola or canned beer, watching TV or listening to music on the radio. Progress has been monumental, but it also has been uneven.

The biggest changes for women in the 20th century fall into three categories: reproduction and life cycle, education, and work participation. Demographic changes are influenced by many factors, among

This essay was first presented as a lecture at the Symposium, "Making Sense of the 20th Century," University of Victoria, British Columbia, September 29–October 1, 1994. This is a revised version.

them urbanization, industrialization, technological innovations and improvements in health care. We can best illustrate this process by looking at some basic facts comparing women in industrial (developed) and industrializing (developing) nations.

In developing nations, women are disadvantaged in nutrition and health and have higher rates of death during their child-bearing years, with the result that there are fewer women than men in the population. (In 1990, there were 95 women for every 100 men in Asia and the Pacific; 106 women to 100 men in the developed regions).[1] Industrial and economic development means an improvement in the average life-span for women. It is an indication of world-wide progress that the average life-span for women has, in this century, risen rapidly everywhere but in Africa. The life expectancy of women has increased worldwide, but the gap between the developed and the developing nations remains wide. (Life expectancy of women in the industrial nations in 1990 was over 80 years; in sub-Saharan Africa and southern Asia it was less than 56 years.) We need to keep in mind that three-quarters of the world's women live in the developing regions.[2]

Reductions in mortality rates make for longer life-spans for both men and women. In developed regions, people marry later, which leads to a decrease in child-bearing rates. In the 20th century, women across the world are having fewer children. In the past twenty years in the industrialized nations child-bearing rates dropped from an average of 2.6 to 1.8 births per woman. In the developing regions the number of births per woman dropped from 5–7 to 3–6, with large regional variations. In the developing regions women have their children early and spend eighteen or more years in child-bearing. In the developed nations women have fewer children over a shorter span (seven years of child-bearing). In general, women in urban areas have smaller families than do rural women. There is also a strong statistical linkage between higher educational levels for women and lower birth rates, although this is not necessarily a cause-and-effect relationship.

Due to millennia of systematic educational deprivation, women have everywhere lagged behind men in attaining literacy. Thus, despite enormous progress in this century in wiping out illiteracy world-wide, in 1985 there were 597 million illiterate women and 352 million illiterate men, that is, nearly twice as many illiterate women as men. This educational deficit is likely to persist for many decades into the next century. Another way of looking at this is to consider different regions. In sub-Saharan Africa illiteracy rates are highest—more than 90 percent of women aged twenty-five and over are illiterate. In eastern and Southeastern Asia more than 40 percent and in Latin America and the Caribbean over 20 percent of women over age twenty-five are illiterate. In the developed nations and wherever literacy rates exceed 95 percent the gender difference is wiped out.[3]

In the developed regions of the world and in Latin America girls, in the 20th century attained parity with boys in secondary education (to age 17). The progress for the younger generation was much slower in Africa and southern Asia, where for every 100 boys 60 girls were enrolled in secondary schools. In southern Asia the ratio was 100:40.[4]

Truly decisive changes occurred in women's access to higher education and to professional training. The percentage of women over age twenty-five having attained post-secondary education was highest in Canada (34.7%) and the United States (28%) and lowest in Africa, where it ranged from 1.7 percent to 0.1 percent.[5] One of the first professional careers open to women is elementary school teaching. By 1984, half of the elementary teachers in the world were women, except in Africa, where the proportion of women teachers increased from 28 percent in 1970 to 39 percent in 1984. Men outnumber women as secondary level teachers everywhere except in Latin America and the Caribbean, where the numbers are equal.[6] In general, the patriarchal principle that the higher the level of education, the fewer the women who teach, remains intact.

Viewed in the perspective of the millennia of educational disadvantaging of women, the 20th century represents a watershed, a period of enormous progress. Yet discrimination remains firmly entrenched in the majority of nations and the effects of past discrimination continue to disadvantage women even under relatively advantageous conditions.

Let me illustrate what demographic change means in the lives of women by giving a more detailed account of changes in the 20th century in the United States. For men and women the century brought above all increases in life-span. In 1900 the life expectancy of a baby girl was 48 years, in 1980 it was 78 years. Since women's life expectancy exceeded that of men by 7 to 8 years, this means not only that women lived much longer, but that they could expect to spend nearly a decade of their old age in widowhood, if they had been married. In 1988, some 77 percent of older U.S. citizens who lived alone were women and the figure is rising steadily.[7]

In part, women's greater longevity was the result of a decrease in maternal deaths rates during the 19th century and of a sharp decrease in infant mortality in the 20th century. With the age of marriage for both men and women remaining stable, there was a decline in the number of children born to women under 45 years of age. Whereas in 1800, U.S. women had on average seven children, the number was down to 3.56 children at the beginning of the 20th century and 1.8 in 1990.

These aggregate figures show the general trends, but we need to note the continuing, significant differences in all of these figures by race. In 1900 the life expectancy of all women at birth was 48 years; it was actually 48.3 years for white women and 33.5 years for black women, a gap of nearly 15 years in favor of whites. By 1989 the gap had narrowed: at birth white women's life expectancy was 79.1 years, that of black women 73.5, a gap of five years. Infant mortality rates at the beginning of the century were for whites 99.9 (per 1000 live births) and 181.2 for non-whites. (A non-white infant was twice a likely as a white infant to die in the first year of life.) By 1990 the figures were 7.7 for whites and 17.7 for non-whites. The survival chances of all infants had greatly improved, but the gap between them had widened slightly. Maternal mortality rates in 1915 were 60.1 for whites and 105.6 for non-whites (a 45.5-point gap). By 1990 this had improved: 5.4 for whites; and 22.4 for non-whites (a 17-point gap). Here we see enormous improvements for both groups, with a narrowing differential.

❧

The demographic shifts in the 20th century had great impact on the life cycles of Americans of both sexes. With greatly increased longevity and fewer births, U.S. women spent a shorter part of their life in child-bearing and child-rearing activities. This fact alone may explain the changes in the workforce participation of U.S. women.

LIFE CYCLES OF U.S. WOMEN[8]

	WIVES BORN 1880–89	WIVES BORN 1920–29
Child-bearing years	11.3	9.7
Child-rearing years	34.6	31.2
Duration of marriage	35.4	43.6
Years of marriage without children present in home	0.8	12.4

The meaning of the figures above is fascinating. It shows that until approximately 1940 the average marriage was devoted to child-bearing and each couple enjoyed less than a year of marriage after the last child left home before one or the other partner died. After 1940, marriages lasted longer (due to greater longevity of both partners); children were fewer and spaced closer together so that, after the last child left home, the married couple still had 12.4 years together before one of them died. Figures for the second half of the century have increased this time to 20 years. The dramatic increase of the divorce rate in the 20th century may thus be, at least in part, a reflection of the new demographics—where in previous centuries marriages after the child-rearing stage ended in the death of one of the partners, in this century they then often end in divorce. (In 1890 the divorce rate was 3.5 percent of marriages, today it is nearly 50 percent.) The great increase in remarriage rates for both sexes supports this interpretation. Today, most divorced persons remarry within five years. But for women there is an added change. Not only do U.S. women now spend only one-fifth of their lives in child-bearing and child-rearing activities, but they can expect to spend nearly that much of their lives as widows.

These demographic facts indicate that the problems posed for women by their changing life cycles made changes in their education and in their work patterns inevitable. It is commonly asserted that feminism is responsible for a weakening of the family, when in fact it is the case that the demands raised by feminism are answers to the problems posed by an already changed family and life cycle. Thus, it should not be surprising to see a world-wide trend for advances in the education of women following upon the basic demographic changes I have outlined above.

At the beginning of the 19th century, elementary education was available to most American girls. High school education was available to girls in urban areas, but there was a large gap between them and their brothers in access to higher education. In 1900 36.8 percent of all students enrolled in institutions of higher education were women; in 1980 they were 51.8 percent[9] Not until 1980 did women gain parity with men in college and university attendance, when women earned 47 percent of the B.A. and 49 percent of M.A. degrees. But they still lagged far behind in obtaining professional degrees, which reflects both the discriminatory obstacles to their admission in the early decades of the century and gender-specific cultural and institutional constraints. Women obtained 6 percent of Ph.D.s in 1900 and 30 percent in 1990. While at the beginning of the century the vast majority of professional schools were still closed to women, their opportunities for professional training greatly improved by the end of the century. In 1910 just 1 percent of all lawyers and 6 percent of all physicians were women; in 1982 women represented 14 percent in both professions.[10] That is progress, but it still falls far short of equity. Women's professional degrees were concentrated in a few fields, most of them in lower-status, lower-paying fields. By the end of the century, women were still severely discriminated against in the sciences and in technology, with women representing fewer than 6 percent of engineering graduates.

During the 20th century women have made greater progress in gaining access to educational resources than in any previous century, but wide gaps between men and women's educational achievements remain. The patterns repeat in women's labor-force participation.

At the beginning of the 20th century U.S. women were 20 percent of the labor force. Working women were typically young, of lower-class origin, unmarried; they worked six to eight years before marriage and contributed their wages to their families. By the end of the century nearly two-thirds of all women, ages 20 to 64, were in the workforce. The typical working woman was married, a mother of school age children, middle class, and she would stay in the workforce for most of her life.

While, by the end of the century, women had made great gains in middle-range business positions, they hit a glass ceiling at upper levels of management. Thus in 1979 women were 1 percent of the managers of the 1000 largest corporations in the country; by 1990 the figure had inched up to 3 percent. Among 986 CEOs (Corporate Executive Officers) there were two females. In general, in all the professions except elementary school teaching, nursing and librarianship, the women were clustered in the lower ranks, and the higher the rank and pay, the fewer women there were visible.

We can gain a better understanding of the limits of U.S. women's economic advances if we look at women in specific occupations. Among the nine occupations with the highest mean earnings, ranging from physician to medical science teacher, women represent from 1 percent—17 percent of the practitioners. Among the five occupations with the lowest mean earnings, ranging from child-care worker to domestic, women represent from 83 percent to 98 percent of the occupation, with 93.4 percent the average. A Rand Corporation study shows that women earned 43 percent of men's pay in 1920 and estimates that by the year 2000 they will earn 74 percent of men's pay. The patriarchal principle that high status, high paying occupations are reserved for men remains intact, despite the considerable educational gains made by U.S. women during the century.

If race were to be factored into these figures, they would show that at all levels of education African-Americans of both sexes fared much worse than white people. Race discrimination has restricted their access to education and delayed their entry into professional training. They have higher illiteracy rates, lower school enrollment- and graduation-rates and face greater obstacles in completing graduate training than whites. Ironically, because race discrimination barriers in employment were always greater against black men than women, black women showed for fifty years (1900–1950) higher professional achievements than black men and white women. Thus, the 1960 Census shows that nearly 8 percent of all black physicians were women, while white women were only 6 percent of all white physicians. Black women lawyers were 9 percent of all African-Americans in the profession, while white women lawyers represented only 3 percent of theirs. One of the major accomplishments of the civil rights movement of the 1960s was in advancing educational opportunities for African-Americans of both sexes, but these gains have been severely eroded by the end of the century. What shows up the complex effect of racism and sexism best are median annual earning figures broken down by sex and race. For 1950–87 they show a persistent pattern of wage differentials in this order: white men earn the best wages, followed by black men, then white women, then black women. This is best explained by the predominance of women of both races in low-paying service jobs.[11]

Returning to the international survey we find that women almost everywhere in the world have increased their labor-force participation. Gendered job segregation and wage discrimination have persisted world-wide, so that there is a big gap between what women produce and what they earn when compared with men. Women's work is concentrated in agriculture, service, clerical and sales jobs, but they are largely excluded from manufacturing, transportation and management positions, depending on the economic development of the region they live in. In general, women remain in the least desirable, most exploited, most disadvantaged economic positions.

Finally, we must consider one other aspect of inequality. Despite the advances of women's workforce participation, time-use studies in developed nations show that women, whether they work outside of the home or as full-time housewives, still do most of the unpaid housework. Women's share of unpaid housework ranges from a low of 64 percent in the United States to a high of 90 percent in Venezuela.[12] Everywhere where statistics are available, women are predominantly responsible for child care and care for the elderly.

To sum up: Increased education and demographic changes have improved women's chances for economic activity, but only slightly. They have improved women's access to political power and representation, but only minutely. They have not appreciably lessened women's responsibility for child care and unpaid domestic labor. Above all, the advances made by women in the 20th century have been grossly uneven, with the majority at the end of the century still living under conditions as bad or worse than those of women in the developed nations at the beginning of the century. If we consider that today three-fourths of all women in the world live in developing countries and that the vast majority of them are non-white, the hopeful story of woman's progress takes on a nasty edge.

Obviously, from the patterns I have discussed, the advancement of women in developing nations is tied to the economic advancement of their nation. In the 20th century many of the previously colonized nations of the world have attained independence and considerable improvement in their economic condition, the big exceptions being the nations of sub-Saharan Africa. Progress has been especially dramatic in China, Southeast Asia and South America. But such national progress has not benefited women equally with men; in fact in some developing nations the situation of women has greatly deteriorated as these nations have entered the world market. In a somewhat similar pattern, the 49 million people who are currently living under abysmally bad conditions as refugees or fugitives in places other than their homelands consist predominantly women and children.

One of the historic preconditions for the advancement of women is the existence of independent women's organizations. The rise of international feminisms has led to a spectacular growth in international contacts, exchanges and cooperation among women, such as expressed by the U.N. Conference on Population, Cairo, 1994, and U.N. World Conference on Women in Beijing, China, in 1995.

Another hopeful and highly significant development is the advance of feminist thought and scholarship in the most highly developed nations. For the first time in history, some women are taking part in defining the content of knowledge and learning. It is difficult to predict how great the impact of this unprecedented development will be and how fast it will spread to other parts of the globe, but in any assessment of the importance of the 20th century it must be considered highly significant. When we also consider the parallel development of formerly subjugated national, ethnic and racial groups, half of them women, acquiring education and independence and challenging the previously predominantly European and North American hegemony over intellectual life, then women's intellectual emancipation takes on added significance.

There are hopeful signs, but there is discouraging slowness in the rate of change in attitudes and institutions. The trends toward the demographic, educational and economic improvement in the status of women are world-wide and of long duration. It is likely that they will continue and accelerate. I am convinced that the changes begun in this century in the direction of greater social justice and opportunity and in the direction of changing hierarchical and discriminatory systems of governance are essential for the survival of humankind in the next century. The demands of feminism and of the world's underprivileged for a fairer distribution of the world's resources and for a world less consumed by militarism not only are morally just but they are pragmatically necessary. We cannot hope to survive in a world of such injustice, such brutality and such mindless destructiveness. We cannot solve the problems of the threat to the ecology, of the exhaustion of natural resources and of the destructive potential of new technologies unless we alter our institutions and change our human priorities. I am hopeful that with the leadership of women and of people who have experienced oppression, it can be done. The emancipation of women, so dramatically advanced in the 20th century, holds the promise of survival of the human race in the 21st century.

8

Looking Toward the Year 2000

hat kind of future can we envision after the year 2000? The state of the world being what it is, one can approach such a question either with profound pessimism, and answer that most likely the world is not going to survive into the 21st century; *or* one can approach it with purely utopian vision. Such an utopian approach may, in fact, be far more practical than the endless repetitions by politicians, statesmen and military leaders of worn-out and utterly inappropriate clichés of 19th-century wisdom. We must act in this worst of all worlds as though it were good; unless we do so we are doomed to alienation, anomie, despair and worse, ineffectiveness. It is from this stance of ambivalence that I want to address the question.

In the 20th century we have lived through the nuclear revolution, the media and cybernetic revolutions, not to mention various political revolutions. World War I signaled the end of the secure world of imperial powers and their dominance over colonial empires. Authoritarian and fascistic regimes of various kinds substituted arbitrary power for the Lockean social contract. The 20th century is marked irrevocably by the Holocaust, an event unique in history. Vicious warfare, the enslavement of conquered people and the brutal suppression of dissenters and those subjugated by dictatorial regimes are as old as human history. What makes the Holocaust unique is that all the technological and political resources of one of the most "civilized" nations of the world were utilized to organize mass killings and to commercialize their prod-

This article was published in translation in the volume edited by Peter Sloterdijk, *Vor der Jahrtausendwende: Berichte zur Lage der Zukunft*, 2 vols. (Baden-Baden: Suhrkamp, 1990), vol. 2, pp. 292–308. This is a revised version.

uct. The linkage of modern industrial complexes, like I. G. Farben and Hoechst, to slave labor and the extermination camps; the marketing of soap made from rendered human fat; the stuffing of mattresses with human hair and the organization of medical experiments on living prisoners in the death camps—these are indeed unique events, unprecedented in history. The Holocaust expressed the unlimited capacity of human beings for evil; it made a reality of "the death of God," and irreversibly undermined the faith of people in the idea of progress which had sustained Enlightenment rationalism.

World War II, while it ended the threat of the world-wide triumph of fascism, brought mass bombings of civilians by conventional means and finally the ultimate and wanton destruction of Hiroshima and Nagasaki. Then followed forty years of "cold war" between the nuclear superpowers which ended in stalemate, disillusionment and the triumph of bureaucratic mediocrity in the developed nations and an ever increasing gap separating the world's rich and the world's poor.

The economies of the nations of the world are more closely linked then ever before. Multinational corporations dominate the economic scene and in actual power transcend the power of national governments. In view of this and the fact that scientific and technological knowledge has become international, the concept of national security needs to be redefined. Excessive military power no longer guarantees political and military hegemony. Major nuclear powers cannot engage in war, for whatever reason, without risking their own and the planet's total destruction. Fundamental social change, consisting of a more equitable distribution of the world's resources among the nations and within each nation is an absolute necessity for human survival. The question is how can such social change be effected under current conditions? Before it can be answered we must consider two other intractable problems of the present.

If the nuclear revolution has brought a limit to military power, the technological revolutions of the 20th century have moved the consideration of a limit to resources from the esoteric speculations of philosophers and nature lovers into the center of political discourse. How long can the production of waste materials continue before it affects our very ability to exist? The danger of the destruction of the earth's ozone layer, the devastation of the forests by acid rain, and the pollution of the rivers, lakes and oceans by industrial wastes demand international solutions.

Scientific and technological advances in the 20th century have enabled us to decipher the genetic code and to reach the moon. We have the potential knowledge for genetic engineering, artificial creation of life, interstellar travel and extra-terrestrial settlement. Our technological and scientific genius has led to advances in health care which reduce prenatal injuries and death and prolong life well beyond what used to be the expected life-span throughout history. Our ability to interfere with life processes and with the process of dying has given rise to a host of new ethical and moral dilemmas.

The major technological and communications revolutions of this century have also basically altered the relation of people to work. A work ethic demanding life-long pursuit of one specialized skill is no longer appropriate to societal needs; it may even be counter-productive. There is not enough work to go around, if all members of society are to work forty hours a week until age sixty. Rapidly changing demands in skills require a work force more readily adaptable to changes in technology than is now created by our educational system. A longer life span with less lifetime devoted to remunerated work demands altered institutions; it also demands people with different values in regard to work.

The dismal catalogue of unsolvable problems and profound contradictions that mark the 20th century signals a profound breakdown of institutions and ideas. We have so far managed to muddle through the challenges of the past decades without making major changes in our thinking, pragmatically trying small alterations in existing ways of acting. Far too often even our limited actions have been ahead of our thinking. An example of this is our pragmatic avoidance of big-power nuclear confrontation coupled with perfectly traditional (and inappropriate) thinking about defense, national sovereignty and security and the imposition of our power on other nations. I see in the current condition of breakdown, ineffectiveness and anomie the necessary precondition for the future.

Under patriarchy, which began for Western civilization with the formation of archaic states in the 3rd millennium B.C. in the Ancient Near East, "progress" or social change has inevitably involved violent struggle. Even reform, the slow process of adjustment of ruling institutions, has been prodded along by the threat, or actuality, of violence. Revolutionary change has been, for most 20th-century people, with the exception of pacifists, the major conceptual paradigm by which we can imagine historical process. Many of us have come to believe—since that is all we know in history—that violent overthrow is the only way large-scale social change is accomplished. The idea of the inevitability of hierarchy has been so pervasive that people cannot think of alternatives to the existing order other than to think in terms of reversal. The oppressed will become the rulers; the former oppressors will, in their turn, be oppressed.

My argument is that these old (19th-century) solutions for social change are utterly inapplicable to the present. The violent overthrow of governments is in the nuclear age less and less feasible. Therefore, revolutionary doctrine based on such theories of overthrow is inappropriate.

The necessity of violent overthrow brings with it the need to subordinate the group that has formerly been dominant. Such repression fosters hierarchy in the revolutionary regime and it fosters the rise of counter-struggle by the newly oppressed group. Violence begets violence; the vicious cycle begins again. The succession of dictatorships in newly liberated colonial countries, the Irish civil war, the Arab-Israeli conflict are all 20th-century examples of the fact that violence in the interest of social change leads to the acceptance of violence and repression as inevitable features of such change.

The emergence of Leninism and Stalinism in the wake of violent overthrow and civil war has proven that a minority ruling over the majority in the name of that majority ("the party as vanguard of the proletariat") can be as vicious, autocratic and destructive as any ruling elite has ever been. Nor have the other socialist systems of the 20th century, insofar as they have survived at all, offered any more promising models of governance. Repression of the opposition, and curtailment or nonexistence of freedom of speech and the press have been the features of each of these regimes. So far, all over the world, socialist humanism has been defeated or it has faltered before it could fully emerge.

In the post-Hiroshima age, ruling elites even in small countries can avail themselves of weapons of such destructive potential that large-scale civil wars cannot be won by revolutionary groups. Major nuclear powers cannot engage in a big-power war, whether to help a struggling revolutionary regime or whether in defense of more basic territorial and economic interests, without risking their own and the planet's total destruction. In the past forty years the great nuclear powers, representing different social and philosophical systems, have stood like paralyzed giants facing each other, unable to move precisely because of their super-weaponry. In face of this stalemate, we are left with the kind of scenario acted out in Vietnam or in the Cuban missile crisis: the nuclear powers do everything short of engaging in a major conflict with one another to defend their ideological or territorial interests. The Vietnam and the Afghanistan wars have shown the limitations of this scenario. In exceptional circumstances, in locations marginal to the territorial interests of the nuclear superpowers, revolutionary regimes can make some gains, but the cost is high and self-defeating. The necessity for engaging in armed struggle against a superpower or its client inevitably leads to the emergence of a centralized, military regime. Such a regime, to be able to survive armed struggle, must become highly bureaucratized and oppressive of dissent within its own country, thereby inevitably giving rise to opposition and struggle.

The development of highly sophisticated technology for surveillance, espionage and thought control of entire populations have given more power to ruling elites than have ever existed before in history. These powers make the long-range survival and possible success of revolutionary groups extremely doubtful. The only kinds of groups which have shown themselves successful in the short range against this array of oppressive state power are terrorists. The emergence of world-wide terrorism in the latter half of the 20th century is a response to the altered balance of power between the rulers and the ruled. The absence of democratic means of dissent and/or the despair of oppressed groups at their inability to change the status quo and to instigate reforms which meet their demands leads to the acceptance of terrorism as the inevitable price to be paid for justice for the oppressed. But, just like the use of mass violence, the use of and acceptance of terrorist means for revolutionary ends distort the persons and movements using such means. Even if we were to postulate the possibility, for which there is not much historical precedent, that terrorist groups can actually overthrow well-established regimes, the former terrorists, now become established, would find it necessary and acceptable to oppress the group they have overthrown. The history of right-wing Zionism and the regimes in some of the new African states illustrate this tendency.

A more frequent occurrence is the establishment of fascistic dictatorships in response to actual or perceived terrorist threats. Given the new technological means at the disposal of ruling elites, the measures used against those seeking fundamental social change have often proved disastrous. The ability of such elites to terrorize and even physically wipe out their opponents has never in history been greater. Nor can we or should we doubt the willingness of ruling elites to wipe out revolutionary groups entirely. In the 16th century, several groups of the left wing of the Protestant Reformation, such as the Anabaptists, were in fact wiped out. Hitler's "final solution" stands as a horrifying 20th-century example of what it is possible for an oppressive regime to do. Hitler was not defeated because he wiped out twelve million people, among them six million Jews and nearly the entire Gypsy population of Europe; he was defeated because his territorial ambitions threatened the security and economic interests of other large powers. It is unfortunately possible and realistic to conceive of a ruling class wiping out its opposition without interference from other countries.

In order to avoid the inevitable disasters of nuclear warfare, decisive social change has to be made in the major nuclear states, in the most technologically advanced countries. Any doctrine of social change which does not address that reality cannot be seriously considered. A few examples of a party or movement attempting a combination of reform and revolutionary tactics exist, i.e. the Italian Communist party and the Chilean government under Allende. These parties have been flexible enough in their tactics to avoid violent confrontation and have sought to come to power by democratic means. In both cases the United States intervened in the development of the process of democratic ascension and in the case of Chile, the intervention resulted in the actual destruction of the regime. It is difficult to imagine conditions of social change in which similar intervention would not occur. Still, this remains the most hopeful scenario for revolutionary change, except for the fact that it does not address the question of how such change is to occur within the very centers of the nuclear superpowers.

But social change consisting of a more equitable and just distribution of the world's resources among the nations is a necessity for human survival. Such social change implicitly demands an end to ideologies of hierarchy, such as racism and sexism. Without the abolition of sexism, none of the other hierarchical concepts and systems can be successfully ended. No matter how changed economic and social relations may become, as long as sexism constantly re-creates inequality in the family and in the consciousness of men and women, hierarchy will be reborn. Therefore, men committed to making social change, have a self-interest in foregoing the benefits bestowed upon them by patriarchal dominance over women. What such men want cannot be achieved without mobilizing the long-latent force of women. It is my belief that the feminism and the tactics appropriate to it offer the single most appropriate transformational philosophy and practice available to women and men.

On the other hand, the goals of feminism cannot be achieved without a vast cultural revolution, involving every institution of society, in particular, the family. The magnitude of the social change needed presupposes the diffusion of the forces of change into every aspect of society. No other oppressed group except women is so located as to be able to effect such changes.

Women as a group stand in a different relation to those who dominate them than do other groups. Because of their sheer numbers and their distribution in every class of society, they cannot be treated as ruling classes treat subordinate and revolutionary groups. Women are everywhere. They cannot be ghettoized; they cannot be wiped out. On the other hand, because of their intimate connection with members of the group that dominates them—fathers, brothers, husbands, sons—women cannot use violence in order to reach their emancipation. They must and will rely on tactics that induce, by persuasion and social pressure, a new consciousness in men and women. *The feminist revolution will not be an overthrow, it will be a transformation.*

There are historic precedents for such transformations in the revolutions made by early Christianity and the Protestant Reformation. While these great transformations were accompanied by violence and bloodshed, this was on the whole violence by an established religion, trying to prevent the new faith from becoming established. In this, the established religions inevitably failed. One hundred years of devastating warfare in Europe ended in 1648 with the coexistence of a vastly transformed Catholicism and a number of Protestant churches, far different in character than had been envisioned by their founders. In this age, when warfare involving major nations has become unthinkable, the theories and practice of transforming social movements offer the only real hope for social change. Feminism represents such a movement.

It would be unrealistic to think that women alone can transform patriarchy and create less hierarchical and divisive forms of societal organization. It will be necessary to build a series of coalitions and alliances among a number of movements whose goals entirely or partially overlap, such as the world peace and the ecology movements and the gay liberation movements of men and women. All of these are characterized by their cross-class, cross-national character, their marginality to current political institutions, their enmity to militarism, nationalism, exploitation, injustice and prejudice. They are natural allies, and I am suggesting that feminist theory can provide a coherent common philosophy for forming coalitions that can endure. Feminist practice, in its non-hierarchical model, its merging of feeling and action, its making the personal political and its dedication to inclusiveness and humane transformation, offers a good model. This is not to ask for or advocate women's dominance over others in such a coalition. In fact, any such social movement will be viable only if it learns how to replace power over others with the empowerment of all participants for the attainment of the common good.

The seeds of the future are already in our hands. Those most dangerous to the survival of humankind are *macho* men in positions of power, regardless of which bloc of antiquated social structures they command. They are as dangerous in the governments of East or West, in highly developed and in developing countries; they are as useless in military as in corporate leadership or in that of the trade-union movement. Since all they know is how to maximize their short-range advantages over others and hold on to whatever illusory power they now hold, they cannot adapt quickly enough to the changes that must be made in order for humanity to survive. (I am, by the way, including in this metaphorical category the few women in power in public life, who have made it to where they are by thinking and acting like men. Until all the institutions of society are staffed in equal numbers by men and women in leadership positions, we will not be able to know what an alternative model of female leadership looks like.) But we do already know that the qualities of leadership needed by persons of both sexes in the coming period of transition will be closer to those developed by women over the centuries, due to their historic marginality to power: sensitivity to others and the ability to persuade, patience, peacefulness, and a non-confrontational style of authority, the ability to be nurturant and to care for conservation, protection of the earth and its resources and of people in need of help. Such qualities and such leaders are already among us, but we must learn to recognize them, to value them and to set them up as role models for others.

We can draw on the experience of the peace movements to learn about alternatives to war and peaceful conflict resolution. We can learn from the ecology movements how to be less wasteful and to think smaller. We can learn from people of other races and other cultures as well as from gay/lesbian movements to be more humble in the face of human diversity and to appreciate the variety and richness of human possibilities. Whether we can learn all of this soon enough and well enough to stave off disaster, I do not know. All I know is that we must act as though we could.

Which brings me finally to the question: What strategies do individuals use to reach toward the envisioned future? I can here only speak for myself. As a feminist scholar I strive for clarity, an improved analysis of past and present which will meet the demands of integrity and applicability. I believe all hitherto created systems of ideas—religions, philosophies and systems of explanation—were created with unacknowledged patriarchal assumptions and therefore marginalize women. In striving to free myself from such assumptions, I am trying to be eclectic and based in reality. I seek theoretical explanations which assume the centrality of women and men to all events in human history and I test each theoretical assumption to see whether it so assumes. If it does, it still may or may not be true; if it does not, it cannot be true.

I try, in my private life, to live as simply as possible and to be mindful of conserving resources and respecting nature. I try to be part of and build community in the various aspects of my life and to move from self-absorption to altruism. In none of this am I sure that I can succeed, but I can and must strive to succeed. As a survivor of several major disasters I remain, as I said at the outset, a skeptical, and at times despairing optimist. As all such creatures, I need an utopian vision— mine is a world in which women and men will have freed their minds from patriarchal thought and which will therefore be free of dominance and hierarchy, a world that will be truly human.

9

The Necessity of History

There is no adequate preparation for writing a presidential address. Trying to choose among the many urgent themes that demand attention, one is painfully aware of the wisdom of one's predecessors and one's own limitations. The audience to be addressed is the most critical and important one will ever face: a national audience of colleagues. For a woman, following a long line of male presidents, there is an added responsibility: one wishes to be representative of the profession as a whole and yet not neglectful of those long silenced.

Behind me stands a line of women historians, who practiced their profession and helped to build this organization without enjoying equality in status, economic rewards and representation. Even the most exceptional among them, whose achievements were recognized and honored by the profession, had careers vastly different from their male colleagues. For example, of the leading female academic historians who practiced in the early decades of this century, only one was employed at a major university, four worked in women's colleges, the others in outside institutions. The medievalist Nellie Neilson, president of the American Historical Association in 1943 and to this day the only woman to hold that office, spent her entire career in Mount Holyoke College. Louise Kellogg, president of the Mississippi Valley Historical Association in 1930, worked at the Wisconsin State Historical Society. Helen Sumner Woodbury made her major contribution to labor history in the Children's Bureau. Martha Edwards, like Sumner a holder of the Ph.D. in history from the University of Wisconsin, spent her career

This essay is the presidential address delivered to the Organization of American Historians in Philadelphia, April 1, 1982. Gerda Lerner is Robinson-Edwards Professor of History at the University of Wisconsin, Madison. Original title: The Necessity of History and the Professional Historian.

first in the Wisconsin State Historical Society, then as a teacher in the extension division. Florence Robinson, who held an M.A. in history from Wisconsin and earned the Ph.D. there a few years prior to her death, was unable to find a teaching job in history and headed the home economics department of Beloit College during her entire career. It was she who endowed the Robinson-Edwards chair I now hold, in memory of her father "who believes in professional opportunities for women and of my friend Martha Edwards, who deserved such professional opportunities."[1]

They and dozens of others did the best they could under the circumstances, opening the way for later generations. To remember them today is to honor their inspiration and to acknowledge their often distorted and diminished careers.

I would not be standing before you today, if it were not for the vision and perseverance of the 19th-century feminists, who treasured and collected the records and documents of female activity during their time. They laid the foundation for the study of women's history. This field would not have developed as rapidly as it did, if it were not for those determined intellectuals, not connected with any academic institution—Elizabeth Schlesinger, Miriam Holden, Mary Beard, Eugenie Leonard—who understood the need to preserve the record of the past of women in archives and who worked tirelessly for the inclusion of the history of women in academic curricula. The significant contributions to women's history scholarship of nonacademic historians, such as Elisabeth Dexter and Eleanor Flexner, also deserve to be remembered.[2]

I would like to encompass as well the sensibilities and views of the present generation of women historians, who assume equality as their right and who expect to pursue their careers without experiencing economic disadvantaging, patronizing attitudes and other forms of sex discrimination. They are the first generation of women professionals truly freed from the necessity of choosing between career and marriage. Having equal access to training and education at all levels, they enjoy the intellectual support offered by collegiality within their departments and by a network of women sharing common concerns. How am I, who have come from such different experiences, to speak for them?

As a Jewish refugee and an immigrant, I have never been able to take freedom and economic security for granted. As a woman entering academic life late, as a second career, I regard access to education as a privilege as well as an obligation. Having been an engaged participant in women's work in society all my life, I could not accept the truncated version of past reality, which described the activities and values of men and called them history, while keeping women invisible or at best marginal. My craft and my profession are inseparable from the road I have come and the life I have led.

You have bestowed upon me the honor of presiding over this organization at a time when the profession is in a crisis. Student interest in history is waning; the academic job market is contracting. A generation of young Ph.D.'s, having completed their education in a period of scarce financial aid and spiraling costs, are competing for too few tenure-leading jobs, while they face years in short-term, revolving-door appointments. Others, unable to see careers in academe, are retooling and using their skills as historians in journalism, business, government, and organizational work. Established academic historians, comparing themselves with their peers in other professions, are painfully aware of their deteriorating status. A recent editorial in the *Wall Street Journal* described the Ph.D. in history as having "low or negative returns" and questioned its worth. Respected senior members of our profession have publicly proclaimed their disillusionment with the state of scholarship, deploring a lack of coherence and unifying vision and what one termed the "disarray of the discipline" and a "dissipation of the core fund of knowledge" through over-specialization.[3]

In our institutions and professional organizations we have sought pragmatically to meet these problems by short-range adaptations—adjusting or contracting graduate programs, embracing new fields of study, extending our definition of the professional historian to include those working outside of the academy. These are constructive measures, but they have not alleviated the malaise many of us feel in our professional lives. This personal crisis may be symptomatic of significant changes that go well beyond individuals and institutions, changes in the way our society relates to the past. And so, speaking from the vantage point of a person long defined as marginal, I would like to address the issues I consider *central*: the necessity of history and the role of the professional historian.

To speak of the necessity of history is to say that history matters *essentially*. Human beings, like animals, propagate, preserve themselves and their young, seek shelter, and store food. We invent tools, alter the environment, communicate with one another by means of symbols and speculate about our mortality. Once that level of social consciousness has been reached, we become concerned with immortality.[4] The desire of men and women to survive their own death has been the single most important force compelling them to preserve and record the past. History is the means whereby we assert the continuity of human life—its creation is one of the earliest humanizing activities of *Homo sapiens*.

But history is more than collective memory; it is memory formed and shaped so as to have meaning. This process, by which people preserve and interpret the past, and then reinterpret it in light of new questions, is "history-making." It is not a dispensable intellectual luxury; history-making is a social necessity.

History functions to satisfy a variety of human needs:

1. *History as memory and as a source of personal identity*. As memory, it keeps alive the experiences, deeds, and ideas of people of the past. By locating each individual life as a link between generations and by allowing us to transform the dead into heroes and role models for emulation, history connects past and future and becomes a source of personal identity.

2. *History as collective immortality*. By rooting human beings on a continuum of the human enterprise, history provides each man and woman with a sense of immortality through the creation of a structure in the mind, which extends human life beyond its span.

3. *History as cultural tradition*. A shared body of ideas, values and experiences, which has a coherent shape, becomes a cultural tradition, be it national, ethnic, religious or racial. Such a "symbolic universe" unites diverse groups. It also legitimates those holding power, by rooting its source in a distant past.[5]

4. *History as explanation*. Through an ordering of the past into some larger connectedness and pattern, historical events become "illustrations" of philosophies and of broader inter-

pretative frameworks. Depending on the system of thought represented, the past becomes evidence, model, contrast to the present, symbol or challenge.

Making history means form-giving and meaning-giving. There is no way to extricate the form-giving aspect of history from what we are pleased to call the facts. As Carl Becker said: "Left to themselves, the facts do not speak . . . for all practical purposes there is no fact until someone affirms it. . . . Since history is . . . an imaginative reconstruction of vanished events, its form and substance are inseparable."[6]

Insofar as the historian chooses, evaluates, analyzes evidence and creates models in the mind that enable us to step out of our own time, place and culture into another world, his or her mental activity is akin to that of scientists and mathematicians, who "pop in and out" of different conceptual systems.[7] But the construction of a coherent model of the past partakes of the imagination as well. The model created by the historian must not only conform to the evidence, it must also have the power to capture the imagination of contemporaries, so as to seem real to them. It shares this quality with the work of fiction. For both writer and historian, form is the shape of content.

History-making, then, is a creative enterprise, by means of which we fashion out of fragments of human memory and selected evidence of the past a mental construct of a coherent past world that makes sense to the present.

"Necessity," wrote Leopold von Ranke, "inheres in all that has already been formed and that cannot be undone, which is the basis of all new, emerging activity. What developed in the past constitutes the connection with what is emerging in the present."[8] We learn from our construction of the past what possibilities and choices once existed. Assuming, as Henri Pirenne says, that the actions of the living and those of the dead are comparable, we then draw conclusions about the consequences of our present-day choices.[9] This in turn, enables us to project a vision of the future. It is through history-making that the present is freed from necessity and the past becomes usable.[10]

History as memory and as a source of personal identity is accessible to most people and does not depend on the services of the professional historian. It is the story of one's life and generation; it is autobiography, diary and memoir; it is the story of one's family, one's group of affiliation. As Wilhelm Dilthey wrote: "The person who seeks the connecting threads in the history of his life has already . . . created a coherence in that life . . . [which represents] the root of all historical comprehension. . . . The power and breadth of our own lives and the energy with which we reflect on them are the foundation of historical vision."[11]

By tracing one's personal roots and grounding one's identity in some collectivity with a shared past—be that collectivity defined by race, sex, class, ethnicity, religion or nationality—one acquires stability and the basis for community. Recognizing this, conquerors have often destroyed historical monuments and the preserved record of the past of the conquered; sometimes, they have also destroyed the intellectuals who remember too much. Without history, no nation can enjoy legitimacy or command patriotic allegiance.

The necessity of history is deeply rooted in personal psychic need and in the human striving for community. None can testify better to this necessity than members of groups who have been denied a usable past. Slaves, serfs and members of subordinate racial or national groups have all, for longer or shorter periods of time, been denied their history. No group has longer existed in this condition than have women. Groups so deprived have suffered a distortion of self-perception and a sense of inferiority based on the denigration of the communal experience of the group to which they belong. Quite naturally, each of these groups, as it moved closer to a position of sharing power with those ruling society, has asserted its claim to the past. Mythical and real heroes were uncovered; evidence of the group's struggle for rights was collected; neglected sources were made to yield information. In the process, inevitably, the established version of history has been revised. In the American setting, this has been the case in regard to African-American history and Native-American history, both fields that have moved from marginality to the mainstream and have, in the process, transformed and enriched our knowledge of the nation's past.

While at first sight the case for women appears to be similar, it is in fact profoundly different. All the other groups mentioned, except for colonials, although of varying sizes, have been minorities in a larger whole. In the case of colonials, subjects of imperial powers, who often are majorities dominated by powerful minorities, there has always been a legitimate past prior to the conquest from which the oppressed group could draw its identity and historical perspective. Jews, ethnics, African slaves could look back on a heroic, though distant, past, on the basis of which they could make claims to the future. During the time of being "out of history" oppressed groups have also been "out of power" and therefore have felt solidarity among themselves as victims of oppression.

Women have had a historical experience significantly different from that of men. Women are not a minority, although they have been treated as if they were members of minority groups. Women appear in each class and rank of society, and they share, through the connection they have with males of their family groups, the fate, values and aspirations of their class or race or ethnic group. Therefore, women frequently are divided from other women by interests of class, race and religion. No other subordinate group with a common experience has ever been so thoroughly divided within itself.

Women have participated in civilization building equally with men in a world dominated and defined by men. Thus, women have functioned in a *separate* culture *within* the culture they share with men. Mary Beard wrote in 1932 that women "have never been solely on the side lines observing passively or waiting for men to put them to needed work. In every crisis women have helped to determine the outcome. . . . No story of cultural history is adequate which neglects or minimizes women's power in the world."[12]

Yet women's culture has remained largely unrecorded and unrecognized. It must be stressed that women have been left out of history not because of the evil intent of male historians, but because we have considered history only in male-centered terms. We have missed women and their activities, because we have asked questions of history that are inappropriate to women. To rectify this we must, for a time, focus on a woman-centered inquiry, considering the possibility of the existence of a female culture within the general culture shared by men and women.[13] As we ask new questions and consult formerly neglected sources, we uncover the record of women's unrecognized activities.[14] For example, when we ask the traditional question, "What have women contributed to reform activities, such as the abolition movement?" we assume that male activities are the norm and that women are, at best, marginal to the male-defined movement. In answer to such a question we learn that abolitionist women demanded the right to lecture in public and to hold office in antislavery societies and thereby, in 1840, provoked a crisis that split and weakened the antislavery movement. What is ignored in this interpretation is the fact that the increased participation of women and their greater activism actually strengthened antislavery ranks. Had we asked the question, "What was women's role in, perception of, and experience in the antislavery movement?" the answers would lend themselves to a somewhat different interpretation. If one looks at the impact of the antislavery movement solely in terms of voting behavior and politics (male activities), the contribution of women may seem unimportant. But reform movements in antebellum America can also be seen as efforts to adjust personal values and public morality to the demands of a rapidly industrializing society. Moral reform, sexual purity, temperance, and abolition became the symbolic issues through which women expressed themselves in the public sphere. Antislavery women's activities—organization building, the spreading of literature, petitioning, participation in slave rescues—helped to create changes in the climate of opinion in the North and West that were essential to the growth of the political antislavery movement. Men and women, even when active in the same social movements, worked in different ways and defined issues differently.[15] As historians are uncovering the record of women's activities and correcting the bias in the interpretation of the past, which has assumed that man is the measure of all that is significant, we are laying the foundation for a new synthesis. Women's History is a tool for allowing us to see the past whole and entire.

Such an enterprise, however, exciting as it is, lies some time ahead. Meanwhile, women must live with the effect of having been deprived of a usable past. As we have noted, history as memory and history as a source of personal identity have presented women with a world in which people like ourselves were, with a few exceptions, invisible in all those activities valued highly as "contributions" to civilization. The actuality—that women, as Mary Beard so confidently asserted, have always been a force in history and have been agents, not subjects, in the process of civilization building—has been obscured.[16] Thus, women have been deprived of heroines and role models and have internalized the idea of their own victimization, passivity and inferiority to men. Men, similarly miseducated through a distorted image of the past, have been reinforced in their culturally created sense of superiority and in the conviction that a sex-based division of labor justifies male dominance.

Speaking of the psychological tensions under which African-Americans have existed in a white world, W. E. B. DuBois described this "peculiar sensation, this double-consciousness, this sense of always looking at one's self through the eyes of others. . . . One ever feels his two-ness—An American, a Negro; two souls, two thoughts, two unreconciled strivings; two warring ideals in one dark body."[17] Although in many decisive respects the condition of women cannot be compared with that of African-Americans, all women have partaken of a kind of "double-consciousness," a sense of being central and yet defined as marginal, essential and yet defined as "the Other," at the core of historical events and yet left out of history.[18]

The complexities of the experience of black women, who are subject to discrimination both as women and as members of a racial minority group, cannot be discussed here. All women have in common that their history comes to them refracted through the lens of men's observations and refracted again through a male-centered value system. The historic condition unique to women is that, for over five thousand years, they have been excluded from constructing history as a cultural tradition and from giving it meaning. In the period when written history was being created, shortly after the formation of the archaic states, women were already in a subordinate condition, their roles, their public behavior, and their sexuality defined by men or male-dominated institutions. From that time on, women were educationally deprived and did not significantly participate in the creation of the symbol system by which the world was explained and ordered. Women did not name themselves; they did not, after the Neolithic era, name gods or shape them in their image.[19] Women have not held power over symbols and thus have been truly marginal to one of the essential processes of civilization. Only in the last two hundred years have the societal conditions been created that would afford women equal access to educational opportunity and, later, full participation in the definition of intellectual fields and disciplines. Only in the past two hundred years have groups of women been able, through organized activities and social sharing, to become conscious of their group identity and with it the actuality of their historical experience, which would lead some of us to begin to reclaim our past. For women, all history up to the twentieth century has truly been prehistory.

If the bringing of women—half the human race—into the center of historical inquiry poses a formidable challenge to historical scholarship, it also offers sustaining energy and a source of strength. With the case of women we can best illustrate that history matters. By contemplating, in the case of women, the consequences of existing without history, we can renew our faith in and commitment to the work of the professional historian.

Today, what does it mean to be a professional historian?

The world in which we now practice our profession is a vastly different world from that in which our profession was first institutionalized. It might be well to remember that written and interpreted history is, of itself, a historical creation, which arose with the emergence of ruling elites. From the time of the king lists of Babylonia and Assyria on, historians, whether priests, royal servants, clerks and clerics or a professional class of university-trained intellectuals, have usually ordered the past within a frame of reference that supported the values of the ruling elite, of which they themselves were a part. The grand unity of design so evident in the history writing of the past has always been based on the commonly held values of those in power. In Western civilization, for many centuries, Christianity provided the common context for the cultural tradition. Later as nationalism developed, national history provided the needed coherence and legitimizing ideology. A teleological framework, in which history was the working out of God's consciousness, gave way to an evolutionary framework, in which history became a story of progress. For American history, manifest destiny and mission long provided an ordering framework, as did confidence in laissez-faire economics and liberal politics. Other commonly held assumptions, such as white superiority and male supremacy, were implicit in the culture, but unacknowledged.

Recent American historiography has reflected the breakdown of commonly held values in the assertion by previously submerged and invisible groups of their right to be heard and to have their own past recorded and interpreted. New technology, which has produced the tape recorder and the computer, has opened new fields, such as oral history and cliometrics. New conceptual frameworks, such as those provided by the social sciences and by psychology, have added to differentiation and specialization.

Historical scholarship has never been more sophisticated, more innovative and more interesting. Specialization and a multiplicity of conceptual frameworks have not weakened historical studies. On the contrary, new groups that have hitherto been "out of history" but are now entering historical inquiry as objects and subjects, have invigorated academic life and form a link to new constituencies outside of the academy. Yet many thoughtful observers have noticed the gap between academic historical scholarship and the public's seemingly insatiable appetite for popular history in its various forms. This phenomenon began early in this century with the media revolution—the dramatic change in the way the society related to past and current events due to the technological innovations embodied in the mass media.[20]

Photography as a mass art form, popular journalism, radio, film and television have profoundly affected the relationship of people to the past. This has never been more sharply evident than in recent decades, when the first generation of youths entirely raised in the age of television have begun to enter adulthood and public life. Members of the "TV generation," and probably all generations succeeding it, connect more readily with the visual symbol than with the written or spoken word. They are discouraged from giving sustained and thoughtful attention to the past by being daily exposed to the mass-media way of perceiving the world.[21] The rapid succession of superficial problems instantly solved, which is the mainstay of both television fare and the advertising that sustains it, induces the viewer to assume that there are simple and readily available solutions to every problem. The constant reiteration of "news," presented in flashes and headlines, induces in the public a present-mindedness, which finds reinforcement in the other mass media and in advertisement. The short-range interpretation of events by television pundits and journalists discourages perspective and in-depth analysis. Present-mindedness, a shallow attention to meaning, and contempt for the value of precise definition and critical reasoning are characteristic attitudes produced by mass media culture. All of them run counter to the mind-set of the historian and to the values and perspective historical studies provide.

Yet the beneficial aspects of education by television—the enormous increase in accessible information, the stimulation and immediacy of entering other lives, the exposure to the variety and richness of human societies and cultures—all feed the public's hunger for a meaningful understanding of the past and for coherent explanations of present-day phenomena. A variety of beneficial historical activities are manifestations of this public interest: genealogy, the vogue for historic spectacles, the popularity of historic-site reconstructions, the search for "roots" through family or ethnic group history. On a shallower level, there is the mass appeal of historical fiction and of new forms that deliberately challenge the boundaries of fact and fiction, such as the docudrama and the docu-film. The public's interest in the past is also reflected in shoddy and surrogate cultural manifestations, such as the nostalgia craze for old records, films and magazines, or in the fashion industry's endless recycling of a past, which it neatly divides into decade-long units. We may deplore the quality of the end product, or we may seek to influence and improve it, but we dare not ignore the concern, interest, enthusiasm of broad new audiences for history.

Without relaxing our standards of accuracy and our commitment to scholarship, we must accept that there are many roads to historical understanding. We must be open to the ways in which people now relate to the past, and we must reach out to communicate with them at their level. We should rejoice at the surfacing of the lost past of women, nonwhite people, and minorities and use every opportunity open to us to encourage members of these groups to participate in the definition of their past with the best skills academic training can provide. In turn, we should allow our own thinking and interpretations to be enriched by the viewpoint and perspective they bring to historical scholarship. We should continue to broaden our definitions of training and accreditation to include applied fields, such as museum and preservation work, train specialists equipped to work as historians in government and business and strive to train biographers and historian/writers, expanding that concept to include writers in the mass media.

A broader understanding of our professional roles is already under way. It is reflected in the increasing participation at all levels of our own organization by historians employed outside of the academy. We may, in time, welcome a new model of professional life in which one can, at various stages of one's career, move freely in between the academic world and the public sector, literary freelance work or business consultancies. Restructuring careers so as to allow historians to move in and out of academe *by choice* might strengthen and energize us.

As we adapt to changing public needs and explore various modes of communication, we must hold fast to our commitment to scholarly and theoretical work. Most of us have and will continue to spend part or most of our lives as scholars. If society increasingly devalues such work and inadequately understands it, we must reaffirm our dedication to scholarship with increasing confidence and assertiveness. Each of us individually, and through our organizations, must be effective publicly in defense of scholarship and of the priceless archival resources on which it rests. Our nation's heritage and its very future are threatened, when shortsighted political decisions undercut the funding for historic documentary projects, for record preservation, and for the National Archives. Freedom of information for scholars and open access to records of government and bureaucracies are causes we must defend with as much vigor as we defend our right to free speech.

As we examine our relationship to the society at large, we see that insofar as we function as fact finders about the past and as re-creators of past worlds (or model builders), the need of society for our skills is as great as ever. It is our function as interpreters of the past, as meaning givers, that has become most problematical. History as cultural tradition and legitimizing ideology and history as explanation have increasingly come under questioning. Again, the causes are societal and historic. The scientific revolution of the 20th century has undermined the claim of history to being, together with philosophy, the universal field of knowledge for ordering the human experience. The facile slogan of the 1960s, which declared history "irrelevant," reflected a perceived discontinuity between industrial and postindustrial society. The explosion of scientific knowledge and of technical control over the environment has made it possible to envision a future dominated by scientific knowledge and technical expertise. For such a future, it appears, the past cannot serve as a model. In its most pragmatic manifestation, this kind of thinking has led to the substitution of "Social Studies" for history in many American school systems.[22] At a more advanced and theoretical level, this kind of thinking is evident in a debate among sociologists, philosophers and historians, some of whom argue that history has been superseded by science as a means of ordering human experience and orienting the individual within society.[23] Most historians would answer that, despite great strides in science and technology, human nature has not essentially changed. Historically formed institutions continue to provide the structures within which the new knowledge and technologies are organized. Historically determined political institutions continue to allocate labor and resources to science and technology, so that those holding and organizing "the new knowledge" operate within the constraints of tradition.

Those arguing the irrelevance of history define history too narrowly, by focusing on history as the transmitter of tradition, as the means for legitimizing the status quo, as the ideology of a ruling elite. But history, as we have discussed earlier, has many other than merely legitimizing functions. It is possible that what we now perceive as "the crisis of history" is merely the coming to an end of the function of history as elite ideology.

Another important strand of 20th-century thought can help us in reorienting history in the modern world. The major upheavals of our time—wars, the Holocaust, the nuclear and cybernetic revolutions, and the threats to the ecological balance—have made us aware of the limited use of rational thought in politics and social planning. Irrationality in political and social behavior may make it more urgent than ever to understand the process of Becoming and the limits placed upon the present by past decisions and choices. Psychoanalysis has directed our attention to the power of the irrational and unconscious in motivating human behavior. Sigmund Freud showed us how the past of the individual, suppressed and made unconscious through faulty interpretation, can exert a coercive force over present behavior. "Healing" of such compulsive behavior occurs through the mental process of bringing past events to awareness and reinterpreting them in light of a new—and better—understanding derived from present circumstances.[24] This process is akin to the work of the historian in reinterpreting past events in light of present questions. The denied past of the group, as well as of the individual, continues to affect the present and to limit the future. We, as historians, might take up the challenge offered by analytic theory and seek to work toward a "healing" of contemporary social pathology, using the tools of our craft imaginatively and with a new sense of direction. We are, after all, not a small group of clerks and mandarins guarding secret knowledge in the service of a ruling ideology, but people with special skills, who translate to others the meaning of the lives and struggles of their ancestors, so that they may see meaning in their own lives.

We do this best in our function as teachers. Most of us, for much of our professional lives, are teachers; yet this activity is the one we seem least to appreciate in ourselves and in others. Our habitual performance at the lectern has, in some aspects, been superseded by the intervention of printing, and many of us, sensing the basic incongruity of the manner in which we conduct our work, have fallen back on being performers, seeking to catch the reluctant attention of an audience more accustomed to the frenetic entertainment style of the mass media.

In fact, the teacher as performer acts within an ancient and valid tradition. Above all, we seek to tell a story and tell it well—to hold the audience's attention and to seduce it, by one means or another, into suspending disbelief and inattention. We seek to focus concentrated attention upon ourselves and to hold it long enough to allow the students' minds to be directed into unexpected pathways and to perceive new patterns. There is nothing shabby about this performance aspect of the teacher's skill, this trick of the magician and the artist. When we succeed in our performance role as teachers, we extend the learner's thoughts and feelings, so that he or she can move into past worlds and share the thoughts and values of another time and place. We offer the student the excitement of puzzle solving in our search for evidence and the sense of discovery in seeing general design out of the mass of particulars.

Lastly, we also teach, as master craftsmen and craftswomen, imparting particular skills to the uninitiated. The ability to think and write with clarity, the habit of critical analysis, the methodology of history, the painstaking patience of the researcher—all these skills are transmitted by the ancient method of transference from master to apprentice. As we allow students to see the historian at work, we become role models, and if we are so inclined, we lighten the students' task by demystifying our knowledge, sharing its "tricks" and openly acknowledging its shortcomings. The craftsmanship aspect of teaching connects us with the craftsmanship of other workers, those who labor with their hands and those who work with their minds. As teaching and researching historians, we work as did the master stonemasons and woodcarvers on the great medieval cathedrals and the ancient Mayan or Buddhist temples or the women who wove the great Bayeux tapestry:

we do our own particular work, contributing to a vast, ongoing enterprise. In our own performance and in the standards we set for students we can represent dedication to understanding the past for its own sake and in its own light. In an age of alienation we can impart a sense of continuity to the men and women we teach. And we can help them to see the discontinuities in a larger perspective.

The problem of discontinuities has never loomed larger than in this generation, which is the first generation in history forced to consider the possibility of the extinction of humankind in a nuclear war. The possibility of discontinuity on such a vast scale staggers the imagination and reinforces the need of each individual to know his or her place in history. Now, as never before, we need to have a sense of meaning in our lives and assurance of a collective continuity. It is history, the known and ordered past, that enables us to delineate goals and visions for a communal future. Shared values, be they based on consensus or on the recognition and acceptance of many ways of form-giving, link the individual to the collective immortality of the human enterprise.

The historian professes and practices such knowledge and imparts it to others with passion and an abiding confidence in the necessity of history. In these times, more than ever, it is good to be a historian.

PART III

RE-VISIONING HISTORY

10

Differences Among Women

The development of women's history in the past twenty years has not only helped to bring new subject matter to history, but has forced us to deal with the concepts and values underlying the organization of historical studies and of all intellectual fields. It has forced us to question not only why certain content was previously omitted, ignored, and trivialized, but also to consider who decides what is to be included. In short, we have begun first to question and then to challenge the conceptual framework for the organization of traditional knowledge. We challenge it because of its omissions: it leaves out the

This article was first prepared for delivery as a keynote address for the Lowell Conference on Women's History, sponsored by the Lowell National Historical Park, the Harvard Graduate School of Education, the Massachusetts Department of Education, the New Hampshire Department of Education and the New England Center for Equity Assistance, held at Lowell, Mass., on March 2, 1988. I benefited from the discussion and comments by over two hundred high school and college teachers attending this conference.

I am grateful also for the comments and suggestions made by Professor Nellie Y. McKay, Afro-American Studies Department, University of Wisconsin-Madison, and by Professor Nell Painter, Princeton University. Over the years, I have learned much from discussion of my ideas on "differences" with my colleagues Florencia Mallon, Steve Stern and Steven Feierman, who helped me to sharpen my thinking in the light of their expertise in Latin-American and African history. Finally, the concepts on which this article is based were tested and applied in an undergraduate lecture course "Sex, Gender, Class and Race in Comparative Historical Perspective," which I have twice given at the University of Wisconsin-Madison. The interest and enthusiasm of my students for this conceptual framework encouraged me to write this article.

I am indebted to the participants of the Conference on Graduate Training in U.S. Women's History, held at Wingspread, Racine, Wisc., October 21–23, 1988, who shared their course syllabi and experiences in attempts to reconstruct Women's History and U.S. History survey courses along nonracist, nonsexist lines.

experiences, activities, and ideas of half or more of humankind. We challenge it because it is elitist: it leaves out not only all women, but most men, those of non-white races, those of various ethnicities, and, until quite recently, those of lower classes. In so doing, it defines all the groups omitted as less significant than the groups included. Patently, this is untrue and therefore it is unacceptable. We challenge it because what traditional history teaches us denies our own experience of reality. We live in a world in which nothing happens without the active participation of men and women and yet we are constantly being told of a past world in which men are presumed to act and women presumed to be acted upon. Women's history, even in its short development, has proven this judgement to be false, for the past as well as the present. Women are and always have been active participants in the shaping of events. One of the basic errors of patriarchal thought has been to make claims of universality for descriptions of the activities of a small elite group of upper-class white males. Traditional historians have described the activities of this group and called it the history of all of humankind. They have subsumed all women under the term "men" and have ignored the actual differences that exist among people by asserting that the small group whose activities they describe can stand for the rest of us. It obviously cannot. In rejecting this androcentric distortion of the past, we have opened the way to other insights and challenges.

Historians of women have long ago come to see that "women" cannot be treated as a unified category any more than "men-as-a-group" can.[1] Women differ by class, race, ethnic and regional affiliation, religion, and any number of other categories. Thus, historians of women have stressed the need for using such categories as tools for analysis.[2] What we mean by that is that whenever we study a group of women, past or present and make generalizations about them, we must take not only the similarities but the differences among them into consideration. We must ask, does this hold true for women of different races? for women of different classes? It simply will no longer do to design a research project or to teach without taking the differences among women into account. Anyone can, of course, study any particular group of women, but then one is not entitled to making claims of universality based solely on the study of that particular group.

The problem one encounters when using race, class, ethnicity, and gender as tools of analysis is that one seems to add endless variation to any problem without gaining greater analytical clarity. One drowns in illustrative detail regarding the various groups. The traditionalists describe this as losing sight of the unity of events in the past, the so-called "common core."[3] Different groups of the population may have experienced the Civil War in different ways, but the common core was provided by the political and military events, which is, they say, what we should be teaching. I would argue that we should be teaching both the common core and the particular in all its variations, and that we distort reality and the truth if we do not.

The problem is that we have an inadequate conceptual framework for dealing with "differences." The model we have is the model of liberal pluralism, according to which America represents not a melting pot but a salad bowl.[4] Presumably this is an advance over the "melting pot" which assumed a national identity into which all alien elements— alien by race, ethnicity, religion, and sex—would need to "melt." The liberal pluralism of the salad bowl assumes not a "melting" but a sharing of space by multiple parts which add up to a whole. This is indeed a conceptual advance, but it is insufficient as a model of reality because it ignores power, dominance, hegemony. It assumes that the process of doing justice to "differences" is additive—leave the whole concept intact and add the infinite variety in which humankind appears in society and history.

If one ignores "differences" one distorts reality. If one ignores the power relations built on differences one reinforces them in the interest of those holding power. I would like to propose a different conceptual model for dealing with "differences."[5]

When men discovered how to turn "difference" into dominance they laid the ideological foundation for all systems of hierarchy, inequality, and exploitation. They found a way of justifying such systems and of keeping them functioning with the cooperation of the dominated. This "invention of hierarchy" can be traced and defined historically: it occurs everywhere in the world under similar circumstances, although not at the same time. It occurs when the development of militarism due to the technological innovations of the Bronze Age coincides with the economic shifts occasioned by the agricultural revolution. Small groups of men, usually military leaders, usurp power in their domain, usually following some conquest of foreigners, and consolidate such power by ideological and institutional means. These means always rest upon the discovery that "difference" can justify dominance. For Western civilization, these events occur in the Ancient Near East in the third and second millennia B.C. and take the form of state formation.[6]

States formed through the consolidation of early military conquests by tribal chiefs or kings become legitimized by the creation of myths of origin which confer divine or semi-divine power upon their rulers, and by the formation of laws, which set up rules increasing hierarchy and regulating dominance. Everywhere, the first step toward turning "difference into dominance" is the institution of patriarchal privileges of men over women.

A small group of men dominate resources and allocate them to the women they have acquired as sexual property and to their children, to other less powerful men, and to a newly created underclass of slaves. The texture of power relationships thus created balances privileges and obligations for each group in such a way as to make the whole arrangement acceptable and to continue it in the interest of the dominant male group. Women and their children, in an age of rampant militarism and constant warfare and in an age of high infant and maternal mortality, needed protection in order for the tribe as a whole to survive. Such reasoning led women in the first place to accept and cooperate with the "patriarchal bargain"—in exchange for their sexual and reproductive services to one man, they will be guaranteed protection and resources for themselves and their children. Slavery, which develops at a time when men first acquire sufficient resources to keep captives alive instead of killing them, initially starts with a similar bargain. Slave women and later men accept that bargain the moment they accept the gift of their life after military conquest in exchange for their enslavement.[7]

It is no accident that everywhere the first slaves known are women of foreign tribes. Often such tribes are racially and visibly different from their conquerors, which makes it easier for the conquerors to designate them permanently as an underclass. But where such racial differences do not exist, it is possible to create them by "marking" the slaves—with a brand, a peculiar way of cutting the hair, a special way of dressing or other means. Always, what is accentuated is "difference." The slave is different from the master and because he is different he can be designated as inferior. Because he or more likely she is designated as inferior she can be exploited, commodified, and designated as in some way sub-human. The institutionalization of militarism as a way of life presupposes hierarchical thinking—some people who dominate have the right to dominate because they are superior; the dominated must accept being dominated because they are inferior.

How can one tell who is to be dominant and who is to be dominated? By force, first of all—the victors dominate; the conquered are dominated. But rule by force alone is untenable in the long run. Even the fiercest warriors could not long enslave other warriors unless they had several conquerors watching each conquered warrior day and night. Dominance is only possible if it can be justified and accepted both by the dominant and the dominated and by the large majority of people who are neither. And, historically, what makes dominance acceptable, is putting a negative mark on difference. This group or that group is different from us; they are our "Other." And because they are our "Other" we can rule them. It is upon such ideological foundations that class dominance was made acceptable even to people who did not directly benefit from it. At the time of the formation of the archaic states non-slaveholding men accepted the bargain of being dominated and exploited in regard to resources by more powerful men of their own group because they were simultaneously offered the chance to dominate and control the resources of others, the "different" others, namely the women and children of their own class. Even to men who did not themselves hold slaves, the existence of an underclass raises their own sense of status and made them accept their own relative inequality as a fair arrangement.

Once the system of dominance and hierarchy is institutionalized in custom, law, and practice, it is seen as natural and just and people no longer question it, unless historical circumstances change very dramatically. For the dominated, the benefits the original bargain conferred upon them are lost, once slavery becomes hereditary—it is then simply exploitation based on arbitrary power.

What I have briefly outlined here is a pattern of development which took many hundreds of years to consolidate. What is important is that this analysis shows, in its simplest and rudimentary form, the connectedness of various forms of difference-turned-into-dominance. It shows that sex, class, and race dominance are interrelated and inseparable, from the start. The difference between men and women was the first, most easily notable difference and therefore dominance by men could first be acted out on that terrain. But class and race dominance (in the form of the enslavement of conquered foreign people) developed almost immediately upon this first human "discovery" of how to use power so as to benefit people unequally. The function of all designations of "Otherness" or deviance is to keep hierarchy in place for the benefit of the dominant. I am not here trying to set up priorities of oppression. Which system of oppression came first and which second is insignificant, if we understand that we are dealing with one, inseparable system with different manifestations.

But we do need richer, more complex, and more relational definitions of terms with which we usually work, such as "class" and "race." In Marxist terms "class" is defined, as a group "who play the same part in the mechanism of production" or, alternatively, "men's relationship to the means of production." The Weberian definition is "people who have life chances in common, as determined by their power to dispose of goods and skills for the sake of income."[8] No matter what the definition, class has been so defined that women are subsumed under the category "men." Males and females are considered as belonging to the same class, without definite distinctions between them. But "class" never describes a single set of locations, relations, and experiences. "Class" is genderic, that is it is expressed and institutionalized in terms that are *always different* for men and women. For men, "class" describes their relationship to the means of production and their power over resources and women and children. For women, "class" describes their relationship to the means of production *as mediated* through the man to whom they render sexual and reproductive services and/or the man on whom they are dependent in their family of origin. In the case of women who enjoy economic independence, "class" still describes not only their relationship to the means of production, but their control (or lack thereof) over their reproductive capacity and their sexuality.

The concept "race" will similarly have to be expanded and redefined. The definition of "race" as a mark of difference and, thereby, inferiority antedates the formation of Western civilization, as I have shown. From its inception, "race" as a defining term was created genderically, that is, it was applied in a different way to men and women. Men of oppressed races were primarily exploited as workers; women were *always* exploited as workers, as providers of sexual services, and as reproducers. Dominant elites, once they had institutionalized slavery, acquired the unpaid labor of enslaved men and women, but they also acquired the sexual and reproductive services of slave women as a commodity. That is, the children of slave women became an actual commodity to be worked, sold, and traded; the unrewarded sexual services of slave women to their master enhanced the master's status among his peers, as in the form of harems; slave women's sexual services were and could be commodified in the form of prostitution.[9]

The binary gendered opposition (male/female) which is so firmly rooted in our culture and cultural product as well as in our language and thought, makes it difficult for us to see the complexity of other structural relationships in society. We have thought of classifications such as "class" and "race" as being vertical boxes into which to sort people in history, but it has been difficult for us to conceptualize the overlapping boundaries of the two concepts.[10] When we think not in terms which compare two separate oppressive systems which may show some overlap, but in terms of one system with several, fully integrated aspects which depend for their existence one upon the other, a truer relationship can be visualized.[11] We can then discuss not "priorities" of oppression or primacies (is a black woman more oppressed because of her sex or of her race?) but we can show the inter-relatedness of both aspects of oppression and their interdependency. Once we do that, a richer description, more closely related to actual relationships, can be drawn.[12]

The system of male dominance over resources and women, called patriarchy, depends for its existence on creating categories of "deviants" or "Others." Such groups, variously constituted in different times and places, are always defined as being "different" from the hegemonic group and assumed to be inferior. It is upon this assumption of the inferiority of presumed "deviant" groups that hierarchy is instituted and maintained. Hierarchy is institutionalized in the state and its laws, in military, economic, educational, and religious institutions, in ideology and the hegemonic cultural product created by the dominant elite. The system which has historically appeared in different forms, such as ancient slavery, feudalism, capitalism, industrialism, depends, for its continuance on its ability to split the dominated majority into various groups and to mystify the process by which this is done. The function of various forms of oppression, which are usually treated as separate and distinct, but which in fact are aspects of the same system, is to accomplish this division by offering different groups of the oppressed various advantages over other groups and thus pit them one against the other. Racism, antisemitism, various forms of ethnic prejudice, sexism, classism, and homophobia are all means to this end. If we see these various forms of creating "deviance" and "Otherness" as aspects of one and the same system of dominance, we can demystify the process by which the system constructs a reality which constantly sustains and reinforces it.

Let me illustrate this by a concrete example. In the antebellum South lower-class white males, whose long-range economic interests were actually opposed to the economic interests of the planter class, derived psychological and status benefits from racism. They had control over the sexuality and reproduction of women of their own class and enjoyed sexual privileges over Black women. This combination of sexual and status privileges made them cooperative with the planter's hegemonic system, despite the fact that they were deprived of educational opportunities, had limited access to political power and had to subordinate their economic interest to that of the planters.[13]

White and Black women of all classes in the antebellum South were also denied political and legal rights and access to education. Although neither group controlled their sexuality nor their reproduction, the differences between them were substantial. White women, regardless of class, owed sexual and reproductive services to the men to whom they were married. Black women, in addition to the labor extracted from them, owed sexual and reproductive services to their white masters and to the Black men their white masters had selected for them. Since the white master of Black women could as well be a white woman, it is clear that racism was for Black women and men the decisive factor which structured them into society and controlled their lives. Conversely, white women could offset whatever economic and social disadvantages they suffered by sexism by the racist advantages they had over both Black men and women. Practically speaking, this meant that white women benefited from racism economically, insofar as they owned slaves; that they could relieve themselves of child-rearing (and at times even childbearing) responsibilities by using the enforced services of their female slaves; that they were relieved of doing unpaid domestic labor by using slave labor. In addition white men and women of all classes derived a sense of higher status from the racist system which decisively affected their consciousness.

Another way of saying this is that dominant elite, white, upper-class men benefited from all aspects of their dominance—economic and educational privilege, sexual and reproductive control, and higher status. Women of their own class benefited sufficiently from racist and economic privilege so as to mask for them the disadvantages and discrimination they experienced because of sexism. Whites of the lower classes benefited sufficiently from racism and (in the case of males) from sexism so that they supported the system, even in face of obvious economic and political disadvantages. For those dominated and oppressed by racism, classism and sexism, all aspects of the oppressive system work to make their emancipation more difficult.

The fact that in the case of antebellum slavery the dominant elite understood the importance of all aspects of the oppressive system to the continuance of their privileges is shown in the increasing severity with which laws against educating slaves were enforced in that period and in the continuous existence of unequal laws in regard to sexual crimes. From the middle of the 18th century on, sexual crimes of Black men against white women were punished by death, while sexual crimes of white men against Black women were not only not considered crimes but were considered white male rights. The denial to African-American men not only of sexual privilege over women of their own race, but of their ability to protect women of their families from the attacks of white men was a further means of dehumanizing them, defining them as "Other" and forcing them to accept lower-status self-definitions.[14] Racism never succeeded in actually making Black men internalize such self-definitions; yet dominant whites never gave up the attempt to impose them on slaves and later on freedmen.

That African-American men were well aware of the intended effect of this strategy can be seen in the Reconstruction period when they first claimed male privilege over their women as a symbol of their "manhood." Black women were to render domestic and nurturant services to their own families only (a goal many of them understandably supported); black men were to be breadwinners; black men were to be able to protect their women from sexual assault by whites.[15] One of the

139

marks of the failure of Reconstruction and of the continuing existence of the racist system was precisely that these goals were not realizable in the 19th-century South.

The importance of sexism as a means of enforcing racism can also be seen in the way racist double standards were used in the post-Civil War period to keep freedmen and later all southern Blacks in subordinate status despite the end of slavery. The rise of violence against black males and the sharp increase in lynchings, always excused as being "in defense of white womanhood," served to intimidate the free black community in the post-Reconstruction period and again at the turn of the century, when Blacks in the South were virtually disfranchised. It was African-American women in their clubs, and especially Ida B. Wells, who first uncovered the workings of this sexist-racist double standard and who exposed the falsity of the charge that white women needed protection from black men.[16] Similarly, the history of the U.S. trade union movement abounds with evidence of the ways employers were able to exploit ethnic and racial differences among their work force in order to retard or prevent unionization, sometimes for decades. Racially or ethnically defined status privileges often induced white workers to act against their best economic self-interest, as did lower-class whites in the antebellum South.[17]

The inter-relatedness of distinctions based on race, class, ethnicity, and sex is not so clearly demonstrable in contemporary industrial society as it is in the society of the antebellum South. Gender relations have undergone considerable change, and some of the more obvious male sexual privileges have altered under the impact of women's political struggle and economic changes. Men no longer have property rights in women and children; women have, at least on a formal level, equal access to education and are entitled to equality of political representation, even if they do not actually enjoy it in practice. Large numbers of women, except for the poor, now have access to economic resources directly, that is, not mediated through a man, although this does not hold for married women who are full-time homemakers. The control of women's reproductive resources is no longer exerted by individual men but instead by male-dominated institutions such as the courts, the state, the churches, and the medical professional establishment.

Still, in contemporary U.S.A, white males of elite groups continue to control the major corporations, the legal and political establishment, the news media, the academic establishment (despite some inroads made by women), the trade union movement, the churches. The economic dependency of women (and, with it, the basic inequality in access to and control of resources) continues. It is secured through the definition of heterosexuality as the norm; through gender-indoctrination; the continued existence of women's unpaid domestic labor and child-rearing services; the gender-based wage discrimination against women and their concentration in low-paid, temporary or dead-end service jobs. Male dominance and privilege are further expressed through the definition of professionalism to fit the male model and through the denial to women of professional career patterns suited to their life cycles. It also is manifested in sexual harassment on the job as a means of keeping women out of better jobs. Male control of women's sexuality and reproduction is now exerted through the politicization of issues of reproductive choice, the continuing growth of the pornography establishment, the sex industry and of prostitution, which, as it has been for millennia, is predominantly an occupation of lower-class women. The ever growing phenomenon of violence against women and children is another distorted and perverted form of male dominance.

All whites derive tangible benefits from racism, but such benefits vary by class and sex so that upper-class males benefit more from racism than do lower-class people of both sexes and upper-class women. Racism, by splitting people from one another, helps to prevent alliances of lower-class people which might effectively challenge the system. Racism gives the illusion of superiority to lower-class whites, which convinces them to support the dominant elites, often against their true economic interests.

The benefits to upper-and middle-class women of the race/class system are so tangible that it is easy for them to overlook and disregard its oppressive aspects, even to themselves. The gains made by women over a century of struggle have benefited upper-class women disproportionally. This group has control over its own property; it reaps the economic benefits of racism and classism and shares them with upper-class men. Women of this group share, even if on a lower level, the benefits of education and of opportunities for professional careers. Class and race privileges allow such women to fulfill their domestic and child-rearing services by substituting another woman for themselves. Their economic independence allows them to define sexual relations in their own interest and to secure divorces without great economic loss. In short, it is their class privilege which helps them offset any disadvantages arising from their subordinate status as women.

The women less privileged economically are more vulnerable since they are in a worse bargaining position. For many middle-and lower-class women, gaining some economic independence by working means assuming the burden of a double working day. Such women are usually not in a position to support themselves and their children in case of divorce, which means they are unable to bargain for better conditions within their marriages or to make other choices. This is the large group of women of whom it can be said that they are "one man away from poverty." This is also the group of white women most committed against feminism since their security and economic opportunities seem to them entirely to rest on the maintenance of their marriages and the good will of the men with whom they are affiliated. Such women have a direct economic investment in maintaining their "respectability" against people of other races or ethnicities or against the most danger-ous "Other"—non-respectable women. Black women of this economic group do not necessarily expect black men to support them and their children; thus, their attitude toward a feminism of their own definition is more positive than that of white women of the same economic class.[18]

In modern industrial society, the majority of the poor are women and children. The "feminization of poverty" is the modern expression of the multifaceted system of patriarchal dominance. Women become poor because they are abandoned by men; because they are oppressed by being in a lower class or a nonwhite race; because they are members of a "deviant" group (lesbians, drug users, handicapped, "immoral," single mothers) or because they are old. Modern society has created new adaptations for the old definitions of "Otherness," but the function of defining "Otherness" as deviance has not changed. It helps to raise the status of dominant males to define themselves against despised outgroups; such raised status perceptions secure the collaboration of middle- and lower-class people in the system that robs them of equity and justice.

Historians who understand the inter-relatedness of the various as-pects of the system of patriarchal dominance are in a better position to interpret the history of women than are those who continue to regard class, race, and gender dominance as separate though intersecting and overlapping systems. The intellectual construct of separate systems inevitably marginalizes the subordination of women.

Race, class, and gender oppression are inseparable; the construct, reinforce, and support one another. The form which class first took historically was genderic and racist. The form racism first took was genderic and classist. The form the state first took was patriarchal. These are the starting points for re-conceptualization.

Above all, historians and teachers must consciously attempt to step outside of the vertical boxes of patriarchal thinking. We are not going to have an integrated history by being additive, nor by structuring a history of "upstairs and downstairs," "private and public," "production and reproduction." We will need to re-think the ways we organize what we teach in order to do justice to "differences" by making them central to our thinking. Just what does that mean concretely?

It means first of all, as I have shown in my example of antebellum history, that we should always vary our generalizations by creating an interactive contextual model which considers the ways in which factors of race, class, ethnicity, and sex are expressed in regard to men and women of the groups under discussion. It means also that we must use new strategies to organize the content of our teaching so as to make these issues visible.

If we teach a U.S. survey following a traditional textbook, the text will barely mention women. If we then simply "add" women, we have improved on this outline but not by much. The women we have added will either be women much like the men we talk about or they will look inferior by comparison with the men. To make women central to our conceptual framework, we must assume that what they do and think is equally important with what the men do and think. If we make such an assumption, we will ask about every unit we teach: what were the women doing while the men were doing what we are teaching? and, going an analytical step further, how did the women interpret what they were doing? This immediately changes the whole unit: we are now talking not only of a world populated by male actors and evaluated according to male standards, but we are talking of a world populated by male and female actors and evaluated by male and female standards.

Now let us see what happens when we make "difference" central to our analysis. We can, of course, be additive, and I would guess that in most cases people who want to do justice to the varieties of ethnic and racial experiences are now teaching in that way: it was like this for European immigrants to the colonies, and it was like that for Native Americans, and like that for African-Americans—the old salad bowl approach. But what if we told the story of settlement not from the moment Columbus "discovered America," a statement and organization which immediately tell the students that what happened on American soil before that time was insignificant and that the arrival of this particular group of Spaniards is of more significance than earlier arrivals or the lives and activities of native peoples? We might start, instead, with the earliest records of Native Americans on this continent, with the way they lived and thought and acted, with their social organization—which was, in many cases, not patriarchal—with their religions, their economies, their values. We might then talk about the various groups of invaders consecutively, and we would be giving students a totally different perspective on the significance of the arrival of the little Spanish flotilla, which made its discovery only because of a navigational error. Following such an approach—which, by the way, already exists in some texts—we might then tell the story of the various decisive events in U.S. history with an equally-handed view.[19] We would want to present not only different points of view—in each case drawing as much as possible on primary sources of the relevant groups—but we would want to represent accurately the power relations existing between the various groups as they interacted in the same place and time. Some teachers have already experimented with organizing women's history survey courses by starting with native American women and then moving, not from East to West, as traditional historiography does, but from West to East. Since settlement in the West actually antedates the development of English settlement in the East, this method has distinct advantages. It also builds a comparative approach into the very structure of the course.

All re-conceptualization must start with a new conceptual framework. We must have our goal firmly in mind and approach our task by finding new analytic questions. If we do this, the integration of new materials will not have to come at the expense of omitting something else of importance. Rather, the question will arise: why is this important and not that? It is not an easy task, and it will challenge the best of our collective minds and energies. But it is a worthwhile enterprise from every point of view. What we are trying to do is to create a holistic history in which men and women, in the various aspects of their lives, interact in various ways, reflecting the differences among them. The textured richness of such a reconstruction of the past depends on our ability to embrace difference, hear many languages, and see interdependencies rather than separation. Learning from female language and modes of perception, we will need to be relational, existential, and aware of our own involvement even as we use the male mode to categorize, order and analyze. The point is that the two modes always have been coexisting and complementary. We must adapt our own craft to that reality by ourselves becoming conscious and accepting of it.

1 1

Rethinking the Paradigm

I. Class
II. Race

In the past ten years, the new and often still embattled field of
Women's Studies has made an enormous intellectual contribution
to transforming thought and reconfiguring curricula by making the
question of power and "differences" among women the focus of serious
debate. Because it has been cross-disciplinary and has mostly taken the
form of articles in specialized scholarly journals, the broader significance of this debate has not always been visible. When looked at from
the vantage point of a single academic discipline, the debate has seemed
disjointed, divisive and fragmented. In fact, the debate on "differences"
represents the most serious challenge to traditional thought and traditional ways of organizing knowledge so far. A tentative consensus is
emerging on a number of issues, as new definitions and holistic modes
of thinking are being applied to centuries-old problems.

The dominant system of ideas in Western societies for nearly four
thousand years has been derived from and in turn supportive of the
social system of patriarchy. Patriarchy is a hierarchical, militaristic so-

This essay was first presented at the American Historical Association meeting in
December 1985 in a much simpler form. I then rewrote it several times and presented
versions of it to different audiences. The final version was greatly improved by the
critical comments of Alice Kessler-Harris, Ann Lane, Kenneth Lockridge, Elizabeth
Minnich, Peggy Pascoe, Ruth Rosen and the sixteen members of the Stanford Women's
History/Women Historians Group who devoted a session to the discussion of the
section on "class." The section on "race" was greatly helped by the critical comments
of Bonnie Johnson, Jan Simpson, Steven Feierman, Nellie McKay. I owe a debt of
gratitude to all of these commentators.

cial organization in which resources, property, status and privileges are allocated to persons in accordance with culturally defined gender roles. Its forms have changed vastly over time and vary with place, but the essence remains: some men control property and hold power over other men and over most women; men or male-dominated institutions control the sexuality and reproduction of females; most of the powerful institutions in society are dominated by men. The persistence of this system was illustrated by the 1994 UN Conference on Population in Cairo. On the subject of women's reproductive health it was not women, but government representatives, mostly men—the Vatican's celibate male clergy and the Islamic fundamentalists—who claimed the right to make decisions. The central prerogative of patriarchy, the male right to control female reproduction was as much at stake as was the health of women and the well-being of children.

Patriarchy is a system of dominance based on the "invention" that arbitrary differences among people can be used to construct categories by which the unequal distribution of resources and power by small elites over large and diverse populations can be justified, explained and made acceptable to those exploited. In short, "difference" can be used to create and maintain power. The differences used can be based on race, class, sex, physical makeup or any other arbitrary distinction, body image, sexual preference.

The debate around "differences" has for long been cast within the framework that assumes that differences are real and significant; that they mark separate identities and that in fact the various categories of "difference"—sex, race, ethnicity, class—are comparable with each other. In other words, the debate so far has stayed within the framework of binary thought. The categories are considered valid, but their placement is disputed. What is needed, it is said, is to decenter the dominant white male and to bring the marginals—women, colonial, people of color, ethnicities etc.—into the center.[1] This is indeed transformative thinking and a valid critique of patriarchal thought. But it is, I think, insufficient. We must question the very categories and arrive at a more nuanced understanding of their relation to each other.

My premise is that the categories are *arbitrarily* selected in such a way as to conceal overlapping features of each and to obscure their true relation to each other.

It has long become obvious that women cannot be subsumed under one term or category and that they vary along lines of class, race, ethnicity, religion, region. Yet the exact relationship of these "aspects" or categories has been puzzling and bewildering. Are these categories separate structures of social organization? If so, are some predominant over others? That is, is class more important than race? Is gender more important than class? If they are not separate structures, but "aspects" of the construction of hierarchy, how exactly do the different aspects relate to one another?

In Women's History other questions pertaining to class and race have long been unanswerable and disturbing. If men and women belong to the same class, why are women's interests within the class always subordinated to those of men? If and when lower classes gain ascendancy, with women participating actively in "the revolution," why is it that with the consolidation of power by the revolutionaries women's interests are deferred and later submerged? If race is the significant divide, why are lower-class men or men of oppressed racial and ethnic minorities oppressive to women of their own group and just exactly how are they so oppressive? If sisterhood is truly a possibility, how can it emerge between women of different classes or races?

Let us then look more closely at the "mantra"—sex, race, ethnicity, class—and see how useful it is or is not for purposes of analysis. I personally don't like the "mantra" because it is linguistically awkward. I also don't like it because it continues the practice of sorting, putting people into vertical boxes labeled "sex", "class" etc., as though doing so would illuminate the complexity of their inter-relatedness. The categories, although inextricably intertwined, are actually not of the same order. If I were to assert that we must take into consideration women's weight, family history and taste in music, before proceeding to any generalization about women, it would immediately be obvious to the reader that the categories cited have nothing to do with each other. Weight is a physical characteristic, family history is an attribute arbitrarily selected from the person's background, and taste in music is an equally arbitrary category describing the person's predilections. It is not so different with our "mantra" categories.

Each of them consists of some noticeable distinction from an imaginary norm. And each category also consists of a powerful mental construct based on that distinction. The construct, in turn, can be positively or negatively evaluated, according to who it is that does the defining. Let's see how that works.

Sex (not gender) is a physical inborn characteristic. Sex—the physical differences between men and women—is a biological given, on top of which culture and power have developed elaborate mental constructs. In the case of sex, the constructs are: the definition of sexuality; the definition of roles and activities deemed proper for each designated sex. We have termed this construct *gender*. As Joan Scott expressed it: "Gender is the social organization of sexual difference . . . the knowledge that establishes meanings for bodily differences."[2] The term "gender" alerts us to make distinctions between the given, actual differences and the ideology or mental constructs built upon it.[3]

Class is a term which sorts people according to their relation to resources (the means of production) and to power. Class, like race is then a social construct, but unlike race it is based on actual differences. The resources that distinguish a rich man from a poor are tangible. They may be elaborated culturally and defined in various ways, but they are quantifiable and real.

Race is a socially constructed term, built on perceivable differences which are culturally elaborated. I will discuss this in more detail in a separate section below (pp. 184–198). For purposes of comparison, we can look upon it as somewhat similar to the case of sex, only we do not have at our disposal two separate terms to distinguish actual differences from cultural constructs. The characteristics that distinguish a white woman from a black woman may be visible to the naked eye, but they become significant only in a system in which difference is used to justify dominance. Otherwise, the visible distinction would not matter any more than does the color of hair or eyes. Perhaps it would be useful to distinguish between different characteristics and "race" (in quotes to indicate the cultural construction), the way we do with sex and gender.

Ethnicity on the other hand, is not defined by physical properties. It is an affiliation by cultural, historical characteristics. The categories by which people are sorted into "ethnicities" are quite obviously imprecise and arbitrary. Is a woman with an Irish father and a German/French mother Irish/German/French? Irish-German with some addition of French? What is a Latin-American? Who is a Hispanic? Are we talking of language affiliation, of cultural affinity, of common history?

Are Spanish-speaking Mexican-Americans Latinos or Hispanics or what? The categories of ethnicity shift with U.S. domestic policies and with the shifting judgment of the Census Bureau, but that does not make them accurately descriptive. On the contrary. Perhaps, if we used food and lullabies as criteria of ethnicity, we would come up with an actual category. On what lullabies was the person raised? What lullabies does she sing to her children? What kind of food does she cook and eat? Ethnicity as a sorting device is obviously arbitrary and unreliable, as is recognized even by the Census Bureau in its efforts to create new categories. In the 1980 Census each individual was required to identify him/herself as a member of a single race and there was no category for "mixed race." Thus, two-third of Hawaiians felt compelled to designate "other" as their racial category. The 1990 Census required either/or responses in the race and "Hispanic" section, but allowed people to acknowledge multiple ancestries in the "ethnic ancestry" questions. Increasingly, organizations made up of multiracial people have urged the abandonment of all "racial" categories in the Census and their replacement by "ethnic" categories.[4]

If we assume that persons should be given designations or named according to their own choice, then what are we actually doing by asking people to so designate themselves? In the case of ethnicity, as well as in the case of sex, once a person decides which label to stand under, he or she is also affected by the mental construct created under that label. In the 19th-century U.S.A. to belong under the label "Irish" was to be an outcast, a member of the lower classes, an undesirable. The same label in the 20th century does not carry such connotations.

Influenced by postmodern and deconstructionist theory, some contemporary scholars have developed the challenging view that "ethnicity" is a modern, constructed identity. They speak of the "invention of ethnicity." Pointing to the overlapping of concepts of ethnicity and nationalism and to the historic origins of both concepts in the revolutions of the 18th century, these scholars argue that ethnicity is reinvented and newly interpreted in each generation.[5] In the wake of the American and the French revolutions, which destroyed a social order based on inherited aristocratic rank, nation-states needed to consolidate their power and create cohesive communities by appeals to ethnic or racial homogeneity. The creation of national, ethnic literatures, the historicizing of invented folkloric traditions, the celebrations of "folk" festivals, the promotion of traditional costumes (often highly inauthentic), all furnished symbols to sustain the new ethnicities. Similarly, in 19th-century U.S., as various ethnic immigrant groups struggled for economic and political power, they consolidated their claims by using these symbols of ethnicity.[6] This postmodernist approach is promising because it reveals the tension between lived historical experience and social construction, which in the case of sex and gender is linguistically explicit, but which, in relation to class, ethnicity and race, is obscured.

My purpose in this essay is to dissect the "mantra"—sex, race, ethnicity, class—and re-define the relationships among the various aspects of dominance in a holistic, functional way. For class, I focus on the process whereby class is first constituted historically and then maintained over time, and show that this process always involves gendered relationships. Surveying these gendered relationships—homogamous marriages, gendered inheritances and unequal obligations of families toward sons and daughters—I depart from the traditional Marxist and Weberian concepts of class and re-define class as a process over time through which hierarchical and exploitative relations are created and maintained in a patriarchal system.

Then, in a separate section, I re-define race and show its intrinsic linkages to class and gender. I hope by this discussion to conceptualize all three categories as aspects of one and the same system and to arrive at a conceptual model which has both analytic and transformative power.

I. RETHINKING THE PARADIGM: CLASS

Feminist theories concerning the relationship of gender and class have covered a wide spectrum of opinion: from those ignoring or downgrading economic class in formulating theories of sexual oppression to those adopting and revising a Marxist or Weberian conceptual framework.[7] In the more recent period, theories centered on the concept "gender" have also encompassed a wide range of positions: from feminist thinkers using the concept as an analytical tool in studying social and intellectual history, to those using a deconstructionist and those using a postmodernist framework.[8]

My own work has not neatly fitted into any of these divisions, although there are aspects of each approach that I have at times found useful. This essay rests upon thirty years of my work on class and race. I have included these categories of analysis in all my work as a historian.[9] As a post-Marxist at the time I became a feminist, I early on concluded that the Marxist and Weberian approach to class were inadequate and did not accurately describe the situation of women, although Weber, in introducing "status" as an aspect of power did at least make room for a consideration of women's role in society. Explanatory systems that ignore the fact that women are half of the population to be described and do not consider the subordination of women as central cannot accurately describe the situation of women or provide liberating theory. For a time I experimented with a dual systems approach, but finally found it inadequate. On the other hand, the theoretical work of radical feminists with its focus on the sexual and reproductive oppression of women had a great impact on me, although I could not accept the tendency to ignore both class and race. Not all women are white, middle-class or Protestant; attempts at broad coalitions based on concepts of "sisterhood" have faltered on such false generalizations.

My research in archival sources of the history of white and African-American women in the 19th century convinced me of the existence of a distinct "women's culture" and "female experience," although I could not decide whether it was based in biologically determined experiences, such as motherhood, or caused by centuries of living under patriarchal oppression. For nearly a decade, in my own work, which was always based on a comparative approach, I thought to combine both the radical feminist and a class-and-race-conscious analysis.[10]

As did my colleagues in Women's Studies I fretted under the inadequacies of the patriarchal conceptual frameworks with which we had to work. I expressed that frustration in a number of my essays, which called for a change in the ruling paradigm. But it was not until I completed my work on the origins of patriarchy that I realized I needed altogether to step outside of the patriarchal edifice of thought and dedicate the rest of my life to the task of re-definition.

Now I am taking a syncretic approach: I believe the insights of the various "feminisms" have added to our understanding of class for women and have been steps in the right direction, even when they seem contradictory. Different approaches have helped us to illuminate different aspects of the problem of re-definition.[11]

As a historian, I must base my thought on the firm belief in the existence of social reality, in the past as well as in the present. To create a conceptual framework of thought which assumes that women and men were and are equal partners and agents in the creation of society, one must, for the time being, be woman-centered, in order to compensate for the overwhelmingly androcentric bias in our culture. Once that bias is eliminated, I foresee future generations who might be able to take a "gender-neutral" approach to their work.[12]

My central concern in recent years in thinking, writing and teaching has been to find a better set of concepts to deal with the differences among people than we now have. I assume there is a complex linkage of the various systems of discrimination by which, historically, various groups in society have been marked as "deviants" and persecuted for such deviance at various levels, which have ranged from harassment to annihilation. In my article "Reconceptualizing Differences Among Women" (Chapter 10), I proposed an inter-active conceptual framework for dealing with the differences among women: gender, class and race are not separate categories, but different aspects of systems of hierarchy and dominance. They are interdependent, interrelated and inseparable, in both their origin and their continuing function.[13]

No theoretical framework for conceptualizing the situation of women can be constructed without taking race as well as class fully into consideration. I will here attempt to discuss the way both concepts can be transformed by putting them into an interactive framework, and how such re-definition has transformational power.

When I began to write this essay, more than ten years ago, I still thought of class in Marxist terms as the relation of men to the means of production. I wanted to show how and why this definition did not fit women and did not do justice to their class position. As I continued to work through the historical material I realized that this definition of class also did not fit men adequately. To my amazement I arrived at a much more radical re-definition of class than I had initially intended. The essay reflects the growth and changes in my thought. I hope to take the reader through the evidence as I was taken and show her/him why my redefinition is preferable to the old way of thinking about the subject.

I will argue the following propositions:

Class in its historical origins was not and is not now a separate construct from gender; rather class was and is expressed in genderic terms. This means:

■ 1. The commodification of women's sexual and reproductive capacities formed one of the major sources for the creation of private property, on which class is based. Historically, class was constructed out of gender relations which advantaged men over women.

■ 2. Classes were formed and maintained by gendered marriage arrangements and inheritance practices.

■ 3. Class must always be defined differently for men and women and has historically always been different for men and women. Men and women never belong to the same class in the same way. Class describes multilayered locations, relations and experiences, differing according to sex, race, nationality and stage in the life cycle.[14]

To elaborate on these propositions I will briefly discuss their origins in the Ancient Near East and, focusing on points 2 and 3, give examples from medieval Europe and then show the continuity of these organizing principles in the development of early capitalism. I distinguish between class formation and class maintenance as two different processes in which elites pursue different strategies.

■ 1. The commodification of women's sexual and reproductive capacities formed one of the basic sources for the accumulation of private property on which class is based. Historically, class was constructed out of gender relations which advantaged men over women.

Patriarchy is a system, created by men and women in a process which in the Ancient Near East took nearly 1500 years (*ca.* 2100-*ca.* 600 B.C.). Patriarchy is not a historically unchanging social construct, but rather all historically known economic and social systems have incorporated the basic principles of patriarchy. Historians must study the ways in

154

which the application of these patriarchal principles have changed over time, how they have been constructed and institutionalized at different periods and how and why they have so long remained invisible.

In its earliest form patriarchy appeared as the archaic state. Long before its formation in the 2nd millennium B.C. gender had already been created and defined.[15] Gender—the different roles and behavior deemed appropriate to each of the sexes—was expressed in values, customs, and social roles. During the long period that led to the establishment of patriarchally organized archaic states, gender definitions became institutionalized in laws, the organization of hierarchies and in religion. Gender was also expressed in leading metaphors that shaped the culture and entered the explanatory systems of Western civilization.

The sexuality of women, consisting of their sexual and their reproductive capacities and services, was commodified, even prior to the creation of archaic states. The development of agriculture in the Neolithic age fostered the inter-tribal "exchange of women," not only as a means of avoiding incessant warfare by the cementing of marriage alliances, but also because societies with more women could produce more children. In contrast to the economic needs of hunting/gathering societies, agriculturists could use the labor of children to increase production and accumulate surpluses. The first gender-defined social role for women was to be those who were exchanged in marriage transactions. For men, the obverse gender role was to be those who do the exchanging or define the terms of the exchanges. As a result of such widespread practices, men had rights in women which women did not have in men. Women themselves became a resource, acquired by men, much as the land was acquired by men.[16]

After the establishment of class societies, women of elite groups shared in their husbands' power in their gender-defined role of "deputy-husband."[17] Fulfilling this role meant that elite women, in the temporary absence of their husbands, could substitute for them in their public functions. Such women also provided connections and linkages between elite families and alternately represented their fathers' and their husbands' interests. They had considerable power and privileges, but their power depended on their attachment to elite men and was based on their satisfactory performance in rendering these men sexual and reproductive services. If a woman failed to meet these demands, she was quickly replaced and thereby lost all her privileges and standing.

155

The wife as "deputy-husband" appears as early as 1790 B.C. in royal documents from the mesopotamian city of Mari. They detail the activities of Queen Shibtu, who, in the absence of her husband during warfare, reigned as his deputy, but who had to follow his orders to select from among captive women he sent home a number of the most attractive for his harem.[18]

■ 2. Classes were formed and maintained by gendered marriage arrangements and inheritance practices.

From the inception of class structures, class was formed *genderically*. That is, some men accumulated land and wealth and controlled the reproduction of the females under their tutelage in such a way that ownership of resources was not threatened. But property accumulation, by itself, does not lead to class formation. *What turns property into class is a set of institutional practices that perpetuate property holdings within a small elite and assure the maintenance of this propertied elite over time.* The main instruments for this process are homogamy and gendered inheritance practices.

It is worth noting how crucial marriage settlements were to the stabilization of classes. Homogamy, the practice of restricting marriages to people within the same propertied group, assures the continuity of property holdings within that group. If men could marry beneath their own group, their property would not increase in marriage and quickly be depleted through the demands of impoverished kin. To secure homogamous marriages the propertied must control the sexuality of their children, but particularly that of their daughters. Homogamy is further reinforced by inheritance arrangements that assure patrilineal control over property.

In the Ancient Near East, homogamy and gendered inheritance practices developed simultaneously and in support of each other. Among the propertied group, marriages were contracted by negotiations between the fathers of bride and groom. The father of the bride received a bride price from the father of the groom. This bride price was offset by a somewhat smaller "settlement" or dowry, given by the father of the bride to the groom after the marriage had been consummated.

Bride price and dowry were material binders of the promise of the bride's virginity. If the bride turned out not to be a virgin at marriage, the bride price was returned and no dowry was given. If the bride was a virgin and the marriage was consummated, the dowry was given to the husband in usufruct, but it was understood that it or its equivalent would be returned to the donor should the marriage fail. Thus the couple had a joint property interest in the success of the marriage. At the death of the husband, the dowry constituted the main source of the widow's support. On her death, it was given to her sons as heirs. Thus, marital property passed from men to men *through* women.

In elite families the bride price received for a daughter frequently enabled the bride's family to secure more financially advantageous marriages for their sons, thus improving the family's economic position. This arrangement again helped to consolidate class formation within the elite.

At the very inception of patriarchy, Babylonian wives of the propertied classes had many civic and economic rights, even some rights in regard to decisions about their children. They could sign contracts, buy and sell land and slaves, and transact business in their own right. But their sexuality was strictly regulated. Thus, female adultery was punishable by death, whereas male adultery was not even considered a crime. Men could take second and third wives and use slave women for sexual services without any societal censure.

For the upper classes judicious management of the bride price and upwardly mobile marriages of sons guaranteed that property would stay and grow within the kin group. The acquisition of slaves would further improve the family's wealth, for female slaves produced textiles, which were a major export item, and their children could be sold or hired out profitably. The product of the commodification of women's sexuality—bride price, sales price and children—was appropriated by men.

If a family had a surplus of daughters they could and did designate one or more of them as priestesses. The dowry a priestess brought to the temple would revert back to her family upon her death, thus furthering the family's class position by not scattering its wealth to other families through marriage.

In Babylonian families of middle or lower range, where usually the only available property consisted of land, the bride price received for a daughter was essential in order to marry off the son. When no daughters were available, the couple often resorted to adoption of a girl. If marriage arrangements for daughters were unfavorable or impossible, the family would go into debt to hold on to its land. If a husband or father could not pay his debt, his wife and children could be used as pawns, becoming debt slaves to the creditor. These conditions were so firmly established by 1750 B.C. that Hammurabic law made a decisive improvement in the lot of debt slaves, by limiting their terms of service to three years, where as earlier it had been for life. The improvement in the lot of debt slaves coincided with a hardening of the conditions of slaves acquired by conquest.

For lower-class families the sexuality of their daughters became their one tangible and negotiable asset if their land failed to produce subsistence. Daughters were bartered for a favorable bride price, if and when possible; they could serve—together with their brothers—as debt slaves, and they might, with luck, become concubines. To the very poor, who had no movable property or land, marriage transactions for profit were not possible, but during bad times the daughters of the poor were sold into marriage or prostitution in order to advance the economic interests of their families.

We see here how the patrician or upper class was formed genderically and maintained through gendered marriage and inheritance practices; how the middling class or burghers maintained their position in the hierarchy through sexual politics; and how the lower classes, peasants and slaves, used male sexual privileges to maintain their precarious class position.

If we look at medieval Europe, we find similar processes of class formation on the basis of gendered family arrangements at work. This can best be discerned by studying the changes in marriage patterns and property arrangements among the warrior aristocracy, usually occurring when simpler forms of tribal organization gave way to more hierarchically organized states, led by a king and his bureaucrats. In western Europe, in the Frankish kingdom, the shift from Merovingian rule (481–751) to Carolingian society (768–884) offers a good vantage point for comparison. In England in the time prior to and past the Norman conquest (1066 A.D.) we find a comparable process.

The transition from tribe-and kinship-focused social organization to bureaucratic, hierarchical states occurred in western European countries somewhat earlier than it did in England, but with similar results for women. Clovis I, the first of the Merovingian line, after assassinating his rivals, made himself King of the Franks in 481 A.D. and expanded his realm by annexation of the disintegrating provinces of Roman Gaul. After his death Frankish royal power was weakened through the division of his land among his four sons and it remained weak under succeeding Merovingian rulers. Following upon the ascension of Charlemagne as King of the Franks in 768, the expansion of his realm through wars of annexation resulted in the creation of the Frankish Empire, and the crowning of Charlemagne as Holy Roman Emperor in 800. During his reign close cooperation between Church and state centralized power and strengthened the authority of both institutions.

By comparing conditions for women in the Frankish kingdom and in England we can observe a similar process of development: as royal power and Church power became bureaucratically institutionalized in national states, opportunities narrowed for women and their sexuality was more rigidly controlled than previously. Their access to property became more limited and their control of property weakened. Society increasingly viewed them as lifelong dependents of their fathers or their husbands, celebrated their role as mothers, nurturers and domestic care-givers, but restricted their public and political roles. These generalizations hold mostly for aristocratic women. Peasant and serf women were not as dramatically affected by these social changes.[19] (See Comparative Chart, pp. 160-161.)

As in Anglo-Saxon England, so in Europe, polygamy, concubinage and forced marriage of windows by male kin were wide-spread among the nobility early in the Christian era. King Clovis's Salic law, issued between 507 and 511, was based on Germanic law, which valued women highly as child-bearers. Later Merovingian law codes also incorporated Roman law, which placed a married woman entirely under her husband's power.[20]

The Merovingian nobility increased and consolidated its wealth, i.e. it became a class, by conducting homogamous marriages and by manipulating the marriages of dependents so as to keep as far as possible the inheritance of land intact. Marriages were contracted without regard to the wishes or inclinations of the couple. Daughters were frequently forced into marriages by raw power and physical chastisement.

The marriage settlement was made by an exchange of gifts and a contract. The bride gift similar to the Mesopotamian bride price was given by the groom's kin to the male kin of the bride and was then wholly or in part turned over to the bride, to provide economic security for her in case she was repudiated. The betrothal followed and was considered binding, even if it was made when the bride was a child, which was often the case. Young women were strictly bound by the betrothal, but young men could repudiate it with ease, by forfeiting the bride gift. At the time of marriage, the bride's parents gave her a dowry, which would later serve as her dower in case of widowhood. Under Merovingian law, the husband controlled the wife's property. Wives were obliged to produce male heirs; failure to do so was always regarded as the wife's fault. She could be divorced; the marriage could be annulled; she could be set aside or imprisoned. Bride gift and dowry formed the basis of the widow's share of the estate, which was to pro-

COMPARATIVE CHART

PERIOD	STATE	CHURCH	MARRIAGE	WOMEN'S STATUS
Frankish Kingdom under Merovingian Rule				
481–751	weak; authority diffuse; kinship-focused	weak	polygamy, concubinage; quasi-marriage possible	Married women's property cannot be alienated; women have equal share in inheritance; widow is head of household.
Frankish Kingdom under Carolingian Rule				
768-884	strong; authority centralized in king and bureaucracy; Empire after 800	stronger; authority more centralized; celibate clergy (9th-11th c.)	indissoluble marriage; more rigid homogamy; no concubinage	Women's legal status declined; widows get one-third of husband's property.

PERIOD	STATE	CHURCH	MARRIAGE	WOMEN'S STATUS
England Pre-Conquest				
ca. 800-1066	weak; tribal society; authority diffuse; kinship-focused	weak	consensual divorce possible; polygamy, concubinage, forced marriage	Women could bequeath property to children of both sexes; widow receives one-half of husband's property if had children; widow under male guardianship.
England Post-Conquest				
1066-*ca*. 1300	strong; royal bureaucracy	stronger	end polygamy; illegitimate children disinherited; end of forced marriage for women	Widows free of guardianship; primogeniture; husband becomes lord of wife; decline in women's property rights.

vide her maintenance and that of her dependent children, but at her death it went either to her sons or to the male members of her family of origin. Note, that here, too, as in the Ancient Near East, wealth passed from men to men *through* women.

Over time, the economic independence of women improved under Merovingian rule. A husband managed the wife's property, but he could not alienate it without her consent. Some women were given land and real property and gradually, under the influence of Roman law, daughters were able to claim an equal share with their brothers in their inheritances.

Some Merovingian women could escape forced marriage, by entering a quasi-marriage (similar to a common law marriage of later periods) without the consent of their parents. Such an arrangement, in which an unmarried woman lived with a man of her choice, deprived her of any economic rights in case her male partner abandoned her. Her parents could also deny her an inheritance. Still, such arrangements were socially recognized as valid marriages and the children were considered legitimate. It is significant from the point of view of tracing the connection between marriage regulation and class formation that in both Roman and Germanic laws unions of free and unfree partners were forbidden and punished with severe sanctions. The dilution of boundaries between free people and slaves threatened the foundation of class formation and was therefore to be avoided. Yet, noblemen often circumvented or ignored laws against the marriages of free persons to slaves, by offering land to free women who were willing to marry the slaves in their realm. Since by such marriages the free women became the lord's retainers, contributing their labor to his household, narrow economic interests prevailed over larger class interests.[21]

The conditions of widows were better under Merovingian law than under Roman, under which she remained a lifelong legal minor. As a widow she had all her husband's rights and became head of the household, which included having guardianship of minor children. She had to give up these rights when she remarried, in which case she also lost her dower rights.

It is noteworthy that dowry and dower (the money due a widow as her portion) are tied to gendered inheritance. In most of Europe, with the exception of the Germanic realms, present-day Italy and the southern provinces of France—Aquitaine—the oldest son inherited all or the largest portion of the land (primogeniture), while the daughters received their shares in the form of dowry. In an economy based on land, this seriously advantaged sons over daughters.[22] Giving daughters some or all of their inheritance in goods and jewels tended to keep family landholdings intact and thus furthered class formation. By contrast, an older system of inheritance prevailed in the Scandinavian countries and in Brittany, in which all children inherited equal shares of land, regardless of sex. This led to the existence of economically independent landholding women and generally a more favorable position for women.[23]

Historically, there had been various forms of property transfers connected with marriages: the Roman marriage settlement, given by groom's kin to bride's kin; the Germanic *dos*, a gift from groom to bride prior to the marriage; and *Morgengabe,* a gift from husband to wife after the consummation of the marriage. These begin to blend in the early Middle Ages in an exchange of gifts of nearly equal value which had three functions: to assure property stayed within the propertied class; to give the bride's family some stake and leverage in the well-being of the bride; and to secure the wife's support in case of abandonment or widowhood. In the later Middle Ages this system will give way to marriages based on dowry, that is, the giving of a large sum of money (or land) by the bride's kin to the groom without reciprocal donations on the part of the groom.

The causes of the change from bride price and bride gift to dowry, that is from a system of the groom's kin giving money or land to the bride's kin to one in which the reverse took place, are complex and difficult to trace. Obviously, what changed was the concept of the function of women in the family of origin. In the bride-price concept, the bride's parents were being compensated for the cost of rearing her and for the anticipated loss of her contribution to the household. In dowry, the bride's parents were paying a price to the groom and his kin for the future upkeep of the daughter. This change and its significance for the status of women and for class formation need to be more fully studied before sound generalizations can be made.[24] But it is clear that in either case, the emphasis was on both families' creating a property fund on which the couple could base their marriage and from which the husband derived greater benefits than the wife.

The situation of the lower orders, free peasants, serfs and slaves, was characterized by their dependence on their lords. Although they had life-long tenancy of their huts and fields, they were bound to the manor and its lord. Peasant women were obliged to get the lord's permission for marriage, but were otherwise free to chose the particular man they wanted. Male and female peasants had to pay the lord a marriage tax, known as *merchet*. Serfs could not contract marriage outside of the lord's realm. Free peasants and serfs owed military and economic tribute to their lords, usually in the form of several days' free labor each week. Since these obligations always included the labor of their wives and children, the nobility as a class directly profited from the marriages of their serfs and peasants.[25]

Within their own class, peasant women enjoyed greater equality with their men than did women of the nobility. Women made essential contributions to the family economy by weaving, spinning, and raising livestock, and their labor was highly regarded both by their men and their lords. Peasant women could improve their status by upwardly mobile marriages and even slave women could rise from concubine to legitimate wife.[26] Still, lower-class women had to bear the typical class burden of women: neither virginity nor married status protected them from the sexual exploitation of their masters. The nobleman routinely assumed and took advantage of his sexual prerogatives. Lower-class women routinely were subject to the demand for sexual services on the part of their masters and had few defenses against sexual assault.

It is also worth noting that when the peasantry began to evolve as a class out of serfdom, peasants began to adopt primogeniture or ultimogeniture (inheritance of the land by the youngest son), with daughters getting goods and tools for their dowry. This is another example of the way in which gendered inheritance, disadvantaging women, functions to create class.

If we now turn, for comparison, to pre-Conquest Anglo-Saxon England, we find a tribal social organization. Warriors acquired land by conquest or by donations to them by a chief or king whose vassal they became. In exchange for their military obligations to that chief, they administered the land and distributed resources to the men and women in their kin group and under their tutelage. Individuals and kin groups advanced in rank by allying with higher-ranking groups through marriages and vassalage.

Marriages were constituted by the payment of a bride price, a gift exchange and, later, by contract. But the contract could be broken by mutual consent and even by the woman alone. A married woman who had a lover, had the option of arranging for a consensual divorce. Her lover would abduct her, pay the husband a fine and buy him a new wife. Married women were entitled to the property they had brought into the marriage and could bequeath it to children of both sexes. Women could ask for a divorce and have it granted. When widowed, Anglo-Saxon wives received half of their husbands' property if the marriage had produced children. If the marriage had been childless, the widow got only a child's portion of the inheritance. In either event, the widow was placed under male guardianship and was often forced to remarry. Concubinage among nobles was widespread, which offered an opportunity for lower-class (peasant) women to rise by way of sexual liaisons. Concubines became members of a man's household and their children could inherit, if their father so desired it.[27]

After the Norman Conquest, state power was consolidated, as kings created more royal bureaucracies, and kinship no longer was the chief determinant of advancement. In a development similar to what we have observed in the Carolingian Frankish realm, the legal status of women declined, as did the ability of lower-class women to be upwardly mobile through marriages and sexual unions. After the Conquest, bride price was gradually transformed so that most or all of it was now given to the bride, as a fund which would later supply her widow's portion, but the money remained under her husband's control during his lifetime.[28] By the end of the Anglo-Saxon period the buying of wives seemed to have abated, divorce initiated by women was no longer possible, and female adultery was severely punished. Married women still could engage in property transactions, but only with the consent of their husbands.[29]

In the pre-Conquest period nobles not only negotiated the marriages of their daughters and sisters, but also had the right to negotiate marriages of the widows of their vassals. Anglo-Saxon kings had the right to force widows to marry a man of the king's choosing. After the Conquest, widows were no longer subject to male guardianship and were able to avoid forced marriages. Henry I (reigned 1100–1135) declared that he would not force a widow to remarry and that she could have her dower, but collected fines from the widows for this prerogative. Henry II (reigned 1154–1189) also collected fines from widows both for their use of their dower, and if they refused remarriage.[30]

The concept of the legitimacy of children has long been an important aspect of class formation. By regulating the sexuality of daughters and wives, men can control the legitimacy of their descendants. Patriarchal marriage definitions based on the virginity of brides and the absolute fidelity of wives ensure the paternity of the householder and with it the legitimacy of his sons and heirs. By privileging legitimate offspring over illegitimate, the householder can keep his property from being divided among too large a pool of children. The law codes of the Ancient Near East gave fathers the right to legitimize the children of concubines or slaves by a certain public declaration, thus disadvantaging the children of the first or legitimate wife.[31] In effect this prerogative would have been used mostly if a man sexually tired of his first wife and wished to please or pacify a second or third wife. Women never had this power. This is another instance of the institutionalization of men's control over female reproduction, which made her privileges dependent on the satisfactory performance of her sexual services to her husband.

As we have seen, males of the upper nobility in early medieval Europe enjoyed sexual privileges similar to those of Babylonian men. Merovingian nobles could declare the sons of their second or third wives or even those of a slave concubine to be legitimate heirs.

In its turn the Church of Rome used sexual control over women and men as a primary means for its own consolidation of power. As Christianity advanced in England and on the Continent, the Church sought to assert its control over the regulation of marriages. Beginning in the 9th century the Church gradually secured the abolition of polygamy and gained control over marriage rituals, and insisted, above all, upon the indissolubility of marriages. Secular Carolingian legislation outlawed divorce and brought marriage practices more firmly under Church control. Indissoluble monogamous marriage upgraded the position of wives, but it also increased wife abuse and weakened the economic power of women. With the downgrading of quasi-marriages the road to upward mobility of lower-class women through sexual liaisons was closed.[32]

The success of the Church in winning control over marriage rituals also increased its ability to enforce rules of legitimacy. Any privileges extended to bastard children and their mothers were strongly opposed by the Church. It insisted on the inheritance rights of "legitimate" children (those stemming from a monogamous marriage) over "illegitimate" children (those stemming from concubinage and extra-marital relations), who were to be disinherited. The firmer lines drawn between legitimate and illegitimate heirs tended to strengthen class formation in the nobility and to sharpen class divisions.

Concubinage proved to be most resistant to reform efforts and continued into the 11th century. In the Merovingian period the Church began a systematic campaign for celibacy of the clergy, by insisting that married men who became clerics must abandon their wives and cease having sexual intercourse. In the Carolingian period, the Church, now transformed into a *Reichskirche* (state church), became more tightly organized, and better able to enforce internal discipline. Clerics were forbidden to live with women other than close blood relatives, and thousands of priests' concubines and their children were cast out and abandoned. The aim was the institution of a celibate clergy, which would benefit the Church by keeping its priesthood free from temptation toward the acquisition and holding of property. A celibate clergy free of personal property would not put family interest above the interests of the Church. This aim was not fully realized until the reform campaigns in the 11th century. Noble families, instead of enriching individual priests, would now have an incentive to leave their property to the Church. The connection between sexual regulation and economic power is evident: in enforcing the celibacy of the clergy, the Church vastly increased its landed property until it held nearly half of the land in western Europe.

In the process of the consolidation of Church power, the division between male and female religious sharpened. The secure monopoly of the Church over education enhanced the position of the educated male clergy, while restricting the role of the female religious. By the middle of the 12th century double monasteries, ruled over by female abbesses, had virtually disappeared. Total enclosure of female religious and their supervision by priests had become the norm. The study of Latin by nuns, which had been widespread in the early Middle Ages, became the exception.

Similar to developments in the Church, the consolidation of secular power in nation-states was based, at least in part, on curtailment of the rights of women. Although marital and spousal rights varied greatly by region, we can generalize that by the 12th century women's property and dower rights were more closely circumscribed, their rights as widows curtailed and a number of economic rights which they had enjoyed in the earlier centuries now restricted.[33]

Beginning in the 11th century, European societies were transformed first by urbanization in Italy, Germany, France and England and then by changes in manufacturing and trading. Towns became manufacturing and production centers and marketing centers for long-distance trade. Intense craft specialization, exemption of towns from feudal obligations, the adoption of a money economy and increasing prosperity were characteristics of this period. Merchant capital, based on trade not land, formed the basis for the new economy and for the emergent classes—merchant-capitalists, artisans and a peasantry no longer primarily engaged in agriculture production but tied to merchant-capitalists through the putting-out system.

The formation and maintenance of bourgeoisie as a class depended as much on the manipulation of marriages as it did on more directly commercial ventures. The dowry of a daughter secured for her a marriage within her class or it made her upwardly mobile. Rich mercantile families made favorable political and trade alliances by marriages. Marital connections between daughters of the bourgeoisie with ample dowries and penniless younger sons of the nobility secured benefits for both families, providing the *nouveaux-riches* with the status that comes from connection to landed gentry and taking an idle younger son out of competition for the family's land. Upward mobility, measured not only by wealth but by status, was achieved through carefully planned marriages.

Cash dowries, which became prevalent in the 13th century, tended to rise in value as their significance in the family economy became more obvious. The higher the rank and status of the groom's family, the greater the bride's dowry. Dowry inflation reached such proportions that the Venetian Senate in 1420 placed a limitation on patrician dowries. A hundred years later, dowries had nevertheless doubled in size and the Senate passed another law setting a ceiling.

Earlier, dowries had represented a portion of a girl's inheritance, but by the 15th century, dowries had come to be a girl's entire inheritance. This had the effect of excluding women from land ownership and of favoring sons in inheritances. On the other hand, a girl now had a *right* to a dowry, and many town councils instituted the practice of furnishing public funds for the dowries of poor girls. Dowry inflation is one measure of the importance of women's dowries in the capital formation of the early bourgeoisie. The phenomenon deserves greater notice than it is usually given.[34]

A sizable dowry meant the availability of liquid capital to the groom and his family, which could be used either to extinguish existing debts, or to venture investment in the rising capitalist enterprises. The fact that the new head of household had a large cash sum at his disposal and under his undisputed control, made entrepreneurial risk investments more feasible.

Among the middling sort, artisans, craftsmen and tradesmen, a girl's dowry often enabled the husband to set up shop. The wives of artisans and merchants were expected to contribute not only all household labor and the supervision and feeding of apprentices and journeymen, but also their own skilled crafts labor to the husband's business. On his death, the widow would often continue that business to provide for her young children. Such women were much in demand as wives, since marriage was not infrequently a requirement for gaining guild membership as a master. Thus, young journeymen could gain middle-class status as guild members by marrying the widow of a guildsman, often a woman much older than themselves.

The financial calculations of a groom in the marriage market in colonial America were coolly described by Benjamin Franklin in his autobiography:

> Mrs. Godfrey projected a match for me with a Relation's Daughter, took Opportunities of bringing us often together, till a serious Courtship on my Part ensu'd, the Girl being in herself very deserving. . . . Mrs. Godfrey managed our little Treaty. I let her know that I expected as much Money with their Daughter as would pay off my remaining Debt for the Printing-house, which I believe was not then above a Hundred Pounds. She brought me Word they had no such Sum to spare. I said they might mortgage their House in the Loan Office. The Answer to this after some Days was, that they did not approve the Match; that on Enquiry . . . they had been inform'd the Printing Business was not a profitable one. . . .

169

and therefore I was forbidden the House, and the Daughter shut up.... I declared absolutely my Resolution to have nothing more to do with that Family.[35]

From the early Renaissance on, the growth of capitalism was supported by the marriage market. As usual, the relatively favorable conditions for women in the early phases of the new economic system, gradually became more restricted and disadvantageous. In the 14th century, women could hold membership in about a third of the existing guilds in Paris and in other European cities and were listed in a broad range of craft guilds, but by the 17th century they were excluded from membership in most of the guilds. Even in formerly predominantly female occupations, such as brewing, weaving and work in the silk industry, women were gradually prohibited from using new technologies or new materials. Increasing regulation and gendered restrictions confined women to the least profitable work and technological advances and increased specialization worked to their disadvantage.[36]

As women's autonomous occupations shrank, their dependence on making a prudent and advantageous marriage intensified. The plight of women who through their own actions or because of the folly of a father made imprudent marriages or failed to get married at all is vividly reflected in the fictional literature of the 18th and 19th centuries. Not until the second half of the 19th century would women be able to chose careers and lifestyles that would give them economic independence apart from and outside of marriage.

As one historian has observed:

> Rules concerning married women's property have always functioned to facilitate the transmission of significant property from male to male; entitlements of women have been to provide them with subsistence for themselves and minor children who are dependent upon them. Men want women to have enough to survive ... but not enough to exercise the power that comes with a significant accumulation of property.[37]

Thus, the medieval widow would lose her dower property if she remarried or committed fornication (1285). A wife lost her dower if she eloped or committed adultery. Eighteenth century British and U.S. law hedged widow's dower rights as had medieval law. And even in the 20th century, divorced wives can lose alimony, trust funds or pension benefits if they remarry.[38]

A detailed consideration of European and British inheritance laws and customs in the 17th and 18th centuries is beyond the scope of this essay, but certain patterns can be noted. There is general agreement by historians that for aristocratic families marriages consistently were instruments for improving the landholdings of the family dynasty and for enhancing the family's power. Thus, the prudent management of marriages served the interest of class formation. Class maintenance, on the other hand, demanded the development of strategies which would guarantee that land would not be dispersed among too many heirs and that favorable marriage alliances could be contracted with offspring of the rising middle class. Male inheritance and primogenture had served to keep land together; now trust and marriage settlements were developed to assure that younger children, sons and daughters disadvantaged by primogenture, would have some share in the family income so as to enable them to make upwardly mobile marriages. Eileen Spring has argued persuasively that the purposes of the "strict settlement," an inheritance settlement made at the time of the eldest son's marriage, which came into extensive use in the 17th century and provided for inheritance in the male line, was to preserve estates, patrilineally and in the interests of patriarchy. The over-all effect of changing patterns of marriage arrangements was a "decline of women's rights over land."[39]

In the same period the rising middle class, wealthy professional and businessmen, married into the gentry and followed the gentry mode of class formation by buying land and holding on to it through gendered marriage and inheritance arrangements that strengthened male control over land and wealth.

As we can see, there is a continuity over several millennia in the way gender relations interconnect with class formation and maintenance of class status. Every major historical development in the formation of classes—slavery in the Ancient Near East; the formation of states in the early Middle Ages; the emergence of nation-states; the consolidation of Church power, the rise of bourgeois capitalism—depended on the regulation of women's reproduction and on limiting their direct access to economic power.

■ 3. Class must be defined differently for men and women and it has historically always been different for men and women.

We can best express the complexity of gendered class positions by comparing each woman with her brother and considering how the sister's and the brother's lives and opportunities would differ.[40] Let us compare brothers and sisters in different societies, at different times and of different classes.

A male member of the warrior elite in the early Middle Ages was dependent on a lord of higher rank in a vassalage relationship. He was obliged to perform military services for his lord, which often required him to be absent for years from his land and his family. His education consisted of training for warfare and for the simulated warfare skills represented by jousts. The brother was not free to make his own choice of marriage partner, but had to defer to family interests and the decisions of his father. Once married, he enjoyed full sexual freedom, that is, he could take several wives, keep concubines and cohabit with lower-class women and slaves. He had charge of his property and the property his wife brought into the marriage, with the usual constraints forcing him to set aside a portion for her dower. He could dispose of his property during his lifetime and bequeath it to heirs of his choosing.

His sister had the same education as her brother, and often better literacy skills. She had similar restraints in regard to choice of marriage partners but enjoyed no sexual freedom prior to marriage. Since her virginity was a major family asset, the daughter would be pledged or betrothed at an early age, often in childhood, and would then have to live in the household of her future husband. Once married, her fidelity was enforced with barbaric constraints (such as the use of metal chastity belts), and any infidelity could subject her to the death penalty. If her husband tired of her sexually or if she did not present him with male heirs, she could be set aside for another wife, imprisoned, forced to return to her father. In short, her class status could deteriorate radically if her sexual or reproductive services were considered wanting. As long as she agreed to this bargain, the lady of the manor enjoyed power over her slaves, serfs and servants, both male and female. Heiresses and ladies of the manor were severely limited in their judicial rights and enjoyed political rights only during their husbands' absences, when acting as the husbands' "deputies." But that role was contingent, and dependent on the husbands' pleasure or whim. There are a number of medieval queens who held great power as "deputy-husbands," but were swiftly replaced when their husband became sexually attracted to another woman or when they failed to fulfill what was considered their primary duty, to produce male heirs. Even the most powerful queen could face annulment or divorce, accusations of rebellion and treason and sometimes long years of imprisonment. Their claims to power were mediated through their relationship with powerful men—in their roles as heiresses, wives or as mothers in behalf of sons. The "class" privileges of elite women depended on their familial, sexual and reproductive relationships. This was not the case for men, who held power in their own right. Even the most powerful medieval women, like Eleanor of Aquitaine, Margrethe of Denmark and Isabella of Castile, could not use their power to advance the position of women.[41] They did, however, serve to advance the class interests of the men on whom they depended.

In the case of the medieval warrior-nobility, the brother thus had direct access and control over resources, economic, educational and sexual, and was a member of the power elite. His sister, even in the case of the most powerful noblewomen and queens, could claim access to power and influence only through her mediated role of "stand-in" for an absent husband or as surrogate for her minor son.

For medieval peasants the situation was roughly as follows: the brothers would inherit the family's land, in the case of free peasants, or, in the case of serfs, the family's obligation and rights in regard to the lord. The brother had an obligation to military service in the interest of the lord. He and his sister had no access to education, except that for a few bright peasant lads the Church offered access to education by way of a monastic career which was closed to females.[42] The marital choices of both sexes of the peasantry were less restricted by family interest than those of the nobility, but they were constrained by their obligations to the lord. The lord had to approve all marriages and he taxed the peasants for the privilege. Lord and peasant male alike acquired, on marriage, sole sexual and reproductive rights in their wives, but the lord deprived the male peasant of the patriarchal privilege of benefiting from the unpaid domestic services of their wives. Since peasant women and children owed the same labor obligations to the lord as did the men of the family, it was mostly the lord who benefited from their services.[43]

The peasant sister shared the constrained economic circumstances of the family. She would, however, not inherit land and would be expected to marry for economic support. Marriage choice was a crucial matter for her, since on it depended her economic and physical well-being and that of her children. In marriage, she owed the same sexual and reproductive services to her man as did the noble woman to the lord, but she did not have the class privilege of being able to transfer part of her domestic and child-rearing burdens to servant women. The distinguishing mark of female lower-class status is that it made her subject to and defenseless against sexual abuse by her lord or other men of the nobility.

In the peasantry, men's access to economic resources came second-hand, through their contract or obligations to a lord. Women's access to economic resources came third-hand, through their male family members. Both brother and sister were politically disfranchised and educationally deprived, with the brother enjoying the single loophole offering educational opportunity, the priesthood.[44]

If we now turn to the formation of the bourgeois class in the cities of Renaissance Europe, we find similar differences between the status of males and females. In the upper ranks of the bourgeoisie, among merchants and entrepreneurs, the virginity of daughters and the fidelity of wives were important family assets. Homogamy, dowries and gendered-inheritance customs supported class formation which rested largely on the disadvantaging of daughters in favor of sons.

In the middle ranks, among artisans and tradesmen, marriage, as we have seen, fostered class formation, by adding the wife's work to that of the husband and by providing capital for the start of a business through dowries. Among this group, women had a freer choice of mates than did upper-class women. It is among this group of women we find the phenomenon of older widows marrying younger men.[45]

From the 16th to the 19th century, peasant populations in Europe and England gradually were transformed into industrial workers. During this early stage of industrialization before the factory system, peasant households became part of the "putting-out" system, whereby merchant-capitalists supplied raw materials and tools to the rural workers and marketed their finished products, paying them a pittance. Conditions in the cottage industries broke the power of peasant patriarchs to control the marriages and lives of their children. It also undermined the modicum of financial independence peasant women had been able to gain by selling the products of their domestic labor—eggs, butter, yarn, wool—in local markets. Since family labor, not land, provided the basis of the family's survival, young men and women could found new households, new units of labor, without regard to their parents' wishes. The essence of the putting-out system was the unlimited supply of cheap labor provided by the peasants and their families. With substandard pay for labor, only the work of the entire family could provide the equivalent of one living wage. The self-exploitation of home-industry workers was ensured by their not being paid a wage, but rather, as independent producers, being paid for their product. Child labor became a survival necessity for rural workers. The work of women and children in home industry thus subsidized the profits and capital accumulation on which industrialization was based. We find the same system in different form operating in the early 19th century in the cities of the eastern United States.

It is tempting to think of the exploited home-industrial workers as belonging to the same class, men, women and children. The merchant-capitalist contracted with the male householder for work performed by the entire family. Wife and children thus functioned as unpaid hired help of the father. But the home-weaver's wife, in addition to her own labor as a weaver or spinner, also had to provide the family with children, whose labor in turn could make the difference between starvation and family survival. The reproductive and household labor of women of this class was, as usual everywhere, unpaid, a double burden for the already overburdened woman. When increased fertility led to an oversupply of rural labor and with it a lowering of pay standards, further pauperization ensued. Poor peasants were turned into landless peasants; rural cottage workers became an industrial proletariat.

In the period of mature capitalism, in the 19th and the early 20th century, the continuation of the upper and middle classes depended, as it had earlier, on homogamy and gendered inheritance practices. The passage of women's property-rights legislation in the later half of the 19th century improved the economic position of middle-class wives. But class stability increasingly rested on the gendered availability of another resource crucial to the success of industrialization: education.

I have shown elsewhere that women were systematically educationally disadvantaged in every known patriarchal society, always with the exception of a small group of elite women, whose education served to advance the interests of their kin group in case of the absence of suitable male heirs.[46] Still, as long as informal, household-based education in skills and trades prepared young people for future occupations, gender differences in access to education did not matter very much. But with the rise of capitalism access to education became a precondition for economic success, especially after entry into politics, professions and technical training depended on university training. Universities had, from their inception in the 11th century, been closed to women. In Europe, in England and in the U.S. women's primary and secondary education also lagged far behind that of men, as did their literacy rates.

The systematic under-education of women constituted, in the first place, a maldistribution of resources, which benefited males in every class. Family resources were spent on the education of sons and were withheld from daughters, which constitutes a tangible economic advantage for sons. By it, women were denied economic opportunities that might maintain them independent of marriage. Married women who faced the need for self- or family support were forced into the lowest-paying jobs by their educational deprivation. Thus, the issue of access to education became, for women, the primary and earliest demand in their search for emancipation.

In the 20th century, when in most industrialized nations women's access to education has been won as the result of long and strenuous feminist struggles, women are still everywhere under-represented in the very fields which are most technologically and economically advanced. Women are seriously under-represented in the sciences and in technology, in astrophysics and space exploration, to name just a few fields. Women who do advance into these fields of training often face a barrage of sexual and other harassment and discrimination in hiring and advancement. In general, the lower-paying a profession, the more likely it is to be equally staffed by men and women or to be predominantly female. The reverse is also true: the higher paid and more prestigious a profession or occupation, the less likely it is to have a sizable number of women in it.

The general connection between access to education and class can be stated as follows: Throughout historical time education was, above all, a class privilege. But it also was a male gender privilege, which served to maintain class.

By surveying the allocation of resources and comparing access to them by sex (the comparison of sister with brother), we have been able to highlight variations in the pattern of resource allocation by time and place. But we have also shown that there is an over-all pattern of gendered resource allocation which disadvantages women. The mechanism by which this is accomplished deserves closer attention.

From its inception in slavery, class dominance took different forms for men and women: men were primarily exploited as workers; women were always exploited as workers, as providers of sexual services and as reproducers. The historical record of every slave society offers evidence for this generalization. The sexual exploitation of lower-class women by upper-class men can be shown in antiquity, under feudalism, in the middle-class households of 19th- and 20th-century Europe, in the complex sex/race relations between women of the colonized countries and their male colonizers—it is ubiquitous and pervasive. For women, sexual exploitation is the very mark of class exploitation.

Class for men was first and foremost based on their relation to the means of production: those who owned the means of production could dominate those who did not. The owners of the means of production also acquired the commodity of female sexual services, both from women of their own class and from women of the subordinate classes. Additionally, men were entitled to the domestic and child-rearing services of women in exchange for women's economic maintenance. This labor-for-maintenance arrangement, which characterizes slavery, continued for women through all historic changes in economic systems, from ancient slavery to modern capitalism. In Ancient Mesopotamia, in classical antiquity and in slave societies, dominant males also acquired, as property, the product of the reproductive capacity of subordinate women—children, to be worked, traded, married off or sold as slaves, as the case might be.

For women, class is mediated through their sexual ties to a man. It is through the man that women have access to or are denied access to the means of production and to resources. It is through their sexual behavior that they gain access to class. "Respectable women" gain access to class through their fathers and husbands, but breaking the sexual rules can at once declass them. "Sexual deviance" marks a woman as "not respectable," which in fact consigns her to the lowest class status possible. We find the first institutional vestige of this definition in Middle Assyrian Law # 40 (recorded 1500–1100 B.C.), which prescribes the dress of women. The law distinguished between women who are sexually attached to one man—wives and daughters of burghers and free men, concubine wives accompanied by their mistress and married hierodules (temple servants)—and those who are not—harlots, slave women and unmarried hierodules. The former are permitted to appear in public veiled, the latter are forbidden to wear the veil. The law imposes severe penalties on female violators and equally severe penalties on males who fail to denounce and prosecute female violators. Since the penalties are public and enforced by the courts, we can assume that the enforcing of visible class distinctions among women was considered an important aspect of public policy. It is the earliest instance in which we see proof of such distinctions being mandated by law, although there is considerable evidence that the practice long preceded the law. What is most important about this law is that the factor distinguishing one class of women from the other is whether they are sexually attached to one man or not. From that period forward, that distinction—between sexually respectable and not respectable women—will indeed determine women's class position.

Women who withheld heterosexual services from men, such as single women, nuns, lesbians, were for many centuries in a precarious position. Such women connected to class through the dominant man in their family of origin and through him gained access to resources. In some historical periods, convents and other enclaves created some sheltered space, in which such women could function and retain their respectability. But the vast majority of single women were, by definition, marginal and dependent on the protection of male kin.

As for those women who insisted on being in charge of their own sexuality and reproduction, they were declassed and marked as deviant. Beginning with the prostitutes in the Assyrian state, who were publicly marked by being denied the right to veil, sexually deviant women were identified by their clothing, their location and by surveillance throughout the centuries. Whether they were actresses, entertainers, peddlers or prostitutes, they were objects of persecution, regulation and discrimination. It is only late in the 20th century that these sexual regulations for women have ceased to have absolute prescriptive power.

The possibility of choosing singleness without severe economic loss did not exist for most women until the development of mature capitalism, which allowed them direct access to employment and economic independence. But we need to keep in mind that even today single, self-supporting women are economically disadvantaged compared with their brothers, by operating in a gender-defined and gender-segmented labor market. We will discuss that in more detail below. Here we need simply to note that the "feminization of poverty," a world-wide phenomenon in the late 20th century, is structurally based. Its foundation is the erroneous assumption that every woman SHOULD live in a male-headed household with a male breadwinner. It is this assumption which accounts for the persistent male/female wage and income gap and for the predominance of women in low-paying service jobs.[47]

The formation of the working classes—skilled workers, unskilled workers and the underclass of occasional workers—also proceeded along gender lines. While both female and male workers under capitalism had access to resources only by way of hiring out their labor power, men struggled and succeeded in defining their rights of access along patriarchal lines. The concept of "the family wage," a wage sufficient to support a family, shored up the creation of a sex-segregated labor market in which women's wages were permanently fixed at well below the wages of men. Trade-union struggles, until the 1930s in the U.S. continued to preserve male privileges in the labor market. Gender-specific job definitions, which relegated women to lower-paying, lower-skilled jobs, reinforced these patterns.

In addition, working-class husbands, as "heads of households," had rights over whatever property the household could accumulate. The fact that working-class fathers and husbands could collect and spend the earnings of their daughters and wives illustrates this point. Working-class housewives supplemented their husbands' earnings or substituted for them in times of economic crises by bartering, home-made production of clothing, by taking in boarders or other people's washing. Finally, women were disadvantaged and more heavily burdened than men by their unpaid household and reproductive labor.

The "invisibility" of housework, its repetitiveness and its ahistoricity have made it easy to overlook it as a serious factor in considering the class position of women. Housework is seldom taken into consideration when class is the subject of discussion.[48]

In colonial Maine the midwife Martha Ballard, who had delivered over 612 babies, while running her household and attending to her large family, describes how in her sixties she fell ill. "I am very sick but under necessity of getting breakfast for Mr. Ballard and Cyrus [her husband and grown son]," she wrote in her diary. At another time she described feeling too sick to get out of bed. "My Husband went to bed and not come to see me so I lay there in my Cloaths till 5 hours morn. . . . I got the men Breakfast but was not able to Eat a morsel . . . but I finisht my washing." This in a marriage that was based on close and generally friendly cooperation.[49]

In 1864, the American author of twenty-one books, Lydia Maria Child, who throughout her happy marriage to David Child had supported him and herself by her writing, made a list of her year's occupations. While some of them pertain to her intellectual work, most of them detail her innumerable domestic duties. She "made suspenders" and four shirts for David, made him a dressing-gown and carpet-slippers, repaired six shirts and "pantaloons" and "mended 70 pair of stockings." She recorded that she "cooked 362 break-fasts . . . cooked 360 dinners, swept and dusted sitting-room and kitchen 350 times" and ended the list with "cut and dried half a peck of dried apples."[50]

In 1876, Dr. Mary Holywell Everett, a forty-six-year-old New York physician with a large practice, consulted a male colleague, who had been helpful to her in her career, about a problem. Her sister was very ill and she had been urged to leave her practice to nurse her. "Even at the risk of losing your practice entirely," the male colleague advised her that "duty commands you to remain by the side of your old mother & help her to carry the burden." Such sacrifice would not have been expected of a male physician in the event of his sister's illness.[51]

Regardless of period, regardless of rank and economic position, women's domestic service obligations prevailed over their work, their careers, their ambitions. Whatever class their occupation may have assigned them to, by being women they were also unpaid servants. Working women have a double burden; they have not one job, but two. While this is quite true, it does not adequately explain the situation of women.

It is true that if one adds housework and child-care work to the paid labor of women, women work far longer hours than men do. But the relation between their paid and unpaid work is not merely additive;

their unpaid service work degrades their status and pay in the workforce. The large wage differential between service jobs held by men (for example, garbage collector, building maintenance worker) and those held by women (child-care worker, domestic worker) illustrates this point.[52]

The examples above show that class is *always different for men and women*. Any class theory which regards economic oppression as structurally different from sexual oppression can neither explain the persistence of social inequalities nor offer adequate solutions. Economic oppression and exploitation are based as much on the commodification of female sexuality and the appropriation by men of women's labor power and her reproductive power as they are on the direct economic acquisition of resources and persons. The traditional concept "class" is inadequate to describe the economic/social relations of *both men and women*. What is needed is a concept that illuminates the actual "relations of ruling" in society, a reconceptualization of "class" in the light of gender differences:

Class or "location in the ranking order of hierarchical societies" consists of various sets of relations whereby people gain access to a variety of resources and privileges. These include economic resources, land, political power, education, technology and access to the formal and informal networks through which societies organize power. Power, in patriarchal societies, has always been maintained through gender and/or "racial" dominance.[53] Various groups in the societies are given partial advantages over other subordinated groups, in order to keep them in line with a system that distributes access to resources and privileges in an unequal way. That is the true structural underpinning of hierarchical governance, whatever form it may take.

Several essays in this volume take up the vexing question of the structural connection of the various categories: race, class, gender, ethnicity, religion, which have also occupied other feminist thinkers and social scientists. Susan Friedman proposes "scripts of relational positionality...

[which regard] identity as situationally constructed and defined and at the crossroads of different systems of alterity and stratification." She asks that we understand "race, class and gender as multiple and interlocking systems of oppression."[54]

Peggy Pascoe suggests that we look on race, class, gender as being like the cords on models of DNA—"their elements line up like separate strings reaching from one end to another, but at crucial points the various lines cross into, wind around, or melt into each other, lending strength to the larger structure." If we think of the "larger structure" as "the patriarchal dominance system," this makes good sense.[55] But we also need to make explicit the various ways in which the categories not only "interpenetrate" but "constitute" each other. The educational disadvantaging of daughters over sons allows men not only greater access to technological and scientific resources but also gives them higher status. White-skin privilege not only gives whites greater access to resources and thereby greater economic wealth, but it allows economically disadvantaged white men to feel superior to people of color and thereby helps them to disregard the economic disadvantages to which they themselves are subject.

To help me visualize the complex of relationships I think of the human body, as represented in the usual medical texts. The skeleton is represented on one page, the muscular system on another, then circulation, nerves, organs etc. In fact, all these systems are inseparable and inter-related and they do not make any sense unless they are seen as aspects of a functioning organism. Prioritizing them as to their significance to the organism as a whole is obviously futile. Which is more important, race, class or gender? is a nonsensical question, any answer to which obscures more than it illuminates.

When we have a toothache, all our body and psychic "systems" are affected. All our systems focus on the offending tooth. When we belong to a group suffering pain from the effects of the system of dominance, our "standpoint" obviously and correctly emphasizes our experience. But to make social change in the living organism—society at any given time and place—we must understand the whole system, not only its offending parts. Our re-definition of class must continue.

Class is not only a set of relations whereby people gain access to resources and privileges, but it is a set of relations dependent on other power relations among people. Each person is, so to speak, enmeshed in a variety of relationships all expressive of various aspects of that person's existence. The network of relations defines the person's location on a ranking order of hierarchies in such a way that the person can be at various levels of ranking for different aspects of his/her existence. For example, a black man can be the deacon of his church (high rank and status); a man with a high-school education (middle rank in access to jobs and resources); a highly respected basketball player (high status within a special network); a janitor in a hospital (relatively low rank and income); a tyrannical husband and father. Clearly, a concept of class dealing only with economics cannot do justice to this man's position in society.

The analysis of class I have just offered explains why men of lower classes and men of racial or ethnic minorities, themselves suffering from economic and social oppression, do not necessarily support the emancipation of women of their own class. It is, of course, because the class interests of men and women are different. While women may share the race and class interests of men of their class and therefore have historically supported class-based movements for social and economic improvements, the men of their own economic or racial group have no interest in losing the privileges gender dominance confers upon them. Male peasants, struggling against feudal landlords, do not wish to relinquish the potential property gains to be made by their ability to control the marriages of their daughters. Male artisans and professionals, struggling for upward mobility, organize family resources so as to foster the education of sons, not of daughters. Male workers, seeking economic and political rights in socialist revolutions have no interest in, in fact resist the possibility that wives and daughters may withdraw the unpaid domestic services which men of their class accept as a natural right. We might add to this the psychological advantages men enjoy in being able to consider themselves superior to a whole group of persons unlike themselves, even when, or especially when, they themselves feel and often are powerless to change or improve their own situation.

Sisterhood among women has been impeded from the time of the inception of patriarchy by the way women are structured into lifelong dependency on men, that is by the way class is formed. Class has always offered women of the ruling group economic and educational advantages—never as great as those of their brothers, but considerably greater than those of women of lower classes. Similarly, "racial" privileges provided women of the racially dominant group tangible advantages over men and women of the subordinate group.

Finally, a holistic re-definition of class would move away from all vertical, horizontal and two- or three-dimensional models. Class is not and never has been static.

Class is a process over time through which hierarchical relations are created and maintained in such a way as to give some men power and privilege over women and other men by their control over material resources, sexual and reproductive services, education and knowledge. Such control over others is maintained by a complex weave of social relations among the dependent groups, which offer each group some advantages over other groups, sufficient to keep each group within the dominance system, subordinate to the top elite.

Class is constructed and maintained genderically; class is constructed racially as well. The relationships are not additive, but interdependent and mutually reinforcing. People derive racial and sexual benefits from class and, in turn, class oppression is expressed in different ways for members of different races and sexes.

II.RETHINKING THE PARADIGM: RACE

The word "race" has a long and embattled history. Modern dictionary definitions show that in earlier centuries, the term was used to mean "lineage," derivation from kin and family groupings. For centuries it was almost identical with kin. The term "race" first appeared in the 16th century; only in the 19th century did it become biologized. It was then, that evolutionary thought became the basis on which the "races of mankind" were classified and hierarchically ordered, with whites inevitably at the top of the ranking order. It can be no accident that these ideological constructions roughly coincided with the development of nationalism and colonialism.[56]

There is no denying that human beings come in different shapes, shades and appearances. What is debatable is whether these external physical differences in any way correlate with other inherent characteristics, such as attitudes, talents or psychological makeup. Modern science gives no support to essentialist racial theories. Underneath the skin, all human beings are alike. There is no such thing as "black blood" or "pure blood" and the only distinctions of blood—blood types— have nothing to do with race. Even so, racial definitions to this day, for example, in the Census, attempt to group people by external physical attributes—color, hair, facial makeup—or by "inheritance," i.e. blood.

In fact, the only significant biological differences between people can be proven scientifically to reside in their genetic makeup. But here, too, science offers no support to advocates of racial definitions. Every individual's genetic code though unique, contains sequences passed down from parent to child and reaching back over billions of years of evolution. Using modern technology, researchers have recently been able to trace human linkages over millennia and thus trace the family history of the species. They trace all human beings to a common female ancestress, an original Eve, who lived approximately 200,000 years ago in Africa. While the dating of the common ancestress is still under dispute, one of the implications of these findings is that all human beings originated in Africa and that the essential, "natural" human race is *one*, mutating into different groups over time due to geographical migration.[57]

The detectable differences in human genetic makeup do not follow conventionally defined racial lines. Genetically speaking, there is little difference between an African tribeswoman, a man from New Guinea and a suburbanite from Westchester County, N.Y. Furthermore, 200,000 or more years of intermixing of human groups and geographical displacement have diluted the visible bodily differences between human beings—hair, skin, facial formation—to the point of insignificance, if ever they had significance. Differences in physical makeup and shading are as great within each group designated as a race as they are when compared across race lines. Differences, then, take on meaning only when they are socially constructed as markers of ranking. Biological race is, in fact, a scientifically nonexistent category, constructed solely for the purpose of labeling a designated group as inferior from those doing the designating.

The arbitrariness and irrationality of the designation race are clearly shown in the case of Jews. For nearly two millennia Jews were distinguishable from others solely by their self-imposed religious observances, which differed from those of the people among whom they lived. They were, at times, forced to mark themselves as Jews by items of clothing, such as the pointed hat and the yellow star imposed on European Jews in the Middle Ages. Up until the 20th century, Jews were despised, persecuted and designated as outsiders for religious reasons and each individual Jew could escape his/her plight by converting to Christianity. When the Nazis in Germany looked for a rationale to explain and justify their desire to exterminate all Jews, they designated them a "race." The Nüremberg laws made this designation the law of the land. The definition of who is a Jew—a purely arbitrary definition—no longer had anything to do with religion. Atheists and converted Jews were marched into the gas chambers, as long as their biological ancestry made them fall under the racial designation invented by the Nazis. *Mischlinge*—mixed—"blood" offspring were spared from extermination only if they had two "Aryan" grandparents and did not profess the Jewish religion. The particular mathematical formula used to determine Jewishness was, again, defined in an arbitrary manner.

By a similarly arbitrary definition a person was defined as a "Negro" or a member of the Negro race in Virginia in 1750 if he had a "Negro" mother. Later, the definition was refined to make a person a "Negro" with "one drop of Negro blood." Since no one has ever been able to distinguish "Negro" blood from any other blood by any property inherent in that blood, the definition is unscientific and clearly political. Lastly, let us remember that in Latin America and in South Africa persons of "mixed" heritage are designated as a group separate from "whites" and "blacks."

Challenges to the use of the term "race" go far back in history and have found expression in the thought of a number of African-Americans. W. E. B. DuBois's position on the use of the term changed significantly over his lifetime. Early in his life DuBois already regarded race not as a scientific but as a socio-historical term, descriptive of societal conditions. He wrote in 1897:

> What, then, is a race? It is a vast family of human beings,
> generally of common blood and language, always of common
> history, traditions and impulses, who are both voluntarily
> and involuntarily striving together for the accomplishment
> of certain more or less vividly conceived ideals of life.[58]

At that time DuBois still accepted the existence of "common blood" as scientifically accurate or plausible. He went on to argue that the Negro race had special contributions to make to civilization, and that it must maintain its race identity in the United States. This position on race is still reflected in the title of his path-breaking book, *Dusk of Dawn: An Essay Toward An Autobiography of a Race Concept* (1940).

But DuBois qualified his acceptance of biological race as early as 1911, when he wrote: "It is not legitimate to argue from differences in physical characteristics to differences in mental characteristics" ... and "the civilization of a ... race at any particular moment of time offers no index to its innate or inherited capacities."[59] Even as he continued to advocate black nationalism and race consciousness, DuBois redefined the term. In 1940 he wrote:

> It is easy to see that scientific definition of race is impossible ... [T]he physical bond is least and the badge of color relatively unimportant save as a badge; the real essence of this kinship is its social heritage of slavery; the discrimination and insult ...

In another, even more telling definition DuBois concluded: "Race is the fact that a Negro in Georgia has to ride in the Jim Crow car."[60] This, perhaps his most radical definition, would imply that "race" is nothing else but "racism."

The contemporary scholar Anthony Appiah agrees with that definition: "The truth is that there are no races: there is nothing in the world that can do all we ask race to do for us. The evil that is done is done by the concept." Appiah further refines DuBois's "badge of color" by stating, "What DuBois shares with the nonwhite world is not insult but the badge of insult. ..."[61]

The unscientific nature of the category "race" was legally recognized as early as 1967, when, in *Loving vs. Virginia*, the U.S. Supreme Court ruled miscegenation laws unconstitutional. "Biological race is no longer a significant category in U.S. marriage law."[62]

In recent years many intellectuals have come to similar conclusions. The African-American historian Barbara Fields wrote in 1982:

> The assumption that race is an observable physical fact, a thing, rather than a notion that is profoundly and in its very essence ideological ... the view that race is a biological fact, a physical attribute of individuals, is no longer tenable ...
>
> Class and race are concepts of a different order; they do not occupy the same analytical space, and thus cannot con-

stitute analytical alternatives to each other. . . . Class refers to a material circumstance: the inequality of human beings from the standpoint of social power . . . the reality of class can assert itself independently of people's consciousness, and sometimes in direct opposition to it. . . . Race, on the other hand, is a purely ideological notion. . . . The material circumstance upon which the concept purports to rest—the biological inequality of human beings—is spurious: there is only one human species, and the most dramatic differences of appearance can be wiped out in one act of miscegenation. . . . That does not mean that race is unreal. All ideologies are real, in that they are the embodiment in thought of real social relations.[63]

Henry Louis Gates calls race a "dangerous trope . . . that pretends to be an objective term of classification" and has adopted the practice of putting the term in quotation marks. "Our decision to bracket 'race' was designed to call attention to the fact that 'races,' put simply, do not exist, and that to claim that they do, for whatever misguided reasons, is to stand on dangerous ground."[64] In 1990, Hazel Carby asked academics to stop speaking of "essential races" but rather to speak of "racial formations."[65]

Challenges to the use of the term have been widespread also in Europe. Recently, German scholars, more and more aware of the dangerous consequences of racist thought, have adopted a practice of not using the term at all and substituting for it the term "ethnicity." While their position is understandable in view of their country's history, in which primary targets for persecution and discrimination were Jews and various ethnicities, it does not fit the history of the USA, where race and "ethnicity" have quite separate and often disparate histories.[66]

Every use of an unscientific term based on prejudice and ignorance tends to encourage further use and legitimizes such use. But the arbitrary, socially constructed designation race cannot be simply dropped from our language. Although there are no biologically definable, essential races, the term "race" has become reified in law, custom and historical practice to such an extent that it has acquired a historical existence. If European Jews never were a race, the fact of that designation of them by the German National-Socialist government led to a new reality which profoundly affected every Jewish person. The erroneous term, reified into law, became in fact a death sentence for every person so designated.

In the same way, in the United States to be designated as belonging to the Negro race imposes an altered reality and a different historical experience upon the person so designated. Thus, what we call "race," a social construct, exists on three different levels: (1) as a tool for dominance which has become institutionalized in the United States and in some other countries; (2) as a historic experience, a force shaping the lives of the designated group; and (3) as a distinguishing marker for the oppressed group, transformed into a mark of pride, resistance and a tool for liberation. Jews think of themselves as the "chosen people." Race pride claims race as a marker: Black is beautiful. Black pride; Black liberation.

Because race exists on these three different levels of reality, scholars are obliged to continue to use the term.[67] What would obviously be most desirable is the development of separate terms for the separate levels. One might call level (1) "Institutionalized racism"; level (2) "experiental racism"; and level (3) "resistance formation." Until such terms or better ones find general acceptance, I agree with Appiah and Gates that putting the term in quotation marks indicates its problematic content and alerts the reader to question the term and I plan to adopt this usage in the future. (See Note on Usage, p. viii.)

The identification of "institutionalized racism" has been the best documented and least controversial aspect of the debate on "race." It may be useful to call attention to the fact that institutionalized racism depends not only on the factual manipulation of resources and power, but also on the manipulation of meaning systems and symbols in the interests of white elites.

"Experiential racism" and "resistance formation" have been so closely intertwined that it is often difficult to separate them out. Both aspects of being a member of a designated out-group based on the construction of race have been involved in identity-formation and therefore hold positive values, which often outweigh the negative ascriptions.

Even as we note that gender, class, ethnicity and race are all social constructs, we must be careful not to homogenize these concepts. Their impact on individuals and groups of people in given historical situations and their impact on historical experience is vastly different. As I have shown with the example of European Jews, their construction as an ethnically and religiously deviant group subjected them to discrimination and persecution, but their racialization led directly to their physical destruction.[68] In the American setting the construction of "ethnicities" has not impeded the upward mobility of persons so designated, whereas the construction of race has. The Irish, who in the 19th century were the most persecuted out-group among white immigrants, became transformed into a powerful political in-group in the 20th century. Had it not been for racism, people of African origins might have created ethnic identities for themselves. Had it not been for racism, which lumped all of them together as having one "African" origin, they might have created many different cultural African-derived identities. The negative implications of the construction of race have been a powerful force in shaping the political and economic realities under which people of African origins have experienced history in the USA.

African-Americans' most powerful weapon against racism has been the reclaiming of race as a positive symbol. This has been a prominent feature of the debate on "multiculturalism" and it has been expressed particularly strongly in the black feminist critique of Women's Studies and of the feminist movement. This critique of white feminism for making false claims of "universality," has become widespread in the past ten years. In 1980 Audre Lorde wrote: "There is a pretense to a Homogeneity of Experience covered by the word *sisterhood* that does not in fact exist."[69]

The conviction that such differences are great enough so that one cannot make any valid generalizations without taking "differences" into consideration has found widespread acceptance, both by black and white feminist thinkers.[70]

Many black historians now also claim that African-American women have a historic and cultural experience unique to them, which singularly qualifies them to interpret their own history. Patricia Hill Collins refers to this as the "standpoint" of black women. Their standpoint consists of oppositional consciousness; an oral and dialogue tradition of expression and learning; an ethic of caring and a history of family and community support for their liberation struggles. Other theorists and historians similarly argue that black women define their identities differently from white women, being more community and family-based.[71] Others term this uniqueness the "African-American experience" and define it in cultural/historic terms.[72] An important aspect of that different experience was defined by Karen Sacks as the fact that African-American women have historically experienced domestic labor as waged labor, whereas white women have not.[73] This is an interesting observation, but it ignores class, since up until the 20th century domestic service was the predominant occupation of white women, as well as black.

The arguments for the existence of a different "standpoint," "angle," "cultural experience" are persuasive and they work well in countering tendencies toward over-generalization or "false universalization," which tend to subsume all women under representations mostly applicable to white women. They work well, in other words, as markers of differences among women. But do they actually illuminate how the *system* or systems of dominance operate? I think not.

What is wrong is that these explanations and definitions are still entirely within a static, dialectical framework. They quite accurately describe relations between "oppressors" and "oppressed" or, we might say, they sort people neatly into vertical boxes, but they totally disregard the complexities of other factors that operate outside of that binary system. If African-American women have a unique "standpoint," so do women of different ethnicities; so do women of different religious; so do rural and urban women; so do women of different economic constituencies; so do women who are lesbian or bisexual. The variations are endless and might include age, disability, childlessness. By the time one considers all these "standpoints" everything is relativized to the point of meaninglessness. For historians, this posture adds up to being mired in the particular, unable to make any valid generalizations. This is indeed the position of some deconstructionists and postmodernists. I find it unacceptable, because it is not useful as a tool of analysis.

The argument for a unique standpoint or historical experience is, in fact, a valid and useful argument, *if* it is not used in isolation. What is required is a multilayered approach. We must not only ask what is unique about a particular group, but also what this group has in common with other, comparative groups, keeping both the particular and the general in perspective. The key to such an approach is to understand that people do not define themselves by a single identity but by a number of interacting identities, and that the various aspects of people's identities which are being manipulated by the systems of dominance are interconnected and mutually constitutive.

This has been brilliantly analyzed, as it applies to colonialism, by the anthropologist Ann Stoler. She observed the way in which colonial powers—the Dutch in Indonesia, the French in Indochina, the British in India—constructed a concept of the colonizer versus a concept of the colonized, which shifted over time and varied with the power needs of the colonizers. Race could not here serve as the marker of difference, since the governance of provinces distant from the mainland required that some of the colonized be part of the group in power. It was therefore essential to construct what Stoler labels "cultural racism." In the earliest periods of colonization, white men (colonizers) freely established sexual unions with native women (colonized). These liaisons, recognized in law and custom as "metissage," produced hybrid offspring which "in their very person exposed the arbitrary logic by which the categories of control were made."[74]

In 19th-century Java, European plantations employed only single white men and looked favorably on concubinage with Javanese women. This changed in the 1920s, when plantation owners began to encourage the immigration of married couples and family formation among their white employees by offering higher bonuses and better housing to married couples. It was hoped that the "steadying influence of white women" would lessen tensions and rowdyism. The new and more rigidly defined order of colonial rule demanded that "colonizers" be physically and socially separated from the "colonized." Dress codes, food, clubs and recreation were organized on a segregated basis, stressing the communality of European traditions and experiences. An important aspect of this construction of European-ness was "an obsession with protection of European women from sexual assault by Asian and black males."[75]

From the 1920s on, sexual controls were imposed in such a way as to discourage interracial marriages. In Indochina, children of mixed marriages were left to their native mothers and abandoned by their fathers. In the Netherlands Indies in 1848 access to European status for children of mixed heritage required: "a belief in Christianity; fluency in spoken and written Dutch; training in European morals and ideas and distance from the native environment."[76] Conversely, in both countries white women who married native men lost their social status and citizenship. Such sexual regulation tended to discourage "mixed" marriages. Stoler shows how the sexual regulation of white women shaped them into instruments of "race-culture" in the colonies. Their primary role was motherhood and domesticity, as defined by the rules of racial separation. Single women were viewed as aberrant, and single professional European women were treated as virtual prostitutes. Concurrent with these policies, the presence of unproductive, unemployed European men was discouraged.[77] Stoler concludes that gender inequalities were essential to the structure of colonial racism.

The conditions Stoler described in her essays for Asia existed as well in African colonies. Chandra Talpade Mohanty describes "the ideological construction and consolidation of white masculinity as normative and the corresponding racialization and sexualization of colonized peoples" in the case of Africa. There, too white men were made to embody rule "by literally and symbolically representing the power of Empire," while the physical and symbolic separation of the races reinforced colonial authority.[78] The realization that the gendered white colonizer was socially constructed dovetails neatly with the recent scholarly attention to the social construction of "whiteness." The connection is well explained by Ruth Frankenberg:

> Race is a socially constructed rather than an inherently meaningful category, one linked to relations of power and processes of struggle. . . . Race, like gender, is "real" in the sense that it has real, though changing effects in the world and real, tangible and complex impact on individuals' sense of self, experiences and life chances. . . . White people as much as people of color are racialized.[79]

If "race" cannot be proven on a biological basis in the case of people of color than whiteness is similarly unprovable. White people are defined as the norm against "the Otherness" of people of color. But "whiteness" as a constructed social category within a system of power bestows privileges on whites which are withheld from "Others." One of these privileges is that it is whites who do the defining of the social categories and who can remain unconscious of their own racial construction. The subject is fairly new in academic studies, but I think it offers one of the most promising means of changing people's consciousness on the uses of "difference" for enforcing dominance.[80]

Although the definitions of sex, class, race and ethnicity have proven troublesome and in a way divisive among scholars, there has slowly developed agreement among many scholars that the terms must be treated not as separate "realities," but as inter-related. But just how these aspects of people's lives and identity-formation inter-relate has proven to be more difficult to define and conceptualize. Let us hear a few representative voices in this debate:

Charlotte Bunch argued that various forms of oppression *interact* to shape the particulars of each woman's life. bell hooks stated: "Sexism, racism and class exploitation constitute *interlocking* systems of domination." This view was supported by Karen Brodkin Sacks, who saw "class, race and gender oppression as parts of a *unitary* system. . . . Women's gender identities are not analytically separable from their racial and class identities." Sandra Morgen explained "that these social relations so *interpenetrate* that they are better understood as constituting (rather than simply modifying—or coloring . . .) one another." Linda Gordon asked for a "transformation of the difference slogan into a more relational, power-conscious, and subversive set of analytic premises and questions." Patricia Hill Collins (1991) while speaking from the "standpoint of and for Black women" spoke of varieties of oppression which are part of one over-all form of domination, *interlocking and interdependent*. This recognition of the complex interrelatedness of the various aspects of domination was echoed also in the work of Elsa Barkley Brown and Evelyn N. Glenn and many other scholars of different races and ethnicities.[81]

Several scholars attempted to define the exact "relations" more closely. The black poet and essayist Audre Lorde forcefully illuminated the connections as early as 1980, comparing methods of discrimination and oppression, rather than categories of identities:

> Racism, the belief in the inherent superiority of one race over all others and thereby the right to dominance. Sexism, the belief in the inherent superiority of one sex over the other and thereby, the right to dominance. Ageism. Heterosexism. Elitism. Classism.[82]

I attempted a comparison by categories when I wrote in 1973:

> Feminists have claimed the universality and priority of sexual oppression as an experience common to all women. . . . The study of black women in American history illustrates that generalizations about sex oppression as *universal* are invalid. The nature of sex oppression differs for women of the dominant and the oppressed race. It also differs for women of different classes. . . . The history of black women should be an integral part of all American history. It is indispensable to the study of the history of American women, not only because of its intrinsic value . . . but also as a corrective to class- and race-based generalizations.[83]

The historian Dorothy Roberts, wrote (1993): "Racism is patriarchal. Patriarchy is racist. We will not destroy one institution without destroying the other."[84]

As we can see, despite different vantage points, standpoints and philosophies, a critical number of feminist scholars have reached agreement on some basic concepts and on first steps toward re-definition. In light of this debate, let us see if it is possible to improve on the definitions of the categories of difference. To do so I propose that we shift away from comparisons among and between the oppressed. Let us instead look at the function, the purpose, of the categories from the point of view of those who designate deviant out-groups in order to dominate over them.

Let us trace the process by which dominance is constructed:

1. *Arbitrary Targeting.* One selects a "difference." This can be one or several characteristics or categories by which difference from the norm (which is usually the group that does the defining) is marked. Exx.: A person is female; a person is darker-skinned; a person belongs to a group called Bosnians; a person is a Jew.

2. *Enforced Group Identity.* Negative characteristics are arbitrarily selected and affixed to the group. Then these negative characteristics are ascribed to each member of the group. (All Latinos are lazy. All Jews are money-grabbers.)

3. *Institutionalized Discrimination.* By discriminatory laws and practices the targeted group is deprived of equal access to power, resources and privileges. The observed negative impact on the group reinforces

notions of its inferiority. Institutionalized racism, sexism, antisemitism, homophobia etc. reinforce prejudices and artificially created "deviance."

4. *A Different Historical Experience.* Members of the groups designated as "deviant" and victimized by institutionalized discrimination experience a historical reality different from that of the dominant group. They experience all collective events from the standpoint of the oppressed. But this segregated experience in turn becomes the source of their ability to survive and to resist.

A common group history becomes the basis for positive reaction-formation—the oppressed take pride in their "marker of difference," they use their defamed group identity as the basis for organizing resistance. Group identity and group history are cherished; self-segregation becomes a means of fostering resistance (separatism, nationalism). Slaves and colonial subjects become rebels, oppressed women become feminists, gays and lesbians "come out" and form interest groups.

By looking at the *process* in terms of its function, one can at once see great similarities between the categories. Sex is actualized and expressed through gender, that is, the bodily actuality of sex is given meaning through gender. The irrational and unreal category "race" is reified through "racial formation"—discrimination, terror and contempt—until it becomes the reality of race as experienced historically. Race is not a description of actuality or a marker of static variations among people in society. Race is a process. In the case of ethnicity, cultural, linguistic and historically different experiences are used as the basis of assigned "differences." In the case of class, distinctions in access to economic resources, to education and to sexual privileges mark the "difference."

We can, then, re-define the categories as follows:

Gender, race, ethnicity and class are processes *through which hierarchical relations are created and maintained in such as way as to give some men power and privilege over other men and over women by their control of material resources, sexual and reproductive services, education and knowledge. Such control over others is maintained by a complex weave of social relations among dependent groups, which offers each group some advantages over other groups, sufficient to keep each group within the dominance system subordinate to the elite.*

The categories are therefore not just *inter-related*, they also are mutually *constitutive:*

Class privileges given to elite women, race privileges given to white women, privileges over "ethnics" given to women of the dominant group, make these women complicit with the hierarchical system and undercut their ability to form interest groups with other women. Thus, gender is constructed racially and through class and ethnicity.

Race is constructed generically and by way of class. That is, race never impacts the same way on women and men, and race varies according to class.

Class is constructed racially and generically; gender is constructed by class and racially.

A similar case can be made for all other social formations, such as ethnicity, religion, sexuality, age.

The significance of these re-definitions is that they help us to see the stages by which the discriminatory systems of dominance are constructed. These systems demand the creation of "deviant out-groups" against which the dominant group can define itself. The criteria of selection of these groups defined as "the other" are arbitrary and opportunistic. They may be people of color, ethnics, women, gypsies, heretics, AIDS victims or welfare mothers. Once subject to the process of being turned into "deviants" they can and do serve as scapegoats for all the unresolved problems of the dominant group. That is their function. And since there are limitless groupings of people with "differences" available for "Othering" the system cannot be affected by efforts to end one form of discrimination or the other. By setting them, group by group, against each other, the people in power can maintain their advantages undisturbed by effective challenges.

As long as we regard class, race and gender dominance as separate though overlapping systems, we fail to understand their actual integration. We also fail to see that they cannot be abolished sequentially, for like the many-headed hydra, they continuously spawn new heads. Vertical theories of separate systems inevitably marginalize the subordination of women and fail to place it in the central relationship it has to the other aspects of the system. The system of hierarchies is interwoven, interpenetrating, interdependent. It is one system, with a variety of aspects. Race, class and gender oppression are inseparable; they construct, support and reinforce one another.

This analysis has important implications for practical politics. Instead of engaging in the endless, fruitless and counter-productive activity of prioritizing discriminations and competing among targeted groups for scarce resources, it enables us to see the commonalities among them. New attempts at building coalitions between women separated by their "differences" can succeed if the differences are acknowledged and respected, even as alliances are formed on partial goals on which there is a commonality of interest. As Charlotte Bunch advised in 1985, an understanding of how the various forms of oppression interact is a necessary foundation for the building of valid coalitions. The systems of dominance are mutually constitutive, therefore they cannot be effectively attacked one at a time. The struggles against sexism, racism, antisemitism and homophobia are inextricably linked.

For historians, this more nuanced understanding of the various manifestations of the system of oppression—gender, ethnic, race and class formation—should enable us to put power relations into the center of any analysis we make. Instead of asking only, how true is this statement or observations for members of groups A-D (a merely additive, comparative approach), we can ask, how are the power relations expressed in this particular situation? How do they vary for different groups? How do the benefits of one group disadvantage another? How can the relationality best be expressed?

Lastly, we need to keep a basic principle in mind: It is not "difference" that is the problem. It is dominance justified by appeals to constructed differences that is the problem.

12

Why History Matters

*The power and breadth of our own lives and the energy
with which we reflect on them are the foundation of historical vision.* (Wilhelm Dilthey, *Patterns and Meaning
in History: Thoughts on History and Society* ed. H. P. Rickman [New York, 1962], p. 87.)

All human beings are practicing historians. As we go through
life we present ourselves to others through our life story; as we
grow and mature we change that story through different interpretations and different emphasis. We stress different events as
having been decisive at different times in our life history and, as we do
so, we give those events new meanings. People do not think of this as
"doing history"; they engage in it often without special awareness. We
live our lives; we tell our stories. It is as natural as breathing.

Our self-representation, the way we define who we are, also takes the
shape of the life story we tell. What we remember, what we stress as
significant, and what we omit of our past defines our present. And
since the boundaries of our self-definition also delimit our hopes and
aspirations, this personal history affects our future. If we see ourselves
as victimized, as powerless and overwhelmed by forces we cannot understand or control, we will choose to live cautiously, avoid conflict
and evade pain. If we see ourselves as loved, grounded, powerful, we
will embrace the future, live courageously and accept challenges with
confidence.

Another aspect of history-making, namely, its function in the healing
of pathology, is recognized and ritualized by most systems of
psychology. People traumatized by abuse or negative childhood expe-

riences are helped to recall the traumatizing events and to reenact their responses to them in the light of therapeutic insights. In other words, they are helped to retell their story in a more positive, perhaps in a more realistic framework. The abused child is taught not to take on the guilt of the abuser, to reinterpret her story so that her own healing anger is allowed expression. "Forgotten" trauma is brought to light through therapy and in the retelling is robbed of its evil power. In other healing methods, people are taught to disassociate from their negative memories and focus instead on a different practice in the present. The shy are reinforced in their efforts to be more outgoing; the anxious are encouraged to disregard their negative past patterns. "Cures" are signaled not only by new behavior but by a more positive reinterpretation of the personal past to reflect the new experiences. History-making is an essential aspect of personal growth and healing.

There is another way in which history affects our personal lives. In traditional, rural societies, time and place are stable over a person's lifetime. One is born, lives and dies in the same place. Each person lives in the circle of a larger family encompassing different generations. Life has meaning as a generational passage. In such societies, which means in most societies in the world up to the beginning of the 20th century, religion was a more important factor in creating personal identity and in giving life meaning than was history. In the 20th century the opposite is true.

Urbanization, removal from the land and the spatial mobility fostered by industrialization have deracinated people. Modern woman and man feel alone and anxious in their ever shifting settings, their smaller and smaller family units, their isolation from meaningful and stable communities. In a world in which personal contact with different generations is often severed, history can link people to past generations and root them in the continuity of the human enterprise. People in modern societies express their deep need for history in tracing their own families through genealogies, and in documenting their own generation by means of modern visual technologies—cameras, videos and tape recordings. Today, in each person's life, the record of images gets more and more voluminous, larger and larger, filling walls and shoe boxes and video-screens, but it lacks context, and therefore it lacks meaning.

The media create a false "virtual reality" by packaging the past into boxes neatly labeled by decades and offering these for nostalgic reliving. For a price, we can acquire the packaged decades—music, famous speeches, newsreels, movie revivals—a surrogate history, all form and no content. Romanticized versions of the past in film and fiction are offered the public by the nostalgia industry as surrogates for a meaningful connection with the past. But all such efforts fail. Try as one might, one cannot purchase the past through souvenirs and artifacts; one cannot travel into the past like a voyager on an airplane or even a train.

A meaningful connection to the past demands, above all, active engagement. It demands imagination and empathy, so that we can fathom worlds unlike our own, contexts far from those we know, ways of thinking and feeling that are alien to us. We must enter past worlds with curiosity and with respect. When we do this, the rewards are considerable.

History, a mental construct which extends human life beyond its span, can give meaning to each life and serve as a necessary anchor for us. It gives us a sense of perspective about our own lives and encourages us to transcend the finite span of our life-time by identifying with the generations that came before us and measuring our own actions against the generations that will follow. By perceiving ourselves to be part of history, we can begin to think on a scale larger than the here and now. We can expand our reach and with it our aspirations. It is having a history which allows human beings to grow out of magical and mythical thought into the realm of rational abstraction and to make projections into the future that are responsible and realistic.

These aspects of history also lead to misuse. We construct symbolic communities, based on ethnicity, religion, race or any other kind of distinguishing mark, setting ourselves apart from those different from us, in order to find and enhance our own identity. We look to a past community, our "folk" of whatever definition, and our stories weave a collective myth into our own narrative. These widespread collective myths can serve a creative, harmonizing function, in stressing shared values, ideas and experiences. They offer us heroes in the past, role models for emulation, and provide us with a coherent narrative which gives shape and order to our experience. The story of Christianity, the life of Jesus, the Protestant Ethic, the American Dream—these are some of the collective myths which have sustained generations.

But those kept outside of these myths or those marginalized by them, experience them as destructive. In legitimizing the coherence of the "in-group" these stories and myths reinforce the deviant status of the "out-groups." By making distinctions between "us and them" appear to be natural, they reinforce a sense of alienation and "Otherness" in those excluded.

To those in power, history has always mattered. In fact, recorded history began as a means of celebrating the accomplishments of military chieftains, usurpers and kings. From the engraved descriptions of Urukagina of Lagash and the *stele* of Hammurabi of Babylon to the monuments and inscriptions celebrating the power of King Darius of Persia there goes a straight line of tradition to the officially endorsed histories glorifying the lives and deeds of emperors, kings, popes and various houses of nobility. These stories of the brave and good deeds of powerful rulers serve both to legitimize power and to maintain it by establishing the official version of events as the dominant version. Beginning in the Renaissance, state governments continually used history as a tool for legitimizing power and for creating a common cultural tradition based on that history. National histories, often mythical aggregates of facts and inventions, created a symbolic universe in which various contesting groups could shelter under a shared awning. The stories of the heroic deeds of ancestors supported the imperialist exploits of their 18th- and 19th-century heirs. Similarly, usurper regimes of the 20th century used history for their own purposes. Mussolini's gangs legitimized their accession to power by boasting of Roman roots and transforming the *fasces* of Roman ancestors into their party's name and emblem. German National Socialism created an elaborate official history extoling the mostly mythical deeds of Teutonic ancestors and rewriting more recent history to fit their version of "Aryan" racial superiority. The Communist regimes in Russia and in its satellite countries went to inordinate lengths to create "official" histories in which Marxist reconstructions of the past led inevitably to the triumph of the regime then in power. The United States, in its rise as a world power and in its claim to world leadership after 1945, used the doctrines of American exceptionalism and Manifest Destiny and the myth of the triumphant conquest of the West as a legitimizing explanatory system. George Washington—who could not tell a lie—, benevolent planter Thomas Jefferson, hard-working Ben Franklin, Andrew Jackson and

Daniel Boone, the frontiersmen—these became the heroic figures in the tale of the creation of an exceptional system which could and would combine power with genuine democracy. This story had to omit all mention of race, slavery, conquest of native people and oppressive constraints on many marginalized groups, including women. The history it told was not so much false, as one-sided and distorted.

Today, the nationalist, hegemonic version of state histories are everywhere being questioned and forced to compete with more balanced, complex and sophisticated versions of stories of the past. In the current public discourse about history, this contest over national history is what matters the most. In the U.S., the virtual "culture war" over definitions of the past has surfaced most recently in the bitter debates over National History Standards, the Smithsonian's Enola Gay exhibition and various exhibits on slavery. Traditionalists defend the older version in apocalyptic language as though history were a zero-sum game in which the old heroes would be inevitably demolished and forgotten were new heroes and heroines to enter the scene. Advocates of the new, more inclusive history point out that there is room in the American narrative for a broader range of heroes and heroines than we have hitherto included and that Abraham Lincoln's stature would not be diminished by the inclusion in the narrative of the story of Frederick Douglass. In fact, discussion of contending and contradictory narratives would more accurately reflect the tensions that existed in the lives of ruling elites and ordinary folk under a system in which both slavery and free institutions coexisted. Revisionist historians also point out that rewriting and reinterpreting the past in light of modern ideas and experiences has always been an essential aspect of historical thinking. The new history threatens only the hegemony of the history of the powerful; it does not threaten the essential integrity of the telling of past events.

Another aspect of the history of the powerful has been much under public scrutiny and needs to be considered here. This concerns "forgetting the past" and "selective remembering." After the Holocaust, after Vietnam, genocide in Cambodia, ethnic cleansing in the former Yugoslavia, whole nations, like individuals after trauma, take part in the great forgetting. The victors forget what brought them to victory and, when enough time has passed, they reconstruct a new story, based on selective memory. An entire generation of Germans tried thus to forget the past, "to let sleeping dogs lie," to forget what cannot be altered. Americans have forgotten napalm bombing and the slaughter of Vietnamese villagers. The more recent atrocities mount corpses on the long-past and forgotten atrocities. Muslim peasants in their mass graves supposedly atone for the Serb partisans slaughtered by Croat fascists in the time of their grandfathers. The spiral of bloodshed builds over time, on the principle that the victors control the story of the past until they are overthrown, then the victims tell their story in blood and rape. Civil wars and racist persecutions thrive on selective memory and collective forgetting.

Herein lies the bloodiest of proofs that history matters.

Just as the healing of personal trauma depends on facing up to what actually happened and on revisioning the past in a new light, so it is with groups of people, with nations. Germany's post-World War II recovery depended on its confrontation with its guilt for fascism, Holocaust and war. Restitution to the survivors and some effort at outlawing the racism that made these horrors possible were steps in the direction of healing. By contrast Austria, in maintaining the fiction of its having been "the first victim of Nazism," engaged in massive, collective forgetting, evaded responsibility for its participation in the Nazi regime and its machinery of war and destruction, and managed to exonerate most its war criminals. The result was continuing antisemitism, without Jews, and the rise of proto-fascistic political parties. It is only recently, more than fifty years later, that the Austrian government is attempting to deal more honestly with the past and to address restitution to the victims. The inability of the U.S. to come to terms with its complicity in slavery has made conflict over race a permanent feature of U.S. political life in the 20th century. In the former Soviet satellite nations the seeds of future conflicts lie buried in a great forgetting and in selective memory of the past. In each of these cases, honest attempts at more inclusive remembering would create mental attitudes and political realities that would weaken the power of ancient conflicts to ignite new fires.

What we do about history matters. The often repeated saying that those who forget the lessons of history are doomed to repeat them has a lot of truth in it. But what are "the lessons of history"? The very attempt at definition furnishes ground for new conflicts. History is not a recipe book; past events are never replicated in the present in quite the same way. Historical events are infinitely variable and their interpretations are a constantly shifting process. There are no certainties to be found in the past.

We can learn from history how past generations thought and acted, how they responded to the demands of their time and how they solved their problems. We can learn by analogy, not by example, for our circumstances will always be different than theirs were. The main thing history can teach us is that human actions have consequences and that certain choices, once made, cannot be undone. They foreclose the possibility of making other choices and thus they determine future events. For example, in 1831 the Virginia House Assembly met to discuss the abolition of slavery, which had become unprofitable in the state, but, unable to envision how white Virginians might live peacefully with large numbers of free Blacks, they decided instead to continue the slave system and increase restrictions on free Blacks. Within the next few years, the governments of all the Southern states abridged the freedom of speech and curbed the rights of protest of all those who opposed slavery. Once these decisions had been made, it was impossible for alternatives to the slave system to be publicly discussed in the South. This set of decisions narrowed the range of future choices for the South and made a peaceful solution of the conflict between the North and South virtually impossible.

Nations, like individuals, have to take responsibility for their past actions. The only way to avoid the determinism inherent in past choices is to confront errors made and openly reverse one's course. In the present time, the new South African government has approached its task of reconstruction in a way exemplary of such an approach. It has admitted the racist, oppressive past, explored its consequences and rejected its pattern.

Selective memory on the part of the men who recorded and interpreted human history has had a devastating impact on women. Women are everywhere and have always been at least half of humankind. It is inconceivable that their actions and thoughts were inconsequential in the shaping of historical events, yet women have been presented as though they had no history worth recording. The only women to have entered the historical record are those who were "stand-ins" for absent husbands or brothers, women who did what men did, rulers, queens. In effect, this process of selective remembering has taught both men and women that women did not contribute to the making of civilization in their own right. Thus, women have been taught to think of themselves as persons who cannot make significant contributions to society in the public realm. This massive distortion of the true record could happen because those who did the selecting were ignorant and contemptuous of the activities of women. The value system by which they judged "historical significance" valued the activities of men over those of women. Warfare and the distribution of wealth were considered more important than child-rearing and the building of communities. By accepting such criteria of selection, historians committed the basic error of seeing the half as the whole, remembering one half and forgetting the other. Selective memory deprived both women and men of the ability to construct a truthful picture of the past.

Many groups other than women have been subject to such "forgetting." Slaves, peasants, colonials have been marginalized and deprived of their history. Selective memory and the distortion of history have long been the powerful tools of oppressive regimes. It is worth noting that whenever subordinate groups have come to power they have tried to define and recover their history. This oft-repeated process testifies in its own way to the deeply felt need for a history of formerly oppressed people.

In order fully to understand how and why history matters, let us look more closely at the two groups which have for the longest time in human history been marginalized and oppressed—women and Jews. The persecution of Jews begins with their slavery in Egypt, sometime late in the second millennium B.C. The subordination of women is as old as patriarchy, which we can date as having been firmly established in most of the areas of the Ancient Near East by the middle of the first millennium B.C. While the chronology of their victimizations is not too different, the two groups differ in several important ways. Women are half of any given population; Jews were always a small minority. Women were always fully integrated into the life of the group that subordinated them, while Jews were easily segregated and marginalized. Women's subordination was perceived by them as "natural" since it came to them through family, state and religion. Jews saw their oppression and persecution as coming from outsiders to their own group and could thus use group cohesiveness, nationalism and religion for resistance. But the most important way in which the two groups differ is, I believe, in their relation to history.

Jews once were Hebrew tribes and later on people living in Jewish kingdoms, distinguished from their neighbors solely by different religious beliefs. After the Babylonian conquest and in the diaspora they became religious believers with a peculiar history which set them off from other groups. Jews were early on conscious of their peculiar relationship to history and built this consciousness into their religious ritual. The story of their slavery in Egypt and their deliverance is part of the annual religious observance of Pessach, the reenacted story of Queen Esther and her struggle against Haman, the oppressor of her people, is the substance of the celebration of Purim; and the story of the resistance of the Maccabees to Babylonian oppressors is the essence of the feast of Chanukkah. One can argue that the Jewish religion with its teleological emphasis on the coming of the Messiah incorporated history into religion in a way that earlier religions had not done. Thus, for Jews, their history, which was full of disasters and persecutions, was also a record of heroic figures resisting oppression. Jewish history became a primary tool for the survival of the people.

This was very different for women. Women have lived in a world in which they apparently had no history and in which their share in the building of society and civilizations was constantly marginalized. Women have also for millennia been denied the power to shape the formation of the dominant institutions of society. Whatever impact they were able to have on such institutions as the Church, the State, the Law, the Military had to be made from the margins, through "influence," not power, and through the mediation of men. Most important, women have been denied the power to define, to share in creating the mental constructs that explain and order the world. Under patriarchy the record of the past has been written and interpreted by men and has primarily focused on the activities and intentions of males. Women have always, as have men, been agents and actors in history, but they have been excluded from recorded history.

It is by now quite obvious that this long history of marginalization decisively affected women's self-perceptions, attitudes and group actions, even though it only recently has been properly "named." Denied any knowledge of their history, women were also denied heroines and role models. In the absence of stories of resistance and opposition, women internalized the ideology of patriarchy and participated in maintaining and strengthening it by transmitting its rules faithfully to their children of both sexes. The tiny minority of Jews, persecuted for millennia, expelled from country after country, their communities destroyed, their leaders killed, then in the 20th century subject to the most savage scientifically organized genocide in history, could and did survive and even build a state. Women, half of the human race, subordinated, deprived of knowledge and resources for millennia, raped and often physically abused, could not recognize their own condition and organize to resist it until the last two centuries. People without a history are considered not quite human and incorporate that judgment in their own thinking. Unaware of any possible alternative, they cooperate in their own oppression. *Not* having a history truly matters.

The comparison of women to Jews can illuminate yet another aspect of the importance of history to human life. It concerns the way experience interacts with thought in the formation of personal identity.

Jewish history for several millennia is the history of a people without a geographical center, without a country, and subject to varying cycles of assimilation and expulsion from a great variety of other cultures. Being God's "chosen people" based on one's religious beliefs was one thing; being a people marked by homelessness, diaspora, persecution and exile was quite another historical experience. Whether in a state of assimilation or one of retrenchment and retreat, every Jew, man, woman and child, carried the burden of that history as a shaping force within memory and psyche. Thus, one can speak of the Old Testament Jews as people of one category; the diaspora Jews as people of another. Their knowledge of the possibility of persecution and discrimination, which is imprinted on the consciousness of even the most assimilated Jews, those of Weimar Germany, those in the former Soviet Union and in the United States, makes them sufficiently different from the neighbors among whom they live to be acknowledged and recognized. Thus, what makes Jews "Jews" is their historically developed experience.

I reason that similarly, what makes female persons gendered women in not their biological, but their historically developed experience. There is not only a biological, a bodily difference between men and women, but there is a historically conditioned difference. Throughout the nearly four thousand years of patriarchal society, women have largely been kept out of power; they have been educationally disadvantaged; they have been discriminated against in the allocation of resources. They have been placed in the position of dependents. For the past two hundred years women, in their independent movements, have fought against these restrictions in an organized way and, inch by inch, against great resistance, have gained some ground. But the long historical experience of relative powerlessness and exclusion from the dominant institutions of society has given women a different psychological and attitudinal heritage, which is expressed in a female way of acting and reacting. I reject the biologically grounded argument for female difference, at least in part, but I recognize the historically grounded difference between the sexes as an important factor which must be taken into account in any analysis of the situation of women.

I will go further. The biological difference between men and women became significant as a marker of subordination only by the cultural elaboration of difference into a mark of degradation. In pre-state societies, before the full institutionalization of patriarchy men and women's biological difference found expression in a sexually based division of labor. Women, either nursing babies, pregnant or encumbered with small infants, pursued different economic activities than men did, without this difference necessarily marking them as inferior or disadvantaged. It is the cultural elaboration of "difference" into a marker of subordination, a social construction which is historically determined, which creates gender and structures society into hierarchies. In historical time, which coincides with institutionalized patriarchy, Simone de Beauvoir's formulation that "one is not born, but one becomes a woman" is accurate. But what makes "the woman," i.e., the woman-under-patriarchy, is not her sexual difference but her historically created genderedness.

All of women's history deals with subjects who are gendered women, women functioning under patriarchy and with the weight of a gendered past on their shoulders. It would be nice to have a separate word to distinguish them from female persons living prior to patriarchy, but since we do not have such a word, I use the term "women" with the understanding that it means "women-under-patriarchy." If that is understood, I can say without being mistaken as a supporter of essentialism, that the historically constructed gender differences between men and women are far more important than their biological differences.

In both the case of women and the case of Jews this historically based difference leads to behaviors which are distinguishable from those of members of the dominant group. In this sense, there is indeed a woman's culture, a woman's vote, a woman's way of social behavior and interaction and it is *not* biologically determined.

That women's self-perceptions were diminished by a centuries-old tradition that put them outside of history and denied their agency in building human society and culture has been proven over and over again. Women's ambitions were lowered by the absence of heroines. For generations the most talented women put their energies into realizing themselves through the achievements of a man, be he brother, husband or son. Women expressed the disappointment and frustrations of their situation in their creative writing, the women characters they created and with whom they identified.

One way this found expression was in the struggle to create women's history. For centuries women amassed collections of "women worthies," heroic and achieving figures who, strung along a time chart, could prove the intellectual worth of women. They could and did provide the heroic models women generally lacked. In studying these lists, which occur in every century, I found that women never cite the lists other women had compiled before them, but frequently made use of the lists compiled by men. That was probably due to the fact that they did not know other women had done this particular work before them, for women's books were not reprinted with the frequency or given the length of life of books by men. It also reflected the conviction shared by men and women, that women were not authority figures. For a woman in the 19th century, such as Sarah Josepha Hale, to cite the lists of male predecessors, such as Livy and Boccaccio, was more impressive than to cite the work of then virtually unknown women, such as Christine de Pisan, Laura Cereta and Rachel Speght. The absence of women's history reinforced the absence of female authority in intellectual matters.

When women discover their history and learn their connectedness to the past and to the human social enterprise, their consciousness is inevitably and dramatically transformed. This experience is for them transcendent, in that it enables them to perceive what they share and always have shared with other women.

The new Women's History has undertaken the task of reconstructing the missing half of history and of putting women as active agents into the center of events in order that recorded history might at last reflect the dual nature of humankind in its true balance, its female and its male aspects.

Women's History of the past thirty years has offered a corrective to "selective forgetting," seeking a holistic worldview in which differences among people are recognized and respected and which records the commonality of human striving in all its variety and complexity. In remembering wholly one can fight the system of distortions and half-truths out of which sexism, classism, racism and antisemitism grow like poisonous weeds.

Women's History, the essential tool in creating feminist consciousness in women, is providing the body of experience against which new theory can be tested and the ground on which a feminist vision can be built.

We have now come back to the point at which we started. We live our lives; we tell our stories. The dead continue to live by way of the resurrection we give them in telling their stories. The past becomes part of our present and thereby part of our future. We act individually and collectively in a process over time which builds the human enterprise and tries to give it meaning. Being human means thinking and feeling; it means reflecting on the past and visioning into the future. We experience; we give voice to that experience; others reflect on it and give it new form. That new form, in its turn, influences and shapes the way next generations experience their lives.

That is why history matters.

Notes

1. A WEAVE OF CONNECTIONS

1. Herbert Rosenkranz, *Verfolgung und Selbstbehauptung: Die Juden in Oesterreich 1938–1945* (Wien: Herold, 1978), pp. 1–39.

2. *Ibid.*, pp. 36–38.

3. *Ibid.*, p. 80. The United States never changed its quota numbers and admitted only 1000 famous artists and intellectuals outside the quota numbers.

4. *Ibid.*, pp. 13, 310.

5. NONVIOLENT RESISTANCE: THE HISTORY OF AN IDEA

1. Staughton Lynd, *Nonviolence in America: A Documentary History* (Indianapolis: Bobbs-Merrill, 1966). Introduction. Additional sources consulted were William Robert Miller, *Non-Violence: A Christian Interpretation* (New York: Association Press, 1964); Charles DeBenedetti, *Origins of the Modern Peace Movement, 1915–1929* (Milwood, N.Y. 1978); Lawrence Wittner, *Rebels Against War: The American Peace Movement, 1941–1960* (New York: Columbia University Press, 1969); Alexander Tyrell, "Making the Millennium: The Mid-Nineteenth Century Peace Movement," *The Historical Journal*, vol. XX, no. 1 (1978), pp. 75–95.

2. "But I say unto you, That ye resist not evil; if a man strikes thee on thy right cheek, turn the other cheek also towards him." Matthew 5: 39. "Evil is not checked by evil, but by good." The Buddha.

3. Frederick B. Tolles, "Dyer, Mary," in Edward T. James (ed.), *Notable American Women, 1607–1950*, 3 vols. (Cambridge, Mass.: Belknap Press of Harvard University Press, 1971), I, pp. 536–37; Horatio Rogers, M.D., *The Quaker Martyr that was Hanged on Boston Common, June 1, 1660* (Providence: Prestone and Rounds, 1896), pp. 84–93; records of Dyer's trial are in Nathaniel B. Shurtleff (ed.), *Records of the Governor and Company of the Massachusetts Bay, 1628–1686*, 5 vols. (Boston: W. White, 1853–54), IV, pt. I, pp. 383–90, 419.

4. John Woolman, *The Journal of John Woolman* (Secaucus, N.J.: Citadel, 1972, reprint of 1873 edition), pp. 14-15, 22, 36-40, 52, 59-61.

5. Both quotations from *The Anti-slavery Record*, Vol II, no. 7 (July 1836), pp. 1–10.

6. Dwight Dumond, *Antislavery: The Crusade for Freedom in America* (Ann Arbor: University of Michigan Press, 1961), chaps. 24 and 26; Leonard Richards, *"Gentlemen of Property and Standing"; Anti-Abolition Mobs in Jacksonian America* (New York: Oxford University Press, 1970).

7. *The Anti-Slavery Record* (July 1836), p. 10, both quotes.

8. See Merle Curti, *Peace or War: The American Struggle, 1936–1936* (New York: Norton, 1936), pp. 39–42; Eunice Minette Schuster, "Native American Anarchism: A Study of Left-Wing American Individualism," *Smith College Studies in History*, vol. XVII, nos. 1–4 (October 1931–July 1932), pp. 44–77. Adin Ballou, *Non-Resistance in Relation to Human Governments*, pamphlet, n.p., 1839).

9. "Right and Wrong in Boston," *Report of the Boston Female Anti-Slavery Society . . .* (Boston: Boston Female Antislavery Society, 1836).

10. Walter Harding, *The Days of Henry Thoreau* (New York: Knopf, 1965), pp. 74, 201. Milton Meltzer and Walter Harding, *A Thoreau Profile* (New York: Thos. Crowell, 1962), pp. 176, 191, 193.

11. Leo Tolstoy, *The Kingdom of God and Peace Essays*, trans. Aylmer Maude (London: Oxford University Press, 1936), p. 1.

12. Count Leo Tolstoy, "Garrison and Non-Resistance," *The Independent*, vol. 56 (1904) pp. 881–83, 887. See also Leo Tolstoy, *The Kingdom of God is Within You: Christianity not as a mystic Religion but as a new Theory of Life* (Lincoln: University of Nebraska Press, 1984) chap 1, pp. 1–18. Tolstoy was equally impressed with the fact that Garrison's and Ballou's theories had been ignored and forgotten for fifty years.

Tolstoy's book *What I Believe*, written in 1884, was suppressed by Russian censorship, but circulated in manuscript and in translations abroad. Tolstoy revised it and published it in 1893 under the title *The Kingdom of God is Within You.*

13. Barry Walsh, "The Tolstoyan Episode in American Social Thought," *American Studies*, vol. 17, no. 1 (1976), pp. 49–68. References from pp. 50–51.

14. William Dean Howells, "In Honor of Tolstoy," *Critic*, vol. XXX (Oct. 1898), p. 288, as cited in Walsh, *American Studies*, p. 50.

15. *Ibid.*, pp. 50–54, 60–64.

16. *Ibid.*, p. 60.

17. Addams approvingly used William James's phrase, "A moral equivalent for war." Jane Addams, *Newer Ideals of Peace* (New York: Macmillan, 1907), p. 24.

18. Henry Salt, "Gandhi and Thoreau," *Nation and Atheneum*, vol. XLVI (March 1, 1930), p. 728, as quoted by Walter Harding, *Thoreau: A Century of Criticism* (Dallas: Southern Methodist University Press, 1954), p. 147.

In his *Autobiography* Gandhi states that a copy of Tolstoy's *The Kingdom of God* was sent to him in Natal, South Africa, in 1894. He was deeply impressed with it, but did not apply any of its teachings until 1906, when he launched his first civil disobedience campaign in South Africa. See Mohandas K. Gandhi, *An Autobiography* (Boston: Beacon Press, 1957), pp. 137–38.

19. M. K. Gandhi, *Nonviolent Resistance: Satyagraha* (New York: Schocken Books, 1961).

20. Martin Luther King, Jr., *Stride Toward Freedom: The Montgomery Story* (New York: Ballantine Books, 1958), pp. 40–43.

21. *Ibid.*, p. 67.

22. I am indebted to a former colleague at Sarah Lawrence College, Dr. Roy Finch, for this information.

23. Alfreda M. Duster, ed., *Crusade for Justice: The Autobiography of Ida B. Wells* (Chicago: University of Chicago Press, 1970), pp. 53–56.

7. THE 20TH CENTURY: A WATERSHED FOR WOMEN

1. Unless otherwise noted, all statistics are derived from Linda Schmittroth, *Statistical Record of Women Worldwide* (Detroit: Gale Research, 1991) and United Nations, Statistical Office, *The World's Women 1970–1990: Trends and Statistics*, Social Statistics and Indicators Series K, #8 (New York: United Nations, 1991). This information is taken from the United Nation's *Trends*, p. 12.

2. UN, *Trends*, p. 12.

3. UN, *Trends*, pp. 45–47; Schmittroth, *Statistical Record . . .*, pp. 235–38, 567.

4. UN *Trends*, pp. 45–47.

5. Schmittroth, *Statistical Record . . .*, pp. 231–35. The figures conflate data taken between 1970 and 1980.

6. UN, *Trends*, pp. 48–49.

7. Unless otherwise noted, all data on the United States are from the U.S. Bureau of the Census, *Historical Statistics of the United States, Colonial Times to 1957*, and Supplement, *Historical Statistics of the United States after 1957* (Washington, D.C.: Bureau of Commerce, 1961 and 1991).

8. Chart from Robert V. Wells, "Demographic Changes and the Life Cycles of American Families," *Journal of Interdisciplinary History*, vol. II, no. 2 (Autumn 1971), pp. 273–82.

9. Figures from table in Barbara Miller Solomon, *In the Company of Educated Women: A History of Women and Higher Education in America* (New Haven: Yale University Press, 1985), p. 63, based on the following sources: Mabel Newcomer, *A Century of Higher Education for American Women* (New York, 1959), p. 46; U.S. Bureau of the Census, National Center for Education Statistics, *Digest of Education Statistics* (Washington, D.C., 1980, 1982, 1983).

10. Virginia Sapiro, *Women in American Society: An Introduction to Women's Studies* (Palo Alto: Mayfield Publishing Co., 1986), p. 114; and Solomon, *In the Company of Educated Women*, p. 127.

11. See table in Schmittroth, *Statistical Record . . .* , p. 355.

12. UN, *Trends*, p. 102.

9. THE NECESSITY OF HISTORY

1. Kathryn Kish Sklar, "American Female Historians in Context, 1770–1930," *Feminist Studies*, 3 (Fall 1975), 171–84. Kathryn Kish Sklar's discussion is based on historians listed in Edward T. James, Janet Wilson James, and Paul S. Boyer, eds., *Notable American Women, 1607–1950: A Biographical Dictionary* (3 vols., Cambridge, 1971). Academic historians whose careers she analyzes are: Lucy Salmon (1853–1927); Nellie Neilson (1873–1947); Louise Kellogg (1862–1942); Annie Abel (1873–1947); Helen Summer Woodbury (1876–1933); Mary Barnes (1850–1898); Helen Gardner (1878–1946); and Mary Williams (1878–1944). I have also included Florence Robinson (1868–1926) and Martha Edwards (1865–1926).

2. Typical of the early compilers of women's biographies are Lydia Maria Child, *Brief History of the Condition of Women, in Various Ages and Nations,* 2 vols. (Boston, 1835); Sarah Josepha Hale, *Woman's Record; or, Sketches of All Distinguished Women, from "the Beginning" till A.D. 1850* (New York, 1853); Phebe A. Hanaford, *Women of the Century* (Boston, 1877); Frances E. Willard and Mary A. Livermore, eds., *American Women: Fifteen Hundred Biographies with over 1,400 Portraits* (2 vols., New York, 1897). The most important collection of nineteenth-century sources is Elizabeth Cady Stanton, Susan B. Anthony, Matilda Joslyn Gage, and Ida Husted Harper, eds., *The History of Woman Suffrage,* 6 vols. (New York, 1881–1922). For a discussion of the work of Elizabeth Schlesinger and Miriam Holden, see Gerda Lerner, "Miriam Holden—In Remembrance and Friendship," *Princeton University Library Chronicle,* 41 (Winter 1980), 164–69. Mary Beard's efforts to establish an archive in the history of women are discussed in Ann J. Lane, ed., *Mary Ritter Beard: A Sourcebook* (New York, 1977). See also Eugenie Andruss Leonard, Sophie Hutchinson Drinker, and Miriam Young Holden, *The American Woman in Colonial and Revolutionary Times, 1565–1800* (Philadelphia, 1962); Elisabeth Anthony Dexter, *Colonial Women of Affairs: A Study of Women in Business and the Professions in America before 1776* (Boston, 1924); Elisabeth Anthony Dexter, *Career Women of America, 1776–1840* (Francestown, N.H., 1950); and Eleanor Flexner, *Century of Struggle: The Woman's Rights Movement in the United States* (Cambridge, 1959).

3. "Ph.D. Phoolery," *Wall Street Journal,* Aug. 18, 1981, p. 32; Oscar Handlin, *Truth in History* (Cambridge, 1979), 3–24, quotations at 18, ix.

4. My ideas here are influenced by Ernest Becker, *The Denial of Death*

216

(New York, 1973), 1–24, and Robert Jay Lifton, *History and Human Survival: Essays on the Young and Old, Survivors and the Dead, Peace and War, and on Contemporary Psychohistory* (New York, 1970).

5. The concepts *legitimation* and *symbolic universe* are discussed in Peter L. Berger and Thomas Luckman, *The Social Construction of Reality: A Treatise in the Sociology of Knowledge* (Garden City, 1966), 93–97.

6. Carl Becker, "Everyman His Own Historian," *American Historical Review*, 37 (Jan. 1932), 233–34.

7. The phrase and my ideas are based on Douglas R. Hofstadter, *Gödel, Escher, Bach: An Eternal Golden Braid* (New York, 1979).

8. Leopold von Ranke, "A Fragment from the 1860's," in *The Varieties of History: From Voltaire to the Present*, ed. Fritz Stern (Cleveland, 1956), 61.

9. Henri Pirenne, "What Are Historians Trying to Do?" in *Methods in Social Sciences: A Case Book*, ed. Stuart A. Rice (Chicago, 1931), 435–45.

10. "Intelligent understanding of past history is to some extent a lever for moving the present into a certain kind of future." John Dewey, *Logic: The Theory of Inquiry* (New York, 1938), 239.

11. Wilhelm Dilthey, *Pattern and Meaning in History: Thoughts on History and Society*, ed. H. P. Rickman (New York, 1962), 86–87.

12. Mary Beard, "University Discipline for Women—Asset or Handicap?" *Journal of the American Association of University Women*, 25 (April 1932), 132.

13. These ideas are more fully treated in Gerda Lerner, *The Majority Finds Its Past: Placing Women in History* (New York, 1979). See also Berenice A. Carroll, ed., *Liberating Women's History: Theoretical and Critical Essays* (Urbana, Ill., 1976), and William H. Chafe, *Women and Equality: Changing Patterns in American Culture* (New York, 1977). For examples of historical work that has accepted the concept of a female culture or highlighted aspects of it, see Nancy F. Cott, "Young Women in the Second Great Awakening in New England," *Feminist Studies*, 3 (Fall 1975), 15–29; Carroll Smith Rosenberg, "Beauty, the Beast and the Militant Woman: A Case Study in Sex Roles and Social Stress in Jacksonian America," *American Quarterly*, 23 (Oct. 1971), 562–84; Carroll Smith-Rosenberg, "The Female World of Love and Ritual: Relations between Women in Nineteenth Century America," *Signs*, 1 (Autumn 1975), 1–29; Kathryn Kish Sklar, *Catharine Beecher: A Study in American Domesticity* (New Haven, 1973).

14. The major guide to manuscript sources is Andrea Hinding, Ames Sheldon Bower, and Clarke A. Chambers, eds., *Women's History Sources: A Guide to Archives and Manuscript Collections in the United States* (2 vols., New York, 1979). For a historiographic essay on women's history, see Barbara Sicherman, "American History," *Signs*, 1 (Winter 1975), 461–85. See also Gerda Lerner, *Teaching Women's History* (Washington, 1981), 69–88.

15. Gerda Lerner, "The Political Activities of Antislavery Women," in Lerner, *Majority Finds Its Past*, 112–28. See also Judith Wellman, "To the Fathers and the Rulers of Our Country, Abolitionist Petitions and Female Abolitionists

in Paris, New York, 1835–45," paper delivered at the Berkshire Conference on Women's History, June 1976 (copy on deposit at the Schlesinger Library, Cambridge, Mass.).

16. Mary R. Beard, *Woman as Force in History: A Study in Traditions and Realities* (New York, 1946).

17. W. E. Burghardt DuBois, *The Souls of Black Folk: Essays and Sketches* (Chicago, 1903), 3.

18. The concept of woman as "the Other" is fully discussed in Simone de Beauvoir, *The Second Sex*, trans. and ed. H. P. Parshley (New York, 1953).

19. My thinking here is based on an ongoing debate among feminist scholars, especially anthropologists. See Sherry B. Ortner, "Is Female to Male as Nature Is to Culture?" in *Woman, Culture and Society*, ed. Michelle Z. Rosaldo and Louise Lamphere (Stanford, 1974), 67–87, and other articles in the same volume. See also Ruby Rohrlich-Leavitt, "Women in Transition: Crete and Sumer," in *Becoming Visible: Women in European History*, ed. Renate Bridenthal and Claudia Koonz (Boston, 1977), 36–59; Ruby Rohrlich, "State Formation in Sumer and the Subjugation of Women," *Feminist Studies*, 6 (Spring 1980), 76–102; and Rayna Rapp Reiter, "The Search for Origins: Unraveling the Threads of Gender Hierarchy," *Critique of Anthropology*, 3 (Winter 1977), 5–24. Mary Daly first called attention to the deprivation of women in not being able to "name gods" or shape them in their image. See Mary Daly, *Beyond God the Father: Toward a Philosophy of Women's Liberation* (Boston, 1973), 1–34.

20. For a discussion of the effect of "the graphic revolution" on various aspects of our culture, see Daniel J. Boorstin, *The Image: Or What Happened to the American Dream* (New York, 1962). See also David Reisman, Nathan Glazer, and Reuel Denney, *The Lonely Crowd: A Study of the Changing American Character* (New Haven, 1950), 99–112; Erik Barnouw, *Mass Communication, TV, Radio, Film, Press: The Media and Their Practice in the United States of America* (New York, 1956), 49–97; Marshall McLuhan, *Understanding Media: The Extensions of Man* (New York, 1965), 297–337; Warren I. Susman, "The Thirties," in *The Development of an American Culture*, ed. Stanley Coben and Lorman Ratner (Englewood Cliffs, N.J., 1970), 179–218, 191; Susan Sontag, *On Photography* (New York, 1977), 3–24, 153–80.

21. "It is the total involvement in all-inclusive *nowness* that occurs in young lives via TV's mosaic image." McLuhan, *Understanding Media*, 335. See also *ibid.*, 332–35.

22. Daniel J. Boorstin ascribes this to the influence of the media: "When in our schools the study of 'current events' (that is, what is reported in the newspapers) displaces the facts of history, it is inevitable that the standard of knowledge propagated by newspapers and magazines and television networks themselves . . . overshadows all others. When to be informed is to be knowledgeable about pseudo-events, the line between knowledge and ignorance is blurred as never before." Boorstin, *Image*, 231–32.

23. Alice Kohli-Kunz, *Erinnern und Vergessen: Das Gegenwartigsein des Ver gangenen als Grund-problem historischer Wissenschaft* (Berlin, 1973), 1–117. In discussing needed reforms in the German university system, Helmut Schelsky stresses the changed position of historical studies, which in the 19th and early 20th century were the central carriers of the cultural tradition. Today, he says, the influence and leadership of educated individuals is restrained by the needs of science and technology, and there is no longer a need for historical thinking and understanding as the basis for social action. Helmut Schelsky, *Einsamkeit und Freiheit: Idee und Gestalt der deutschen Universität und ihrer Reformen* (Duesseldorf, 1971), 169. Jürgen Habermas points to the main danger in the supremacy of manipulative technological and sociological techniques over "enlightenment": "Emancipation by means of enlightenment is replaced by instruction in control over objective or objectified processes. Socially effective theory is no longer directed toward the consciousness of human beings who live together and discuss matters with each other, but to the behavior of human beings who manipulate." Speaking from a neo-Marxist position, he urges a fusion of theory and praxis. Jürgen Habermas, *Theory and Practice* (Boston, 1973), 235–57, 265–82. Analyzing the impact of the technological and scientific revolutions of the 20th century from an opposing viewpoint, which he proudly dubs "reactionary," John Lukacs argues for the revival of a teleological interpretation of history. John Lukacs, *Historical Consciousness, or the Remembered Past* (New York, 1968).

24. Kohli-Kunz, *Erinnern und Vergessen*, 66–67, 82–99. See also Robert Jay Lifton, *The Life of the Self: Toward a New Psychology* (New York, 1976), 29–47.

10. DIFFERENCES AMONG WOMEN

1. I first called attention to the need of including class differences among women in any generalization made about women in my 1969 article, "The Lady and the Mill Girl: Changes in the Status of Women in the Age of Jackson," *American Studies* 10, no. 1 (Spring 1969), reprinted in Gerda Lerner, *The Majority Finds Its Past: Placing Women in History* (New York: Oxford University Press, 1979), chap. 2.

For discussion of the problem of "differences" among women, see *ibid.*, chaps. 4–7.

For a review of the historiography of Women's History in the first decade of its 20th-century revival, see Barbara Sicherman, "Review Essay; American History," *SIGNS: Journal of Women in Culture and Society* 1, no. 2 (Winter 1975): 461–85; Mary Beth Norton, "Review Essay; American History," *SIGNS: Journal of Women in Culture and Society* 5, no. 2 (Winter 1979): 324–37. For a review of this topic covering the years 1975–80 see Hilda Smith, "Recent Trends in Women's History," in Paula A. Treichler et al. eds., *For Alma Mater:*

Theory and Practice in Feminist Scholarship (Urbana: University of Illinois Press, 1985).

2. The need for considering race and ethnicity as factors in Women's History was raised in Gerda Lerner, ed., *Black Women in White America: A Documentary History* (New York: Pantheon, 1972). The theoretical implications were discussed in Lerner, *Majority*, chaps. 5–7.

See also: William Chafe, *Women and Equality: Changing Patterns in American Culture* (New York: Oxford University Press, 1977); Sharon Harley and Rosalyn Terborg-Penn, eds. *The Afro-American Women: Struggles and Images* (Port Washington, N.Y.: National University Publications, 1978); Gloria T. Hull, Patricia Bell Scott and Barbara Smith, eds. *All the Women are White, All the Blacks are Men, But Some of Us Are Brave* (Old Westbury, N.Y.: The Feminist Press, 1981); bell hooks, *Ain't I a Woman: Black Women and Feminism* (Boston:South End Press, 1981); Bettina Aptheker, *Woman's Legacy: Essays on Race, Sex, and Class in American History* (Amherst: University of Massachusetts Press, 1982).

For background on issues of ethnicity see: *Frontiers*, Special issue "Native American Women," 6, no. 3 (Fall 1981); *SIGNS*, Special issue on Hispanic-American Women, 3, no. 1 (Autumn 1977); Maria Linda Apodaca, "The Chicana Woman. A Historical Materialist Perspective," *Latin American Perspectives* 4, nos. 1/2 (1977): 74–89; Louisa Ano Nuevo Kerr, *Chicanos* (Bloomington: Indiana University Press, 1978); Alfredo Mirande and Evangelina Enriquez, *La Chicana: The Mexican American Woman* (Chicago: University of Chicago Press, 1979); Magdelena Mora and Adelaida R. Del Castillo, eds. *Mexican Women in the United States: Struggles Past and Present* (Los Angeles: University of California Chicano Studies Research Center, 1980); Verna Abe et al., *Asian American Women* (Stanford: Stanford University Press, 1976).

3. This argument has recently appeared in several influential works in the form of an attack on the "new history." See Gertrude Himmelfarb, *The New History and the Old: Critical Essays and Reappraisals* (Cambridge: Belknap Press of Harvard University Press, 1987); Theodore S. Hamerow, *Reflections on History and Historians* (Madison: The University of Wisconsin Press, 1987). See also the contributions of Theodore S. Hamerow, Gertrude Himmelfarb, Lawrence W. Levine, Joan Wallach Scott, and John E. Toews in "AHR Forum, Perspectives on The Old History and the New," *The American Historical Review* 94, no. 3 (June 1989): 654–98.

4. The concept of America as the "melting pot" became popularized in 1903 through a play by that name by Israel Zangwill, which also had wide distribution in book form. The "salad bowl" metaphor was popularized in the widely used one-volume textbook on American History by Carl Degler, *Out of Our Past: The Forces that Shaped Modern America* (New York: Harper & Row, 1959), 296. Degler states: "A more accurate analogy would be a salad bowl, for, though the salad is an entity, the lettuce can still be distinguished from the chicory, the tomatoes from the cabbage." For a general background

on questions of ethnicity and prejudice, see Gordon W. Allport, *The Nature of Prejudice* (Garden City, N.Y.: Doubleday, 1954); George Eaton Simpson & J. Milton Yinger, *Racial and Cultural Minorities: An Analysis of Prejudice and Discrimination* (New York: Harper & Bros., 1953); Peter Rose, *They and We: Racial and Ethnic Relations in the United States* (New York: Random House, 1964); Albert Memmi, *Dominated Men* (Boston: Beacon Press, 1968).

5. For a forceful argument on the need to make "gender" a primary tool of historical analysis, see Joan W. Scott, "Gender: A Useful Category of Historical Analysis," *The American Historical Review* 91, no. 5 (December 1986) 1053–75. Particularly important is her definition of gender as always connected to power: "[G]ender is a constitutive element of social relationships based on perceived differences between the sexes, and gender is a primary way of signifying relationships of power" (*Ibid.*, 1067). I share her conviction that the connection between these two propositions is "integral," and I am here trying to show that this integral connection embraces relationships of power expressed not only in terms of gender, but of race, ethnicity, and class.

6. The following analysis is based on the research and findings detailed in my book, Gerda Lerner, *The Creation of Patriarchy*, (New York: Oxford University Press, 1986). Since it would be cumbersome to repeat here the extensive documentation of the argument, interested readers are referred to the book, esp. to chaps. 3–6 and 11.

7. This point is elaborated in Orlando Patterson, *Slavery and Social Death. A Comparative Study* (Cambridge: Harvard University Press, 1982).

8. David Sills, ed. *Encyclopedia of the Social Sciences*, (New York: The Macmillan Co. and the Free Press, 1968), Vol. 15, 298 and 300–301. Essay by Seymour Martin Lipset.

9. These generalizations are based on my detailed study of the development of slavery in the Ancient Near East in the second and first millenniam B.C. I tested them out in comparative studies of Chinese and South American slavery and of the slave systems of Antiquity and of medieval Europe. Although most of the generalizations hold for the specific case of antebellum U.S. slavery, this relatively late slave system showed some peculiarities that cannot be detailed here due to lack of space. The development of African slavery, in its early and native form, was quite different.

10. There is a vast literature of modern Marxist-Feminism that tries to reconceptualize the social constructs "class" and "gender," while attempting to retain the basic structure of Marxist thought. The discussion is well summarized in Zillah R. Eisenstein, *Capitalist Patriarchy and the Case for Socialist Feminism* (New York: Monthly Review Press, 1979) and Zillah, R. Eisenstein, *The Radical Future of Liberal Feminism* (New York: Longman, 1981).

For a reconceptualization based on two separate, but interrelated, systems, see Gayle Rubin, "The Traffic in Women: Notes on the Political Economy of Sex," in Rayna Rapp Reiter, *Toward an Anthropology of Women* (New York: Monthly Review Press, 1975), 157–210 and Mary O'Brien, *The Politics of Re-*

production (Boston: Routledge & Kegan Paul, 1981). Joan Kelly came closest to breaking out of the constraints of this approach in her "The Doubled Vision of Feminist Theory," reprinted in Joan Kelly, *Women, History and Theory* (Chicago: University of Chicago Press, 1984), 51–64.

For a flexible analysis that still remains within the Marxist framework, see Heidi Hartmann, "Capitalism, Patriarchy, and Job Segregation by Sex," *SIGNS* 1, no. 3, Part 2 (Spring 1976): 137–70, and her "The Family as the Locus of Gender, Class, and Political Struggle: The Example of Housework," *SIGNS* 6, no. 3 (Spring 1981): 366–94.

11. African-American women have in the past decade expressed their acute unease and dissatisfaction with the racism they experienced in the modern feminist movement and with the inadequacy of feminist theoretical work in regard to race. They have proposed a variety of alternative theoretical approaches and have insisted that the complexity of their own life experience as black women be recognized and expressed in dialogue with white feminists.

Important work in this redefinition was done by Frances Beal, "Double Jeopardy: To Be Black and Female" in Tony Cade, ed., *The Black Woman* (New York: New American Library, 1970), 90–100; Pauli Murray, "Jim Crow and Jane Crow," and Fannie Lou Hamer, "It's in our Hands," both reprinted in Gerda Lerner, ed. *Black Women in White America: A Documentary History*, (New York: Pantheon, 1972), 592–98; 609–14; Angela Davis, *Women, Race and Class* (New York: Random House, 1981); Paula Giddings, *When and Where I Enter: The Impact of Black Women on Race and Sex in America* (New York: William Morrow & Co., 1984); Audre Lorde, *Sister Outsider: Essays and Speeches* (Trumansburg, N.Y. Crossing Press, 1984); Alice Walker, *In Search of our Mothers' Garden: Womanist Prose* (New York: Harcourt, Brace Jovanovich, 1983); June Jordan, *Political Essays* (Boston: South End Press, n.d.), and by bell hooks, Gloria Hull et al., Sharon Harley and Rosalind Terborg-Penn in the works cited in fn. 2.

Michelle Wallace, *Black Macho and the Myth of the Super Woman*, (New York: Dial Press, 1978) confronted the issue of black sexism.

Linda M. Perkins, "The Impact of the 'Cult of True Womanhood' on the Education of Black Women," *Journal of Social Issues* 39, no. 3 (1983): 17–38 compares differing educational goals and self-concepts of white and black women in the 19th century.

12. A model somewhat similar to my own, although restricted to "race" and "gender" is proposed by Althea Smith and Abigail J. Stewart in their "Approaches to Studying Racism and Sexism in Black Women's Lives," in *ibid.*, 1–16. The authors call for a "contextual interactive model" in which all generalizations would be tested on "gender-race groups" (i.e., white women and men, black women and men) to assure a more varied, accurate, and sophisticated analysis. I have added class as a factor in the concrete historical example I am offering.

13. C. Vann Woodward, *The Strange Career of Jim Crow* (New York: Ox-

ford University Press, 1957), chap. 2; W. J. Cash, *The Mind of the South* (New York: Vintage, 1941), discusses the ideology and politics of planter and non-slave-holding whites; Frank L. Owsley *Plain Folk of the Old South* (Chicago: Quadrangle PB, 1965), chap. 4.

My generalizations on the antebellum South are based on extensive readings in slave narratives and primary sources. For specific discussion of the position of women in antebellum society see: Anne Firor Scott, *The Southern Lady: From Pedestal to Politics: 1830–1930* (Chicago: University of Chicago Press, 1970); Catherine Clinton, *The Plantation Mistress: Women's World in the Old South* (New York: Pantheon Books, 1983); Suzanne Lebsock, *The Free Women of Petersburg: Status and Culture in a Southern Town, 1784–1860* (New York: Norton, 1984); Jacqueline Jones, *Labor of Love, Labor of Sorrow: Black Women, Work and Family from Slavery to the Present* (New York: Basic Books, 1985); Deborah Gray White, *Ar'n't I Woman? Female Slaves in the Plantation South* (New York: Norton, 1985); Elizabeth Fox-Genovese, *Within the Plantation Household: Black and White Women of the Old South* (Chapel Hill: The University of North Carolina Press, 1988).

14. The subject is fully explored in Winthrop Jordan, *White over Black: American Attitudes toward the Negro: 1550–1812* (New York: Norton, 1968), and George M. Fredrickson, *The Black Image in the White Mind: The Debate on Afro-American Character and Destiny: 1817–1914* (New York: Harper & Row, 1971), esp. chap. 2.

15. Leon S. Litwack, *Been in the Storm So Long: The Aftermath of Slavery* (New York: Alfred A. Knopf, 1979), 244–45.

16. Ida B. Wells, *A Red Record* (Chicago: Donohue & Henneberry, 1895); Alfreda M. Duster, ed., *Crusade for Justice: The Autobiography of Ida B. Wells* (Chicago and London: University of Chicago Press, 1970).

See also: Mary Church Terrell, "Lynching from a Negro's Point of View," *North American Review* 178, no. 571 (June 1904): 853–68.

17. David Brody, *Steelworkers in America: The Nonunion Era* (Cambridge: Harvard University Press, 1960).

18. According to a *New York Times* poll conducted June 20–25, 1989, eighty-five percent of African-American women questioned supported the women's movement, compared to only 67 percent of white women.

19. Francis Jennings, *The Invasion of America: Indians, Colonialism and the Cant of Conquest* (Durham: The University of North Carolina Press, 1975). This work, with its radically new concept of viewing U.S. history, unfortunately omits women entirely from its consideration. An attempt to write a one-volume U.S. history free from Eurocentric bias is represented by Peter N. Carroll and David W. Noble, *The Free and the Unfree: A New History of the United States* (New York: Penguin Books, 1977).

Three more recent texts succeed in more fully integrating women, race, and ethnicities, and the new scholarship on these topics in their texts: David Burner, with Eugene D. Genovese and Forrest McDonald, *The American People*

(St. James, N.Y.: Revisionary Press, 1980); Mary Beth Norton et al., *A People and a Nation: A History of the United States*, 2nd ed., 2 vols. (Boston: Houghton Mifflin, 1986); James A. Henretta et al., *America's History* (Chicago: The Dorsey Press, 1987). The Henretta and Norton texts handle the invasion better than any of the others, and pay more attention to women and ethnic groups. Yet, I find the treatment of the latter two subjects disappointing, because the authors are still grafting these groups on to a traditional framework.

11. RETHINKING THE PARADIGM: I. CLASS / II. RACE

1. Joan Wallach Scott, in her important essay, *Gender and the Politics of History* (New York: Columbia University Press, 1988), p. 30, pointed out that the categories of what she called "the litany" are not comparable. On decentering, see Elsa Barkley Brown, "African-American Women's Quilting: A Framework for Conceptualizing and Teaching African-American Women's History," *SIGNS* 14, no. 4 (Summer 1989): 921–29; p. 924.

2. Scott, *Gender and the Politics of History*, p. 2.

3. Deconstructionist theory has been useful in pointing up the significance of symbolic discourse and systems of meaning, although several authors have stressed meaning systems at the expense of the actual conditions that give rise to them.

4. Reference to Hawaii: F. James Davis, "The Hawaiian Alternative to the One-Drop Rule," in Naomi Zack (ed.), *American Mixed Race: The Culture of Microdiversity* (Lanham, Md.: Rowman & Littlefield, 1995), pp. 115–31; ref. p. 116.

1990 Census and recommendations on use of "ethnic" classifications: "Testimony of the Association of MultiEthnic Americans Before the Subcommittee on Census, Statistics, and Postal Personnel of the U.S. House of Representatives, *American Mixed Race*., pp. 191–210; ref. pp. 195, 204.

For background on "mixed race," see articles in same source. See also: Naomi Zack, *Race and Mixed Race* (Philadelphia, Temple University Press, 1993); Maria P. P. Root, *Racially Mixed People in America* (Newbury Park: Sage Publications, 1993); Gloria Anzaldua, *Borderlands/La Frontera: The New Mestiza* (San Francisco: Spinsters/Aunt Lute, 1987). For autobiographical accounts of "mixed race," see Ellen Terry, *The Third Door: The Autobiography of an American Negro Woman* (New York: David McKay Co., 1955); Shirlee Taylor Haizlip, *The Sweeter the Juice* (New York: Simon & Schuster, 1994).

5. Werner Sollors, "Introduction" in Sollors (ed.), *The Invention of Ethnicity* (New York: Oxford University Press, 1989), pp. ix-xx.

6. See the articles in Sollors, *Invention*, for examples of this process in the United States. For examples in England, Scotland, Wales and Africa, see Eric

Hobsbawm and Terence Ranger (eds.), *The Invention of Tradition* (Cambridge: Cambridge University Press, 1983).

7. There is a vast literature on the Marxist-feminist debate, which tries to reconceptualize the social constructs "class" and "gender." The earlier debate was well summarized in Zillah R. Eisenstein, *Capitalist Patriarchy and the Case for Socialist Feminism* (New York: Monthly Review Press, 1979) and Zillah R. Eisenstein, *Radical Future of Liberal Feminism* (New York: Longman, 1981). The more recent debate is fully considered and documented in Catherine A. MacKinnon, *Toward a Feminist Theory of the State* (Cambridge: Harvard University Press, 1989). Rather than attempt to give a full bibliography of all the works I have read, I will cite the major trends.

The major contribution made by radical feminist theorists was to locate the cause of female oppression in men's control of women's sexuality and reproductive capacities. While the theorists varied as to stressing biological determinism or societal conditioning, they agreed that women belong to a "class" defined by their sexuality, which they named "sex class." Kate Millet, *Sexual Politics* (Garden City, N.Y.: Doubleday, 1969); Shulamith Firestone, *The Dialectic of Sex: The Case for Feminist Revolution* (New York: Bantam Books, 1970); Ti-Grace Atkinson, *Amazon Odyssey* (New York: Links, 1973); Susan Brownmiller, *Against Our Will: Men, Women, and Rape* (New York: Simon & Schuster, 1975); Robin Morgan, *Going Too Far, The Personal Chronicle of a Feminist* (New York: Random House, 1977); Adrienne Rich, *Of Woman Born: Motherhood as Experience and Institution* (New York: W. W. Norton, 1979), and Mary Daly, *Gyn/Ecology: The Metaethics of Radical Feminism* (Boston: Beacon Press, 1978).

The position of those attempting to fit feminism into Marxist categories is represented in Sheila Rowbotham, *Woman's Consciousness, Man's World* (Baltimore: Penguin, 1973); Juliet Mitchell, *Woman's Estate* (New York: Pantheon, 1974); Angela Davis, *Women, Race and Class* (New York: Random House, 1981); Heidi Hartmann, "Capitalism, Patriarchy and Job Segregation by Sex," *SIGNS* 6 (Spring 1981): 366–94. Other feminists have tended to argue for the existence of two separate systems of oppression which stand in some relation to each other, namely, an economic system of class oppression represented by capitalism and a sexual system of oppression represented by patriarchy. Thus the anthropologist Gayle Rubin defined the "sex/gender system" as a separate structure, paralleling the system of class dominance. Gayle Rubin, "The Traffic in Women: Notes on the Political Economy of Sex," in Reina Reiter (ed.), *Toward an Anthropology of Women* (New York: Monthly Review Press, 1978), pp. 159–210.

Some Marxist-feminists attempted to define parallel systems of "production" and "reproduction," revising the classical Marxist position which made the latter subordinate to the former. Analytically, they wrestled with the difficulty of adding another "structure" to the Marxist dialectical model of class oppression. See, for example, Juliet Mitchell's "four structures" in her *Woman's Estate* (cited above), or Renate Bridenthal's structural model, in "The Dialectics of Production and Reproduction in History," *Radical America* 10, no. 2 (March-April 1976): 3–9. Mary O'Brien took this approach to its furthest reach in her influential work *The Politics of Reproduction* (Boston: Routledge & Kegan Paul, 1981), in which she analyzed the "system of reproduction" as a system co-equal in importance to the system of production.

For a combination of Marxist and feminist "standpoint" theory, see Alison M. Jaggar, *Feminist Politics and Human Nature* (Totowa, N.J.: Rowman & Allanheld, 1983); Nancy C. M. Hartsock, *Money, Sex and Power: Toward a Feminist Historical Materialism* (Boston: Northeastern University Press, 1983); and Dorothy Smith, *The Everyday World as Problematic: A Feminist Sociology* (Boston: Northeastern University Press, 1987).

8. Joan Scott, *Gender* . . . ; Michele Barrett, "The Concept of Difference," *Feminist Review* 26 (July 1987): 29–41; Gayatri Chakravorti Spivak, "Can the Subaltern Speak?," in Cary Nelson and Laurence Grossberg (eds.), *Marxism and the Interpretation of Culture* (Urbana: University of Illinois Press, 1988); Linda Nicholson, *Feminism/Postmodernism* (New York: Routledge, 1990); Patricia J. Williams, *The Alchemy of Race and Rights: Diary of a Law Professor* (Cambridge: Harvard University Press, 1991); Elizabeth Abel, "Black Writing, White Reading: Race and the Politics of Feminist Interpretation," *Critical Inquiry* 19 (Spring 1993): 470–98.

9. Cf. Gerda Lerner, *The Majority Finds Its Past: Placing Women in History* (New York: Oxford University Press, 1979), esp. chaps. 1, 2, 10, 11.

10. For a discussion of "women's culture," see "Politics and Culture in Women's History: A Symposium," with Ellen DuBois, Mari Jo Buhle, Temma Kaplan, Gerda Lerner and Carroll Smith-Rosenberg, in *SIGNS* 6, no. 1 (Spring 1980): 26–64.

11. Important efforts at building a feminist theory on new grounds are: Dorothy Dinnerstein, *The Mermaid and the Minotaur: Sexual Arrangements and Human Malaise* (New York: Harper & Row, 1977); Susan Griffin, *Woman and Nature: The Roaring Inside Her* (New York: Harper & Row, 1978); MacKinnon, *Toward a Feminist Theory of the State*; Carol Gilligan, *In a Different Voice: Psychological Theory and Women's Development* (Cambridge: Harvard University Press, 1982); Dorothy E. Smith, *The Everyday World As Problematic*.

The vast debate on the subject of "difference," which has occupied so much space in recent feminist scholarship, cannot be adequately summarized here. I have found the following to be important highlights of the debate: Hester Eisenstein and Alice Jardine (eds.), *The Future of Difference* (Boston: G. K. Hall, 1980); Elizabeth Spelman, *Inessential Woman: Problems of Exclusion in Feminist Thought* (Boston: Beacon Press, 1988); Michelle Barrett, cited in n. 8 above; Karen Hansen and Ilene Philipson (eds.), *Women, Class and the Feminist Imagination* (Philadelphia: Temple University Press, 1990); Karen

Brodkin Sacks, "Toward a Unified Theory of Class, Race, and Gender," *American Ethnologist* 16, no. 3 (August 1989): 534–50; Linda Gordon, "On 'Difference'," *Genders* 10 (Spring 1991, University of Texas Press): 91–111.

12. I have attempted to make use of the deconstructionist and postmodernist theories now so popular. While I appreciate their deconstruction of fixed verities and concepts and appreciate the sophistication of their methodology, I have not found them helpful in the work I want to do.

13. Historians working in the fields of labor and African-American history have worked toward new definitions of the term "class" and have stressed that class and race and gender are relational, intertwined and interdependent. Many of these authors are cited in the latter part of this essay. For labor history, see "A New Agenda for American Labor History: A Gendered Analysis and the Question of Class," in J. Carroll Moody and Alice Kessler-Harris (eds.), *Perspectives on American Labor: The Problem of Synthesis* (DeKalb: Northern Illinois University Press, 1989), pp. 217–34; and Alice Kessler-Harris, "Treating the Male as 'Other': Redefining the Parameters of Labor History," *Labor History* 34, no. 2 (Spring/Summer 1993): 190–204.

The comment that "class" is not a "structure" but a set of historical relationships was made by E. P. Thompson, *The Making of the English Working Class* (New York: Vintage Books, 1963), pp. 9 and 11, but Thompson concentrated on "consciousness" and did not consider gender, race, ethnicity as constitutive parts of the "relationship."

14. My theoretical speculations are based on empirical data gathered in my historical work on women, especially the two volumes *Women and History:* Vol. I: *The Creation of Patriarchy* (New York: Oxford University Press, 1986); Vol. II: *The Creation of Feminist Consciousness: From the Middle Ages to 1870* (New York: Oxford University Press, 1993).

Since I am, in this essay, primarily concerned with demonstrating the interrelatedness of the various aspects of the system of dominance, I leave out of consideration, when discussing class, an important aspect of maintaining it, namely, "class culture." I do not think that this invalidates any of my claims about class.

15. The discussion of conditions in the Ancient Near East is based on a broad range of primary and secondary sources cited in my *Creation of Patriarchy.* See esp. chaps. 1–3.

16. Claude Meillassoux, "From Reproduction to Production: A Marxist Approach to Economic Anthropology," *Economy and Society*, no. 1 (1972): 93–105, and "The Social Organisation of the Peasantry: The Economic Basis of Kinship," *Journal of Peasant Studies* I, no. 1 (1973); John Moore, "The Exploitation of Women in Evolutionary Perspective," *Critique of Anthropology* III, nos. 9–10 (1977): 83–100; Peter Aaby, "Engels and Women", *ibid.*, pp. 25–53; Maxine Molyneux, "Androcentrism in Marxist Anthropology," *ibid.*, pp. 55–81.

For information on archaic state formation, see Robert McCormick Adams,

The Evolution of Urban Society (Chicago: Aldine Publishing Co., 1966); Carl H. Kreling and Robert McC. Adams, *City Invincible: A Symposium on Urbanization and Cultural Development in the Ancient Near East* (Chicago: University of Chicago Press, 1960); Charles Redman, *The Rise of Civilization: From Early Farmers to Urban Society in the Ancient Near East* (San Francisco: W. H. Freeman, 1978); Elman Service, *Origins of the State and Civilization: The Process of Cultural Evolution* (New York: W. W. Norton, 1975).

17. In my book *Creation of Patriarchy* I used the term "stand-in" wife to describe this role. The term was somewhat confusing, since it might be interpreted as one woman standing in place of another. I prefer to use the term coined by Laurel Thatcher Ulrich in her excellent book, *Good Wives: Image and Reality in the Lives of Women in Northern New England: 1650–1750* (New York: Oxford University Press, 1980) p. 9, since it describes the role more accurately. I am grateful to Peggy Pascoe for pointing this out to me.

18. The incident is detailed in Lerner, *Creation of Patriarchy*, pp. 70–71.

19. My generalizations are based on Suzanne Fonay Wemple, *Women in Frankish Society: Marriage and the Cloister, 500 to 900* (Philadelphia: University of Pennsylvania Press, 1985); Susan Mosher Stuard (ed.), *Women in Medieval Society* (Philadelphia: University of Pennsylvania Press, 1976); Jacques Le Goff, *Time, Work & Culture in the Middle Ages* (Chicago: University of Chicago Press, 1980); David Herlihy, *Opera Muliebra: Women and Work in Medieval Europe*, (New York: McGraw-Hill, 1990).

20. Under Germanic law a woman's *Wergeld*, the sum the family would receive if she were to be killed, was set at twice the amount of that for a man. Reference to Merovingian law: Wemple, *Women in Frankish Society*, p. 31.

21. Wemple, *Women in Frankish Society*, p. 72.

22. Joan Thirsk, "The European Debate on Customs of Inheritance, 1500–1700," in Jack Goody, Joan Thirsk, E. P. Thompson (eds.), *Family and Inheritance: Rural Society in Western Europe, 1200–1800* (Cambridge: Cambridge University Press, 1976), 177–91. See also Jack Goody, "Inheritance, Property and Women: Some Comparative Considerations," *ibid.*, pp. 10–36.

23. Barbara E. Crawford, "Marriage and Status of Women in Norse Society," in Elizabeth M. Craik, *Marriage and Property* (Aberdeen: Aberdeen University Press, 1984), pp. 71–88. Jack Goody ascribes this favorable treatment of daughters in Norse society to the fact that cattle-raising, not landholding, formed the mainstay of the economy and could, as a movable inheritance, be transfered more easily than land. J. Goody, "Introduction," in Goody, Thirsk, Thompson, *Family and Inheritance*, p. 8.

24. It is unclear whether bride gift or dowry contributed more to the well-being of the bride. I tend to think bride gift was a better guarantee of the bride's receiving good treatment than was dowry. Bride gift had to be returned to the bride's family if the marriage failed, and thus it gave the groom and his family an incentive to make the marriage work. The "dowry killings" in 20th-

century India are a horrifying illustration of the way dowry can work against the interest of brides.

25. Chris Middleton, "Peasants, Patriarchy and the Feudal Mode of Production in England: Feudal Lords and the Subordination of Peasant Women," *The Sociological Review* 29, no. 1 (Feb. 1981): 137–54; information on tax, p. 143.

26. Wemple details the practice of polygyny in the Merovingian royal family through three generations. Clothar I (reigned 558–561) had six wives and at least one concubine (slave woman) of which at least two wives, but possibly four, were married to him at the same time. The practice continued through at least four generations of the royal family. Clothar I's great-grandson Dagobert (reigned 632–639) had five wives, at least three of them simultaneously, and many concubines. Concubinage was also common among the Merovingian nobility (pp. 38–41). Chart, pp. xii-xiii.

Three Merovingian kings in the sixth century and four in the seventh century married servant girls and even slaves. Many Merovingian women of the lower nobility served the advancement and alliances of their families of origin by way of securing advantageous marriages with noblemen of the higher ranks or with greater proximity to the royal family (pp. 56–59).

27. General information on the "warrior aristocracy" is based on Joan Kelly, "Family and Society," in Joan Kelly, *Women, History and Theory: The Essays of Joan Kelly* (Chicago: University of Chicago Press, 1984), pp. 100–155; Bonnie S. Anderson and Judith P. Zinsser, *A History of Their Own*, 2 vols. (New York: Harper & Row, 1988), I, 119–50.

For specific issues, see Margaret Clunies Ross, "Concubinage in Anglo-Saxon England," *Past and Present*, no. 108 (August 1985): 3–34; pp. 6–7. Anne L. Klinck, "Anglo-Saxon Women and the Law," *Journal of Medieval History* 7, no. 2 (June 1982): 107–21; p. 109.

Information on inheritance is based on Jack Goody, *The Development of the Family and Marriage in Europe* (Cambridge: Cambridge University Press, 1983), p. 246.

28. W. G. Runciman, "Accelerating Social Mobility: The Case of Anglo-Saxon England," *Past & Present*, No. 104 (August 1984): 3–30; pp. 7, 26 See also Goody cited above, p. 27), p. 246.

I follow Suzanne Wemple's lead in referring to the payment made by the bridegroom or his kin, whenever all or part of it was transferred to the bride, as "bride gift." This is to distinguish it from "bride price," in which the entire amount is given by the groom to the bride's male kin, with the woman having no right in it. See Wemple, *Women in Frankish Society*, pp. 207, 21.

There is a lively and unresolved controversy among historians, Assyriologists, anthropologists as to whether bride price ever was an indication of marriage by sale. From the point of view of my argument what is important is to compare "bride price" with other forms of marriage arrangements which historically evolved at a later stage and to try and ascertain which of the forms allowed wives more freedom and economic self-determination.

29. Klinck, "Anglo-Saxon Women and the Law," p. 118.

30. Janet Senderowitz Loengard, " 'Of the Gift of Her Husband': English Dower and Its Consequences," in Julius Kirshner and Suzanne F. Wemple (eds.), *Women of the Medieval World: Essays in Honor of John H. Mundy* (Oxford: Basil Blackwell, 1985), pp. 233–34. Also Anderson and Zinsser, *A History of Their Own*, I, 325.

31. The story of Abraham, his legitimate wife Sarah, and their "bondswoman" Hagar (Gen. 21:1–21) reflects marriage customs prevalent in surrounding Ancient Near East societies. The infertile couple, Abraham and Sarah, accept as their own son the son of Hagar by Abraham. But then the story deviates sharply from Babylonian practice. Through a miracle, Sarah, in ripe old age, bears a son; she feels herself mocked by Hagar, and, at Sarah's insistence, Abraham banishes Hagar and her son Ishmael into the desert. God saves both from death, but the family line is carried forward only by Isaac, the offspring of the legitimate wife. This may be considered a strong divine endorsement of a new concept—the primacy of the rights of legitimate sons.

32. Jo-Ann McNamara and Suzanne Wemple, "Marriage and Divorce in the Frankish Kingdom," in Stuard, *Women in Medieval Society*, pp. 95–124, and Wemple, *Women in Frankish Society*, chap. 6

33. Shifts and changes in dowry and women's property rights have been thoroughly analyzed in Marion A. Kaplan, *The Marriage Bargain: Women and Dowries in European History* (New York: Harrington Park Press, 1985; originally published by Haworth Press, 1985). See esp. Diane Owen Hughes, "From Brideprice to Dowry in Mediterranean Europe," *ibid.*, pp. 13–58.

The reference to the deteriorating condition of Englishwomen in the 13th century derives from David Herlihy, "The Medieval Marriage Market," in Dale B. J. Randall (ed.), *Medieval and Renaissance Studies* (Summer 1974; Durham, N.C.: Duke University Press, 1976), pp. 3–27; 9.

34. Stanley Chojnacki, "Dowries and Kinsmen in Early Renaissance Venice," in Stuard, *Women in Medieval Society*, pp. 173–91. See also: Anderson and Zinsser, *A History of Their Own*, I, 394–99, 401–2; Hughes in Kaplan, *The Marriage Bargain*, pp. 34–37.

35. Leonard W. Labaree (ed.), *The Autobiography of Benjamin Franklin* (New Haven: Yale University Press, 1964), p. 127.

36. Anderson and Zinsser, *A History of Their Own* I, 376–73; 406–9.

37. Susan Staves, *Married Women's Separate Property in England, 1660–1833* (Cambridge: Harvard University Press, 1990), p. 35.

38. *Ibid.*, p. 37.

39. Eileen Spring, *Law, Land & Family: Aristocratic Inheritance in England, 1300–1800* (Chapel Hill: University of North Carolina Press, 1993), citation p. 93. Spring revises earlier interpretations which regarded marriage settlements as more favorable to women. See Lawrence Stone, *The Crisis of the*

Aristocracy 1558–1641 (Oxford: Clarendon Press, 1965); ———, *The Family, Sex and Marriage in England 1500–1800* (New York: Harper Colophon, 1977); Lloyd Bonfield, *Marriage Settlements 1601–1740* (Cambridge: Cambridge University Press, 1983); Alan Macfarlane, *Marriage and Love in England: Modes of Reproduction 1300–1840* (Oxford: Basil Blackwell, 1986).

40. A woman's status can be properly evaluated only when compared with the status of her brother—that is, holding class, race and time stable and including in the evaluation of status for both the factor of control over sexual and reproductive resources.

41. This interpretation is well supported by Anderson and Zinsser, *A History of Their Own*, I, chap. 3.

42. Women were required to furnish a dowry before being admitted to convents, effectively closing this educational opportunity to poor girls.

43. On peasants' inheritance rights and practices, see Barbara Hanawalt, *The Ties That Bound: Peasant Families in Medieval England* (New York: Oxford University Press, 1986), pp. 68, 110–11. Hanawalt observes that in the case of serfs, although the lord legally was owner of the land, in practice families claimed the right to hold the land from generation to generation.

44. While peasant boys could receive a monastic education and join orders, the requirement of a dowry for women upon entering an order denied peasant girls a similar privilege.

45. Barbara Hanawalt shows that during the 13th and 14th centuries, when land was in demand, widows who had inherited land were sought as marriage partners by younger men. Later, when land was in good supply, men married younger women (pp. 7–8).

Suzanne Lebsock has shown that in colonial Petersburg, Va., wealthy widows refused remarriage in order to hold on to their property and use rights. Suzanne Lebsock, *The Free Women of Petersburg: Status and Culture in a Southern Town, 1784–60* (New York: W. W. Norton, 1984), pp. 26–27, 39.

46. Lerner, *Feminist Consciousness*, chap. 2.

47. Alice Kessler-Harris, *Out to Work: A History of Wage-Earning Women in the United States* (New York: Oxford University Press, 1982), chaps. 2 and 3; Leslie Woodcock Tentler, *Wage-Earning Women: Industrial Work and Family Life in the United States, 1900–1930* (New York: Oxford University Press, 1979).

48. There is a large descriptive literature—sociological, historical, and recently of oral histories—pertaining to housework, which does not concern me here.

The earliest feminist analysis of housework as a determinant of women's status is Charlotte Perkins Gilman, *Women and Economics* (1898; reprint ed., New York: Harper & Row, 1966). Among important Marxist theoreticians are Mary Inman, "In Woman's Defense," in Gerda Lerner (ed.), *The Female Experience: An American Documentary* (New York: Oxford University Press, 1992; reprint of 1977 ed.), pp. 138–43; Mariarosa Della Costa, "Women and the Subversion of the Community," *Radical America* 6, nos. 4–5 (July-Oct. 1973); Eli Zaretsky, "Capitalism, the Family, and Personal Life," *Socialist Revolution,* 3, nos. 1–2 (Jan.-April 1973): 69–125 and *idem.,* vol.3 no.3 (May-June 1973): 19–70; Wally Secombe, "The Housewife and Her Labour Under Capitalism," *New Left Review* 83 (Jan.-Feb. 1974): 3–24; Jean Gardiner, "The Role of Domestic Labour," *New Left Review* 89 (Jan.-Feb. 1975): 47–58; Heidi Hartman, "Capitalism, Patriarchy . . ."; and Heidi Hartman, "The Family as the Locus of Gender, Class, and Political Struggle: The Example of Housework," *SIGNS* 6 (Spring 1981): 366–94.

The most important historical work on the subject is Jeanne Boydston, *Home and Work: Housework, Wages, and the Ideology of Labor in the Early Republic* (New York: Oxford University Press, 1990).

49. Ulrich, *The Midwife's Tale,* pp. 222 and 226. Spellings as in original.

50. Lydia Maria Child Papers, Anti-Slavery Collection, Cornell Library, Ithaca, N.Y., in Lerner, *Female Experience,* pp. 124–26.

51. Samuel Lilienthal, M.D., to Mary Holywell Everett, M.D., New York, Sept. 8, 1876. Everett Family Papers, Newberry Library, Chicago. As cited in Lerner, *Female Experience,* pp. 178–80.

52. Alice Kessler-Harris, *A Woman's Wage: Historical Meanings & Social Consequences* (Lexington: University Press of Kentucky, 1990), chap. 4.

53. The term "racial" is here used as shorthand to describe various groups constructed as "deviant" by race, language, ethnicity or religion.

54. Susan Stanford Friedman, "Beyond White and Other: Relationality and Narratives of Race in Feminist Discourse," *SIGNS* 21, no.1 (Autumn 1995): 1–49; first quote, pp. 16–17; second quote, p. 20.

55. Personal communication, Peggy Pascoe to Author, Sept. 4, 1995.

56. My generalizations on the origins of racism are based on extensive reading in primary and secondary sources on the subject. I have been particularly influenced by W. E. B. DuBois, *The Souls of Black Folk* (Chicago: A. C. McClurg, 1903); Albert Memmi, *Dominated Man* (Boston: Beacon Press, 1968); Winthrop Jordan, *White Over Black: American Attitudes Toward the Negro, 1550–1812* (Chapel Hill: University of North Carolina Press, 1968; and George M. Fredrickson, *The Black Image in the White Mind: The Debate on Afro-American Character and Destiny, 1817–1914* (New York: Harper & Row, 1971).

57. Adam Goodheart, "Mapping the Past: DNA," *Civilization: The Magazine of the Library of Congress,* March/April 1996, pp. 40–47.

58. William E. Burghardt DuBois, "The Conservation of Races," in David Levering Lewis (ed.), *W.E.B. DuBois Reader* (N.Y.: Henry Holt, 1995), pp. 20-27, quote p. 21

For an interesting debate on the development and meaning of DuBois's definitions of "race," see Lucius Outlaw, "On W. E. B. DuBois's 'The Conservation of Races' " and Stephen Protero's 'Conjuring Race'," in Linda A.

Bell and David Blumenfeld (eds.), *Overcoming Racism and Sexism* (Boston: Rowman & Littlefield, 1995), pp. 79–112.

59. DuBois, "Races," *Crisis*, Aug. 1911, pp. 157–58, as cited in *ibid.*, p. 30.

60. Long quote: DuBois, *Dusk of Dawn: An Essay Toward an Autobiography of a Race Concept* (New York: Harcourt, Brace, 1940), pp. 137–38; short quote, p. 153.

61. Both quotes: Appiah, "The Uncompleted Argument: DuBois and the Illusion of Race," in Henry Louis Gates Jr. (ed.), *"Race," Writing and Difference* (Chicago: University of Chicago Press, 1986), pp. 35–36.

62. Peggy Pascoe, "Race, Gender and Intercultural Relations: The Case of Interracial Marriages," *Frontiers: A Journal of Women's Studies* 12, no.1 (1991): 5–18; quote, p. 11.

63. Barbara J. Fields, "Ideology and Race in American History," in J. Morgan Kousser and James M. McPherson (eds.), *Region, Race, and Reconstruction* (New York: Oxford University Press, 1982), pp. 143–77; quotes, pp. 144, 149–50.

Fields pointed insightfully to "the well-known anomaly of American racial convention that considers a white woman capable of giving birth to a black child but denies that a black woman can give birth to a white child" (p. 149).

64. As cited in Kwame Anthony Appiah, "The Conservation of 'Race'," *Black American Literature Forum*. 23, no.1 (Spring 1989): 37–60; quotes, p. 39 and p. 57, fn. 2.

65. Hazel V. Carby, "The Politics of Difference," *MS.*, Sept./Oct. 1990, pp. 84–85.

66. I became aware of this change in the practice of German scholars when I lectured in Austria in 1995. The title of one of my lectures had the word "race" in it and I was asked by the sponsors of the lecture, historians at the University of Vienna, to change the word to "ethnicity." Since I felt this was inappropriate to my topic in American Women's History, I changed the title altogether so as to avoid both terms. My German publisher, Campus Verlag, also confirmed the existence of this practice.

67. Many contemporary thinkers have attempted to better define the various strands of meaning woven into the concept "race" and to disentangle biologically essentialist definitions from socio-historical meanings. Howard Winant and Michael Omi propose to replace the concept "race" with the concept "racial formation," which they define as "an unstable and 'decentered' complex of social meanings constantly being transformed by political struggle." See Howard Winant and Michael Omi, *Racial Formation in the United States* (New York: Routledge & Kegan Paul, 1986), p. 68.

Lucius Outlaw sees "race" as one of many "communities of meaning" which need to be preserved. See Outlaw, "W. E. B. DuBois . . . ," pp. 98–99.

"Race," writes Stephen Protero, ". . . is as historically and socially real as it is scientifically ephemeral." See Protero, "Conjuring Race," p. 104.

68. The destruction of medieval European Jews was justified entirely on the grounds of their being "heretics," that is, on the ground of their religious deviance from Christianity. Since such grounds would have been unacceptable in modern society, the racialization of Jews in 20th-century Europe was a necessity for those who wished to destroy them. We can today observe the workings of such racialization and social construction in the former Yugoslavia, where genocide is once again excused by appeals to racialized stereotypes.

69. Audre Lorde, "Age, Race, Class and Sex: Women Redefining Difference," in *Sister Outsider: Essays and Speeches by Audre Lorde* (New York: The Crossing Press, 1984), pp. 114–23; quote, p. 116.

70. Bettina Aptheker, Angela Davis, Gloria T. Hull et al. (eds.), *All the Women Are White, All the Blacks Are Men, But Some of Us Are Brave: Black Women's Studies* (Old Westbury, N.Y.: Feminist Press, 1982); C. Moraga and G. Anzaldua (eds.), *This Bridge Called My Back: Writings by Radical Women of Color* (New York: Kitchen Table: Women of Color Press, 1983); bell hooks, *Feminist Theory: From Margin to Center* (Boston: South End Press, 1984); Elizabeth V. Spelman, *Inessential Woman*; Barbara Christian, "The Race for Theory," in Hansen and Philipson, *Women, Class and the Feminist Imagination,* pp. 568–79; Evelyn Brooks Higginbotham, "Beyond the Sound of Silence: Afro-American Women in History," *Gender & History* 1, no.1 (Spring 1989): 50–67; Brown, "African-American Women's Quilting"; bell hooks, *Talking Back: Thinking Feminist, Thinking Black* (Boston: South End Press, 1989); Karen Brodkin Sacks, "Toward a Unified Theory of Class, Race, and Gender," *American Ethnologist* 16, no.3 (August 1989): 534–50; Linda Gordon, "On 'Difference'."

In their eagerness to prove the justified charge of "false universalization" against white feminists, the critics committed the same error by forgetting or suppressing those white feminists who for decades had taken "race" into consideration and urged others to do the same. See, for example, Eleanor Flexner, *Century of Struggle: The Woman's Rights Movement in the United States* (Cambridge, Harvard University Press, 1959); William Chafe, *The American Woman: Her Changing, Social, Economic and Political Roles, 1920–1970* (New York: Oxford University Press, 1972) and ———, *Women and Equality: Changing Patterns in American Culture* (New York: Oxford University Press, 1977); Gerda Lerner, *Black Women in White America: A Documentary History* (New York: Pantheon, 1972); and ———, "Black Women in the United States: A Problem in Historiography and Interpretation," in ———, *The Majority Finds Its Past: Placing Women in History* (New York: Oxford University Press, 1979), chap. 5; Catharine Stimpson, "Thy Neighbor's Wife, Thy Neighbor's Servants: Women's Liberation and Black Civil Rights," in Vivian Gornick and Barbara K. Moran (eds.), *Woman in Sexist Society: Studies in Power and Powerlessness* (New York: Basic Books, 1971); Bettina Aptheker, *Woman's Legacy: Essays on Race, Sex, and Class in American History* (Amherst: University of Massachusetts Press, 1982). For a recognition of this error, see Nancy Hewitt, "Reflections from a Departing Editor: Recasting Issues of Marginality," *Gender & History* 4, no.1 (Spring 1992): 3–9.

71. Angela Davis, *Women, Race and Class* (New York: Random House, 1981); Bonnie Thornton Dill, "Race, Class and Gender: Prospects for an All-Inclusive Sisterhood," *Feminist Studies* 9, no.1 (Spring 1983): 131–50; Cheryl Gilkes, "From Slavery to Social Welfare: Racism and the Control of Black Women," in Amy Swerdlow and Hanna Lessinger (eds.), *Class, Race and Sex: The Dynamics of Control* (Boston: G. K. Hall, 1983), pp. 288–300; Patricia Hill Collins, *Black Feminist Thought: Knowledge, Consciousness, and the Politics of Empowerment* (New York: Routledge, 1991); Paula Giddings, *When and Where I Enter: The Impact of Black Women on Race and Sex in America* (New York: William Morrow, 1984).

72. See Bettina Aptheker, *Woman's Legacy*; hooks, *Feminist Theory*.

73. Sacks, "Toward a Unified Theory . . . ," p. 537.

74. Ann Stoler, "Sexual Affronts and Racial Frontiers: European Identities and the Cultural Politics of Exclusion in Colonial Southeast Asia," *Comparative Studies in Society and History* 34 no.2 (July 1992): 514–51; p. 57.

75. Ann Laura Stoler, "Rethinking Colonial Categories: European Communities and the Boundaries of Rule," *CSSH* 31 no.1, (January 1989): 134–61; quote, p. 138.

76. Stoler, "Sexual Affronts," pp. 36–37.

77. Ann Laura Stoler, "Carnal Knowledge and Imperial Power: Gender, Race and Morality in Colonial Asia," in Micaela di Leonardo (ed.), *Gender at the Crossroads: Feminist Anthropology in the Post-Modern Era* (Berkeley: University of California Press, 1990), pp. 51–101; the term "race-culture" is used on p. 83.

78. Chandra Talpade Mohanty, "Introduction: Cartographies of Struggle: Third World Women and the Politics of Feminism," in Chandra Talpade Mohanty, Ann Russo and Lourdes Torres (eds.), *Third World Women and the Politics of Feminism* (Bloomington: Indiana University Press, 1991), pp. 1–47; quotes, pp. 15, 17, 21.

79. Ruth Frankenberg, *White Women, Race Matters: The Social Construction of Whiteness* (Minneapolis: University of Minnesota Press, 1993), pp. 11–12.

80. See also Marilyn Frye, "On Being White: Thinking Toward a Feminist Understanding of Race and Race Supremacy," in *The Politics of Reality: Essays in Feminist Theory* (Trumansburg, N.Y.: Crossing Press, 1983), pp. 110–27; references, pp. 112, 115, 116. Peggy MacIntosh, "White Privilege: Unpacking the Invisible Knapsack," *Peace and Freedom*, July/August 1989, pp. 10–12; Elizabeth Minnich, *Transforming Knowledge* (Philadelphia: Tem-

ple University Press, 1990); David Roediger, *The Wages of Whiteness: Race and the Making of the American Working Class* (New York, 1991); Toni Morrison, *Playing in the Dark: Whiteness and the Literary Imagination* (Cambridge: Harvard University Press, 1992); Shelley Fisher Fishkin, "Interrogating 'Whiteness,' Complicating 'Blackness': Remapping American Culture," *American Quarterly* 47, no.3 (September 1995): 428–66; George Lipsitz, "The Possessive Investment in Whiteness: Racialized Social Democracy and the 'White' Problem in American Studies," *American Quarterly* 47, no.3 (Sept. 1995): 369–87; Vron Ware, *Beyond the Pale: White Women, Racism and History* (New York: Verso, 1992).

For historical examples of the construction of whiteness through miscegenation laws and other racial legislation, see Kathleen Brown, *Good Wives and Nasty Wenches: Gender, Race and Power in Colonial Virginia,* (Williamsburg: Institute of Early American History and Culture, 1996); Pascoe, "Race, Gender . . ."; Mary Frances Berry, "Judging Morality: Sexual Behavior and Legal Consequences in the Late Nineteenth-Century South," *Journal of American History* 78, no.3, (December 1991): 835–56.

81. Charlotte Bunch, "Making Common Cause: Diversity and Coalitions," in Lisa Albrecht and Rose M. Brewer (eds.), *Bridges of Power: Women's Multicultural Alliances* (Philadelphia: New Society Publ., 1990), p. 52; bell hooks, "Feminism: A Transformational Politic," in *Talking Back: Thinking Feminist, Thinking Black* (Boston: South End Press, 1989), pp. 19–27; quote, p. 22; Sacks, "Class, Race, and Gender," pp. 545–46; Sandra Morgen, "Conceptualizing and Changing Consciousness," in Hansen and Philipson (eds.), *Women, Class, and the Feminist Imagination,* quote, p. 285; Linda Gordon, "On 'Difference'," quote, p. 107; Elsa Barkley Brown, " 'What Has Happened Here': The Politics of Difference in Women's History and Feminist Politics," *Feminist Studies* 18, no.2 (Summer 1992): 295–312; Evelyn Nanako Glenn, "From Servitude to Service Work: Historical Continuities in the Racial Division of Paid Reproductive Labor," *Signs* 18, no.1 (Autumn 1992,): 1–43; Ann Russo, " 'We Cannot Live Without Our Lives': White Women, Antiracism, and Feminism," in Mohanty, Russo and Torres (eds.), *Third World Women,* pp. 297–313; Tessie Liu, "Teaching the Differences Among Women from a Historical Perspective: Rethinking Race and Gender as Social Categories," *Women's Studies International Forum* 14, no.4 (1991): 265–76. A useful anthology is Margaret L. Andersen and Patricia Hill Collins, *Race, Class and Gender: An Anthology* (Belmont, Calif.: Wadsworth, 1992). Eilleen Boris, "Gender, Race & Rights: Listening to Critical Race Theory," *Journal of Women's History* 6, no.2 (Summer 1994): 111–24. Italics added by author throughout this paragraph.

Two recent books that exemplify a holistic approach to the problem of the inter-relatedness of various aspects of oppression are Steve J. Stern, *The Secret History of Gender: Women, Men and Power in Late Colonial Mexico* (Chapel Hill: University of North Carolina Press, 1995), and Florencia E. Mallon, *Peas-*

ant and Nation: The Making of Postcolonial Mexico and Peru (Berkeley: University of California Press, 1995).

82. Lorde, *Sister Outsider,* p. 115.

83. Gerda Lerner, "Black Women in the United States: A Problem in Historiography and Interpretation," in Lerner, *Majority,* chap. 5, pp. 81–82. See also chap. 6 ("Community Work of Black Club Women") and chap. 7 ("Black and White Women in Interaction and Confrontation") in the same volume.

84. Dorothy Roberts, "Racism and Patriarchy in the Meaning of Motherhood," *The American University Journal of Gender and the Law* 1, no.1 (Spring 1993): 1–38.

Index

Manifest Destiny, 77, 122, 202
Markers, 189, 191, 209
Marriage: in Ancient Near East, 156–58; and class, 156–76, 183; in colonial America, 169–70; and medieval church, 166–68; in medieval Europe, 158–68, 172, 173; in nineteenth century, 170; and race, 192–93; in Renaissance Europe, 174; in seventeenth and eighteenth centuries, 171; between slaves and free people, 162
Marxism, 70, 136, 151, 152, 202
Media, 83, 123–24, 200–201
Medieval Europe: class in, 158–68, 170, 171, 172–74
Melting pot model, 133
Memorials/monuments, 21–22, 23–26, 32, 118
Memphis, Tennessee: streetcar boycott in, 72
Men. See Domination; Gender; Male; Patriarchy
Meritocracy, 74–75, 83
Merovingian society, 158–63, 166, 167
Middle class: in Ancient Near East, 157–58; and capitalism, 175–76; and differences among women, 141–42; and dowry, 174; marriage in, 169, 171, 174; and origins of patriarchy, 157–58; and race, 141–42; in Renaissance, 169, 174; in seventeenth and eighteenth centuries, 171. See also Bourgeoisie
Militarism, 133–35
Minorities: and American values, 80, 83, 84, 90, 91–92. See also specific minority
Mobs, 63–64, 66
Montgomery, Alabama: bus boycott in, 71–72, 73
Monuments. See Memorials/monuments
Mormons, 80, 87
Multiculturalism, 190
Munich, Germany, 26–31

Nationalism, 13, 16, 122, 184, 203. See also Zionism
Native Americans, 75–77, 81, 84, 86, 118, 143

Nativism, 75, 81, 84–86, 87, 90
Natural resources. See Ecology
Nazism: in Austria, 8–12, 41–42, 50, 51, 204; and history, 202; Lerner's writings about, 41–42. See also Germans/Germany; Holocaust
Negroes. See African Americans
New England Non-Resistance Society, 65
"New humanism," 13
New School for Social Research, 46
Nonviolent resistance: and civil rights, 59, 71–72, 73; and Indian independence, 59, 70–71, 72, 73; in 1930s, 70; and pacifism, 65–66, 67–69, 72, 73; and political theory and practice, 59–73; and religion, 60–62, 65–66, 68; and slavery, 61, 62–67, 71, 72; and women, 66
Northwest Ordinance, 77
Nuclear power, 89, 90–91, 104, 105, 107, 108, 126, 128
Nüremberg laws, 14, 186

Occupations, 99, 100, 170, 176, 179–81, 191
Organized labor, 70, 81, 83, 140, 179
Otherness: and Ancient Near East, 206, 207; and assimilation, 4, 13–14; and Blacks as Other, 138, 139, 142; and differences among women, 142; and domination, 135, 136, 137–40, 142, 194–98; and evil, 30; and gender, 209; and history, 6–7, 15–17, 121, 202, 206–10; and homosexuality, 138; and identity, 208–9; and immigration, 11–13; and Jews as Others, 3–17, 30, 54, 80, 138, 185–86, 206–10; and patriarchy, 137–40, 207–9; and race, 16, 54, 138, 193–94; and religion, 54; response patterns to, 13–15; and scapegoats, 197; and self-definition, 15–17; and sexism, 138; and women as Others, 15–17, 54, 121, 142, 206–10. See also Deviance/difference

Pacifism, 59, 65–66, 67–69, 72, 73, 102, 106. See also Peace movements

If you wanna check my credentials, just ask the last chick I had to beat *down*. She'll gladly show you the stamp I left on her forehead, *okay*?

Soooo. Moving on. As I was saying, I'm from the hood. Lived on the same block, in the same house, all my life. I know these streets like I know the back of my hands 'n' the curve of my hips. They can be mean 'n' dangerous 'n' ohhh, so exciting. And, yeah, the streets might be praising me, but they ain't raising me. So I'm not about to serve you some effed up tale about a chick being lost in the streets, eaten 'n' beaten alive. No, no. I'm a hood goddess, boo. That chick the wannabes bow down to, 'n' the lil thug-daddies worship. But, trust. This ain't no hood love story. So be clear.

No, hun. I wasn't born with a silver spoon hanging from my pouty mouth, but that doesn't mean I can't dream. That doesn't mean I can't want more than what I already have. And, yeah, a chick dreams about getting outta the hood. Traveling the world. Bagging a fine cutie-boo, or two, or three, who I can call my own. And being filthy rich. One day I will be. Trust. But for now, that doesn't mean I can't wear the illusion like a second skin. And, trust. I wear it well, boo.

So if you're hoping for some sob story about some broke-down, busted, lil fast-azz, boy-crazy ho tryna claw her way outta the hood, trickin' the block huggers up offa their paper for a come-up—sorry, boo-boo. Not gonna happen. If you're looking to hear about a chick going hungry or sleeping on some pissy-stained mattress, or having her hot pocket stuffed in some dirty panties going to school smelling like a sewer, then go find you another seat, boo, because you're sitting in the wrong arena. That stage play is being run somewhere else. If you're looking to hear about some fresh-mouthed chick who got beat with fists 'n' locked in closets, that's not gonna be featured here, either. Sorry, hun. I can't tell you a thing about that. Well, I could. But that's not my story. So I'll save that for some other hood chick.

So who am I?

I'm that hot chick, boo.

I'm a diva.

I'm a boss *bish* . . . and *whaaaat*?!